Hosting the Olympic Gam[...]

Hosting the Olympic Games: Uncertainty, Debates and Controversy provides a broad and comprehensive analysis of past Olympic and Paralympic events, shedding critical light on the future of the Games with a specific look at the upcoming Paris 2024 Olympics. It draws attention to the debates and paradox that hosting the Games presents for the contemporary city.

Employing a range of interdisciplinary theoretical and methodological approaches, individual chapters highlight the various controversies of the Games throughout the bidding process, the event itself and its aftermath. Social Science-based chapters place strong emphasis on the vital importance of sustainable strategy for contemporary host cities. Along with environmental concerns whether atmospheric, microbiological or otherwise, many other requirements, costs and risks involving security and public expenditure among others are explored throughout the book.

Including a variety of international and comparative case studies from a range of contributing academics, this will be essential reading for students and researchers in the field of Event studies as well as various disciplines including Tourism, Heritage studies and Urban and Environmental studies.

Marie Delaplace (marie.delaplace@u-pem.fr) holds a PhD (1994) and a *"habilitation à diriger les recherches"* (2009) in economics on the emergence of different types of innovations (IT, biopolymers, transportation, services) in different places. Since 2011, she has been professor of planning and regional development in the Lab'Urba research unit at the "École d'urbanisme de Paris" (Paris School of Urban Planning) within Université Paris-Est Marne-la-Vallée (UPEM). Her works have focused on the wide-ranging effects of high-speed rail on local economic development for more than 15 years and on tourism and local economic development for more than 10 years. She is the co-director of the "City, Tourism, Transport and Territories" Group within the Urban Futures LabEx and represents the university president in the French association AsTRES (Association for Tourism Research and Higher Education). In 2017, she co-founded the Observatory for Research on Mega-Events (ORME) at Université Paris-Est (https://www.u-orme.fr/en/). Alone or with other researchers, she has published almost 60 articles in academic journals and 10 book chapters on these issues.

Pierre-Olaf Schut (po.schut@u-pem.fr) is a Professor of sports history in the research centre "Analyse Comparée des Pouvoirs" (EA 3350) at Université Paris-Est Marne-la-Vallée, France. His main research areas are the development of sports and their relationships with tourism and regional planning, especially regarding sports facilities. He also works on the history of Olympism and the legacy of mega-events. He has co-founded ORME, the Observatory for Research on Mega-Events. He is part of the editorial board of the *International Journal of the History of Sport* and elected in the International Society for the History of Physical Education and Sport council. He recently published in French *Espaces et lieux de sport dans l'histoire* by EPURE.

Routledge Advances in Tourism
Edited by Stephen Page
Hertfordshire Business School, University of Hertfordshire, UK

Destination Marketing
An International Perspective
Edited by Metin Kozak and Nazmi Kozak

Tourism and the Creative Industries
Theories, Policies and Practice
Edited by Philip Long and Nigel D. Morpeth

Positive Tourism
Edited by Sebastian Filep, Jennifer Laing and Mihaly Csikszentmihalyi

Automobile Heritage and Tourism
Edited by Michael Conlin and Lee Joliffe

Scotland and Tourism: The Long View 1700–2015
Alastair J. Durie

Tourism Resilience and Adaptation to Environmental Change
Definitions and Frameworks
Edited by Alan A. Lew and Joseph M. Cheer

Tourism, Resilience and Sustainability
Adapting to Social, Political and Economic Change
Edited by Joseph M. Cheer and Alan A. Lew

Slow Tourism, Food and Cities
Pace and the Search for the 'Good Life'
Edited by Michael Clancy

Lifelong Learning for Tourism
Concepts, Policy and Implementation
Edited by Violet V. Cuffy, David Airey and Georgios C. Papageorgiou

Hosting the Olympic Games
Uncertainty, Debates, and Controversy
Edited by Marie Delaplace and Pierre-Olaf Schut

For more information about this series, please visit:
https://www.routledge.com/advances-in-tourism/book-series/SE0538

Hosting the Olympic Games
Uncertainty, Debates and Controversy

Edited by
Marie Delaplace and Pierre-Olaf Schut

Routledge
Taylor & Francis Group

LONDON AND NEW YORK

First published 2020 by Routledge

2 Park Square, Milton Park, Abingdon, Oxon OX14 4RN
605 Third Avenue, New York, NY 10017

Routledge is an imprint of the Taylor & Francis Group, an informa business

First issued in paperback 2022

Publisher's Note

The publisher has gone to great lengths to ensure the quality of this reprint
but points out that some imperfections in the original copies may be apparent.

British Library Cataloguing in Publication Data
A catalogue record for this book is available from the British Library

Library of Congress Cataloging-in-Publication Data
A catalog record has been requested for this book

ISBN: 978-0-367-22396-0 (hbk)
ISBN: 978-1-03-233811-8 (pbk)
DOI: 10.4324/9780429274695

Typeset in Times New Roman
by Taylor & Francis Books

Contents

Contents

Illustrations

Figures

Maps

Tables

Contributors

Dr Isabella Annesi-Maesano is Research Director (DR1) at the French NIH (INSERM) and Professor of Environmental Epidemiology at Université Pierre et Marie Curie (UPMC) and Université Denis Diderot in Paris. Since 2006, she has headed the Department of Epidemiology of Allergic and Respiratory Diseases (EPAR) at the Pierre Louis Institute of Epidemiology and Public Health of INSERM and UPMC in Paris. Her research includes the explanation of the development of allergic and respiratory diseases and their comorbidities (metabolic diseases, cardiovascular diseases, neurodevelopmental troubles, etc.) through an exposomic approach. She is presently Principal Investigator and Coordinator of the FP7-ENV Health and Environment-wide Associations based on Large Population Surveys (www.health-eu.eu). She is also leading other international and national projects, including the WP Allergic and Respiratory Diseases in the French EDEN Birth Cohort.

Dr Matthias Beekmann is senior researcher at Centre National de Recherche Scientifique. He is working at the Laboratoire Interuniversitaire des Systèmes Atmosphériques (LISA), UMR CNRS 7583, Universités Paris-Est Créteil et Paris Diderot. His main research topic is atmospheric pollution modelling. He codeveloped the CHIMERE chemistry-transport model which today is in widespread use for operational air quality forecast and simulation. He initiated an intensive measurement campaign in the Paris agglomeration in order to better constrain fine particulate matter sources in a European megacity. Matthias Beekmann was president of the French scientific program committee LEFE/CHAT (CHemistry of the ATmosphere). He is president of the Conseil Académique of Université Paris-Est. He is director of the Observatoire des Sciences de l'Univers EFLUVE (Enveloppes FLUides de la Ville à l'Exobiologie).

Jean-David Bernard graduated from Université Pierre et Marie Curie in 2003. Jean-David joined EDF Research and Development with a mission on the management of aqueous effluents from the Renardières R&D site for two years. He then joined the Department of Energy Efficiency for Buildings to work on ventilation technologies. Since 2010, he has led the project on

Building Envelope Technologies and Indoor Air Quality and Ventilation. In parallel, he leads a high-level sporting career in rowing where he ascends to national and international podiums. Until 2010, he had achieved 20 national podiums, two medals at the European championships, two medals at the world championships, four podiums in World Cup and Olympic Finals in Athens.

Pietro Bernardara is currently Director of CEREA (Center of Teaching and Research in Atmospheric Environment), a joint laboratory between EDF and ENPC (Ecole des Ponts ParisTech) and head of the Atmospheric Environment group within the MFEE department (Fluid Mechanics, Energy and Environment) of EDF R&D. He holds an engineering degree from the Politecnico di Milano (2000), with an environmental specialism; he subsequently obtained his PhD in hydraulics and hydrology within the same school (2004). During his first career, he worked on Natural Risks within the research teams of ENPC (CEREVE) and EDF R&D (LNHE). Then between 2013 and 2017 he directed the Environment and Natural Hazards program for the EDF Energy R&D UK Center in London. These experiences have enabled him to promote his research in more than 20 scientific publications and scientific books, the supervision of several theses and the obtaining of the habilitation to lead research at the University Paris La Sorbonne in 2018.

José Chaboche (jose.chaboche@univ-orleans.fr) is an assistant professor in geography, planning and sport management at Collegium Sciences and Technology – UFR STAPS; Sport Management of the University of Orléans, CEDETE (EA 1210). His research focuses on urban and territorial development through sport policies. His recent publications are about major stadiums and urban projects. They also concern the image linked to Olympic Games.

Jean-Loup Chappelet (jean-loup.chappelet@unil.ch) is a full professor of public management at the Swiss Graduate School of Public Administration (IDHEAP) of the University of Lausanne. He was IDHEAP Dean from 2003 to 2011. He previously held management positions at the International Olympic Committee and in one of the big-four international accounting firms. In 1995, at IDHEAP, he launched the first sport management course in Switzerland, which is still held every autumn. For 12 years (1999–2011) he was the director of the MEMOS program, a master's program run by 11 universities for Olympic Solidarity. In 2000, Prof. Chappelet founded the Académie internationale des sciences et techniques du sport (AiSTS) with colleagues from the Universities of Lausanne and Geneva, and the Swiss Federal Institute of Technology (EPFL). He authored many scientific articles and several books on sport management and Olympic governance, as well as on public management and information systems organization. His latest book (2016) was published under the title *The Olympic Games: rekindling the flame*, in French (also in Korean and soon in Japanese). He has attended most Olympic (Summer) Games and Olympic Winter Games since 1972, as well as the first Youth Olympic Games. Prof. Chappelet currently coordinates the Certificate in Football Management, a blended learning program for UEFA (Union of European Football Associations).

Marie Delaplace (marie.delaplace@u-pem.fr) holds a PhD (1994) and a *"habilitation à diriger les recherches"* (2009) in economics on the emergence of different types of innovations (IT, biopolymers, transportation, services) in different places. Since 2011, she has been professor of planning and regional development in the Lab'Urba research unit at the "École d'urbanisme de Paris" (Paris School of Urban Planning) within Université Paris-Est Marne-la-Vallée (UPEM). Her works have focused on the wide-ranging effects of high-speed rail on local economic development for more than 15 years and on tourism and local economic development for more than 10 years. She is the co-director of the "City, Tourism, Transport and Territories" Group within the Urban Futures LabEx and represents the university president in the French association AsTRES (Association for Tourism Research and Higher Education). In 2017, she co-founded the Observatory for Research on Mega-Events (ORME) at Université Paris-Est (https://www.u-orme.fr/en/). Alone or with other researchers, she has published almost 60 articles in academic journals and 10 book chapters on these issues.

Guillaume Delatour is a research professor at the Université de technologie de Troyes (UTT). His research works concern the organization, the cooperation and decision-making applied to the area of risk and crisis management. He managed a research project on the preparation of French municipality for crisis management. He is also an Army reserve officer.

Dr Cécile Doustaly (cecile.doustaly@u-cergy.fr) is senior Lecturer at the Université de Cergy-Pontoise (Greater Paris). She heads the Research Group on Heritage in the AGORA research centre. She created and directs two Masters in International Engineering (Culture & Territories/Heritage & Tourism). After graduating from the universities of Reading and Sorbonne Nouvelle (Sociology/British Studies), she completed her PhD on the genesis of public support for the arts in England 1832–1970 (Sorbonne Nouvelle). Her transdisciplinary research now centres on comparative arts and heritage policies, notably in France and Britain, with special emphasis on their relation with urban change in London and Paris and internationalization.

Nathalie Fabry (nathalie.fabry@u-pem.fr) is an Associate Professor at the Université Paris-Est Marne-la-Vallée. Her recent research focuses on the ability of territories to fix, in the long run, actors and socioeconomic activities. She is studying the attractiveness of destinations, with a focus on the role of institutions, networks, and clusters. She is examining how a destination may develop through tourism in a smart and resilient way. She specifically studies tourism clusters, the process that paved the way to clustering (the cauterization process), and stakeholders' – including inhabitants' – involvements. She is in charge of the

Meeting and Event Industry and Luxury Hospitality streams of the Master's Degree in Tourism Studies at the Université Paris-Est Marne-la-Vallée. She is an active member of the "Cluster de Tourisme Paris Val d'Europe". She belongs to the DICEN-Idf Research team.

Dr Gilles Foret (gilles.foret@lisa.u-pec.fr) is an assistant professor at Université Paris-Est Créteil working at the Laboratoire Interuniversitaire des Systèmes Atmosphériques (LISA), UMR CNRS 7583, Universités Paris-Est Créteil et Paris Diderot. His main research topic is the study of atmospheric pollution either with numerical models or in situ observations. He is in charge of the OCAPI research network attached to the Institut Pierre-Simon Laplace (IPSL). He is also the coordinator of the regional air quality network QI^2 (Qualité de l'air, Impacts Sanitaires, Innovations Technologiques et Politiques) that gathers more than 30 laboratories and institutions working on the topic of air quality.

Dr Bernard de Gouvello is a researcher of the Centre Scientifique et Technique du Bâtiment and the UMR MA 102 LEESU (Champs-sur-Marne, France). His field of expertise is the sustainable management of water at different levels from the building to the city. He is particularly interested in rainwater reuse and usage in terms of development and impacts on urban water management

Martial Haeffelin is a senior research scientist with 25 years' experience in atmospheric remote sensing research. He conducted research on the effect of clouds on the global Earth radiation budget at the NASA Langley Research Center (VA, USA) from 1993–2001. In 2002, he initiated a surface-based atmospheric observation program for CNRS-IPSL, developed a world-class atmospheric observatory located in the École polytechnique, and directed this program for 15 years. He is currently the Deputy Director of Institut Pierre Simon Laplace, in charge of Earth Observations, and acts as scientific director of ACTRIS-FR, a French research infrastructure dedicated to support climate research. Dr Haeffelin conducts research on cloud physical processes and remote sensing, as well as cloud effects on the solar resource for photovoltaic energy production. He is the author and co-author of more than 80 peer-reviewed articles.

Harry H. Hiller (hiller@ucalgary.ca) is Director of the "Cities and the Olympics Project" and Faculty Professor of Urban Sociology at the University of Calgary. He has published extensively on the Olympics from an urban sociological perspective in journals such as *Urban Affairs Quarterly, Research in Urban Sociology, International Journal of Urban and Regional Research, European Sport Management Quarterly, Sociology, Leisure Studies, Urban Affairs Review,* and numerous book chapters. He is the author of *Host Cities and the Olympics: An Interactionist Approach* (Routledge, 2012). Hiller has also made presentations at many Olympic cities and spoken about the Olympics at universities and cities around the world.

Anna Kobierecka (anna.kobierecka@uni.lodz.pl) is an assistant professor in the Department of Theory of International Relations and Security, Faculty of International and Political Studies, University of Łódź. In her research she focuses on the nation branding and public diplomacy. She is author of two books and numerous scientific articles and chapters.

Michał Marcin Kobierecki (michal.kobierecki@gmail.com) is an assistant professor in the Department of Political Theory and Thought, Faculty of International and Political Studies, University of Łódź. His research interests include sports diplomacy, politics and sport, nation branding and public diplomacy with a specific focus on the use of sport. He runs a research project "Consensual and branding role of sport in diplomatic activities of states and non-state actors" funded by the National Science Center, Poland. He is author of numerous books, chapters and scientific articles.

Martin Koning is senior researcher in transportation economics at IFSTTAR (L'Institut français des sciences et technologies des transports, de l'aménagement et des réseaux). His works mainly focus on the negative externalities generated by urban road freight (including traffic congestion, noise and local pollutants) but also on public policies aimed at mitigating the corresponding social welfare losses. He has published various peer-reviewed articles in international scientific journals.

Patrick Laclémence has been professor at the Université de techonologie de Troyes (UTT) since 1988. He is a teacher-researcher under various statutes at UTT, University René Descartes (Paris V), Reims, and multiple other institutions. At the same time, he holds various operational positions at the Ministry of the Interior of France. Doctor in sociology and with a habilitation to direct doctoral research since 1988, he has developed a thematic research area on social risks and security. With the current Director of the National Institute of Advanced Studies of Safety and Justice (IHESI, INHESJ), he has developed, since 2001, the concepts of global security and anticipation. He has set up several higher education degrees with the Universities of Reims, Paris V and Troyes in collaboration with the INHESJ and ENSOSP. He is the Director of the Research Center of the France's National Police College and research advisor to the Center of advanced studies of the home office (CHEMI). He holds the Chair of Crisis Management and directs the Global Security Institute.

Pr. Françoise Lucas (lucas@u-pec.fr) is a microbial ecologist working at the Université Paris-Est Créteil in the UMR MA 102 LEESU. She studies the dynamics and diversity of waterborne pathogens and bacterial communities in urban aquatic systems. She is interested in the fate and distribution patterns of fecal indicators and pathogens (mycobacteria, enteric viruses) during storm events.

Pr. Jean-Marie Mouchel works at Sorbonne Université (Paris, France). He is the director of the UMR 7619 METIS and the co-director of the Zone Atelier Seine. He is an expert in the modelling of contaminant flows. He is interested in estimating the fate and flows of chemical and microbial contaminants in urban and rural aquatic environments.

Dr Laurent Moulin is an expert microbiologist at Eau de Paris (Ivry, France) specialized in the evaluation of the sanitary risk associated with water consumption. He is in charge of the Research and Development laboratories. His research focuses on understanding the distribution and dynamic of pathogens (viruses, bacteria, protozoa) in drinking and surface waters.

Rachel Nadif is an epidemiologist in respiratory diseases and the co-Head of INSERM Unit 1168 "Aging and chronic diseases. Epidemiological and public health approaches". She is pursuing a research program on biological phenotypes and genetic polymorphisms regarding oxidative, nitrosative and inflammatory pathways in interaction with environmental exposures for respiratory diseases. She has published numerous papers, reviews and book chapters in the field.

Olivier Ramalho is a research scientist dedicated to indoor air quality at the Health and Comfort Department from the Scientific and Technical Center for Building (CSTB) in France. He holds a PhD in atmospheric sciences and throughout his 20 years' experience has acquired expertise in various fields such as olfactometry, analytical chemistry, aerosol sciences, gas sensors, ventilation, building materials, volatile and semi-volatile organic compounds and statistical modelling. He currently works for the French Observatory of Indoor Air Quality (OQAI) designing measurement strategies and questionnaires for national surveys in various environments like dwellings, schools, offices, and including less typical buildings like swimming pools or gymnasiums. He has co-authored 68 peer-reviewed articles, 53 conference papers, and one book.

Paul-Henri Richard (paul_henri.richard@utt.fr) is a research engineer at the Université de technologie de Troyes (UTT). After working on a thesis about crisis management in safe cities, he manages and coordinates a chair on crisis management co-founded with the French Academy for Fire, Rescue and Civil Protection Officers (ENSOSP). He is also a volunteer firefighter.

Alain Schoeny (alain.schoeny@univ-orleans.fr) holds a PhD in sports management and communication at the Université d'Orléans. His research focuses on communication process through sports events.

Pierre-Olaf Schut (po.schut@u-pem.fr) is a Professor of sports history in the research centre "Analyse Comparée des Pouvoirs" (EA 3350) at Université Paris-Est Marne-la-Vallée, France. His main research areas are the development of sports and their relationships with tourism and regional planning, especially regarding sports facilities. He also works on the history of Olympism and the legacy of mega-events. He has co-founded ORME, the Observatory for Research on Mega-Events. He is part of the editorial board of the *International Journal of the History of Sport* and elected in the International Society for the History of Physical Education and Sport council. He recently published in French *Espaces et lieux de sport dans l'histoire* by EPURE.

Audrey Morel Senatore is a doctor of law and directs the Centre of Interdisciplinary Research on Civil Safety (CERISC) at ENSOSP.

Pr. Pierre Servais is a microbial ecologist working at the Université libre de Bruxelles (Belgium) where he is director of the laboratory "Ecology of Aquatic Systems". His research interests focus on the bacterial ecology of aquatic systems. He is also expert in health-related microbiology; in this topic, he studies the origin and fate of micro-organisms of sanitary interest in aquatic systems and in wastewater treatment plants. He is also an expert in microbiology of drinking water treatment and distribution.

Thierry Terret is a former Professor in sport history at the University of Lyon and rector of Britannia Region. He works now as a Ministerial Delegate for the Olympic and Paralympic Games for the French Government. His main research focuses on sport and gender, politics and transculturalism. He has published 65 books and hundreds of papers at national and international levels, with a particular interest for the mega-events such as the Olympic Games.

Etienne de Vanssay, is doctor in chemistry of atmospheric pollution and environmental physics and the founding manager of Rincent Air – Cap Environnement sarl. He has over 20 years of experience in the field of air quality and pollutant metrology (research & studies). In 2009, Etienne de Vanssay impelled the creation of the inter-professional federation of trades in the atmospheric environment, FIMEA, of which he is the founding president.

Dr Sébastien Wurtzer is an expert virologist at Eau de Paris (Ivry, France) specialized in the evaluation of the sanitary risk associated with water consumption. He is interested in the fate and diversity of enteric viruses in surface waters as well as in the distribution systems and treatment plants for drinking water.

Sylvain Zeghni (sylvain.zeghni@u-pem.fr) is an Associate Professor at the Université Paris-Est Marne-la-Vallée. His recent research focuses on smart destination governance. He is studying the attractiveness of destinations, focusing on the role of institutions, networks, clusters, and tourist mobility. He is examining the way a destination may develop through tourism. In particular, his work is directed towards tourism clusters, the process that paved the way to clustering (the cauterization process), and stakeholders' involvements. He is in charge of the Destination Management stream of the Master's Degree in Tourism Studies at the Université Paris-Est Marne-la-Vallée. He is an active member of the "Cluster de Tourisme Paris Val d'Europe". He belongs to the LVMT research team.

Dr Geneviève Zembri-Mary (genevieve.zembri-mary@u-cergy.fr) is senior lecturer at the Université de Cergy-Pontoise (Greater Paris), where she created and directs the Master in Transport Studies course. Within the MRTE research centre, her European comparative research in urban studies focuses on uncertainty in urban projects planning and design (housing, sports, leisure, business, transport projects). She holds a PhD from the École nationale des ponts et chaussées and a Habilitation Thesis in Urban Studies from the University of Lille 1.

Foreword: building the Olympic legacy for Paris 2024

Thierry Terret, Ministerial Delegate for the Olympic and Paralympic Games

It is nowadays obvious that the organization of the Olympic Games produces effects that go far beyond the limits of the host-city as their numerous consequences go beyond the few days during which the Games take place. The impacts of the Olympic events are at once local, national and international. Some are expected and even anticipated, others, on the contrary, are unexpected.[1] Such consequences can be positive or negative depending on the position of the observer. A significant impact on local tourism in a region hosting the Games may cause, for instance, a decrease in tourist attendance in a nearby area.

Within the international Olympic community 'legacy' focuses rather on the economic and infrastructural consequences of the Olympic Games, while 'heritage' may embrace a wider perimeter including the expected effects of the Olympic event and bringing together material, immaterial and memorial dimensions. Both concepts are however steadily used on an equal level since the International Olympic Committee adopted a clear strategy in this area and imposed the heritage question as a compulsory part of the applications expected from candidate cities.

Olympic legacy: a long-term and strategic issue

Since the first Games of the modern era in 1896, none of the Olympic events escaped from the explicit identification of diverse expectations by the host cities and the host nations. Yet these expectations noticeably mirror the particular local, national and international context of the time and obviously interfere in the priorities of the decision makers, as witnessed in the latest French Olympic experiences.

As an example, the Olympic Games of Paris in 1924 were presented by their organizers and promotors as a tool for the development of sports in France, but they were actually deeply shaped by the political, socio-economic and cultural issues of the previous years following the Great War.[2] The Winter Games of Chamonix in 1924 and Grenoble in 1968 were seen as an opportunity to develop the winter sports resorts, a way to better perform in the international race for the best equipment technologies and a matter of national prestige. As for the Games in Albertville in 1992, many expectations were expressed in sports, environmental, industrial and cultural fields beyond the given challenge of ending the geographical isolation of the Tarentaise region which dominated in official speeches.[3]

A few years later, the International Olympic Committee tried to give a more ethical orientation to such goals. It launched an internal reflection on the question of legacy, which lead to the first appearance of the concept, yet little detailed, in the Olympic Charter in 2003. It became then one of the fundamental principles of the IOC to "take measures to promote a positive legacy from the Olympic Games to the host city and the host country, including a reasonable control of the size and cost of the Olympic Games, and encourage the Organizing Committees of the Olympic Games (OCOGs), public authorities in the host country and the persons or organizations belonging to the Olympic Movement to act accordingly".[4]

The need for the candidate cities to reflect on legacy during the biding process soon obliged the IOC to clarify its own conception in a document entirely dedicated to this issue and unambiguously entitled *Olympic Legacy.*[5] The text clearly recalled the full responsibility of the organizers of the Games: "To take full advantage of the opportunities that the Games can provide, a potential host city must have a strong vision and clear objectives of what the Olympic Games, and even bidding, can do to for its citizens, city and country".[6]

The IOC thus defined five main aspects of the "positive legacy" that host cities must plan before the Games themselves.[7] At sport level, the potential benefit on infrastructures and facilities was listed. The development of sport practice was of course strongly expected, both in clubs and schools, together with the launching of training programs of sport supervision. At social level, the legacy of the Games was reflected in terms of strengthening collective cohesion, enhancing national culture, integrating the values of Olympism – excellence, friendship, respect – through education, and promoting new and more cooperative approaches in working environment. As for the environmental front, it was expected that the Games would have an impact on the revitalization of urban areas, on the introduction of greener transport, and on a better control of energy expenditure and environmental protection. At urban level, the Games must be able to change the image of the host cities, enrich and modernize their infrastructures, and better integrate the issues of mobility. Finally, in economic terms, an impact on businesses would be all the more significant as it was anticipated and supported both locally and nationally. Effects of the Games on tourist attractiveness within the organizing city, or even at a national level were to be considered. One year after this publication, in 2014, the IOC placed the legacy issue high on its roadmap, known as the Olympic Agenda 2020.

The IOC's Committee on Sustainability and Legacy, now composed of 29 members and chaired by Prince Albert II of Monaco, defined the concept of legacy in 2014: "The Olympic legacy is the result of a vision. It includes all long-term tangible and intangible benefits initiated or accelerated by the

holding of the Olympic Games/sporting events for individuals, cities/terri-
tories and the Olympic Movement."[8] At the same time the IOC set a roadmap for Candidate Cities detailed in four goals.

The first issue concerns the integration of legacy into the Olympic Games
lifecycle, which must be discussed with the Candidate Cities and should also
be included in all the decision-making processes which relate to the Games.
The planning and delivery of legacy are monitored in a transparent manner
and regulatory measures can be proposed. Legacy governance needs to be
operational early in the life cycle, be independent of policy change and rely on
long-term funding. The second issue is to document, analyse and commu-
nicate on the legacy of the Olympic Games. The third issue questions the way
to value the legacy whereas the last one finally emphasizes the necessary
establishment of strategic partnerships

The educative legacy for Paris 2024: the engagements of the French State

For 2024 the candidacy of Paris took place at a time when, for the Olympic
community, the Games could no longer be conceived without a thorough and
anticipated reflection on the control of short- and long-term benefits.[9] The
principle was integrated by all concerned people in the making of the bid, from
sports movement and communities to State, private actors and all stakeholders.

For the French State the framework of the legacy was set up in March
2017, i.e. six months before the vote of the IOC to design the organizing city
for 2024 and right in the middle of the national program called "Year of
Olympism from School to University", which was developed in schools
during the year 2016–2017. In a document co-authored by all the ministries
most directly concerned by the Games, 24 measures were then specified
around six major thematic areas: youth/education/culture; health/disability;
social insertion/employment; gender equality; sport and territories; environmental excellence.[10] National Education was concerned by several of these 24
commitments, including especially the creation of a label for schools and universities called "Generation 2024", and the development of more continuity
between sport in schools and universities and sport in clubs.

On September 27, 2017, on the occasion of the National School Sport Day,
the French Minister of Education Jean-Michel Blanquer relied heavily on this
framework document to set a series of seven measures constituting the Horizon 2024 National Education Program: Appointment of a National delegate
for the Olympic and Paralympic Games 2024, creation of a label "Generation
2024" to develop bridges between the school world and the sports movement,
implementation of sports associations in primary schools, creation of sports
sections and classes with arranged schedules for sport, creation of vocational
training courses targeting the sport market, hosting international school
sports events, and preparing 10,000 additional young sports officials through
the action of the National School Sport Union by 2024.

The objectives pursued through these various measures concern at the same time the school system and the Olympic and Paralympic Games themselves. On the one hand it is expected to strengthen the links between schools and sport clubs by managing on four levels: school sports, arrangements for young talents (Sports Sections, special classes), official agreements between the schools and clubs and between the State and the sport bodies, and implementation of vocational training course for the sport market. On the other hand, the measures are also thought to contribute to increasing the popular success of the Olympic and Paralympic Games in 2024.

The Horizon 2024 program is based on the annual highlights of the June 23rd Olympic Day, the National School Sport Day in September, and the annual Olympic and Paralympic Week in January, which already succeeded in the 2017 and 2018 editions with tens of thousands of pupils. However, the program is intended to settle a long-term dynamic beyond one-off events.

It also includes Higher Education and universities. Thus, reflecting on the legacy of the Olympic and Paralympic Games 2024 concerns primarily the students' life, with an expected effect in the increase of their sport participation. A label for higher education institutions and universities was launched in September 2018 in order to support the efforts made locally to enhance the students' participation in sport and the adaptation of curricula for the sport elite. The objectives also relate to the complex issue of the lack of coherence between the training courses aiming at sport professions concurrently proposed by different French ministries. Finally, the legacy program expands to the research area in sport science, especially for the high potential of new knowledge in elite sport, with the idea of better structuring and financing such researches at a national level.

The Horizon 2024 program is currently in its first stage, obliging the many partners of the Olympic adventure to learn to work together with a common stake: valuing what will remain in the aftermath of the Games.

Notes

1 J.A. Mangan, Marc Dyreson (eds), *Olympic Legacies: Intended and Unintended Political, Cultural, Economic, Educational*, London, Taylor & Francis, 2009.
2 Thierry Terret (ed.), *Les paris des Jeux olympiques de 1924*, Biarritz, Atlantica, 2008, especially the chapter « Les paris des Jeux de 1924 dans la France de l'après-guerre : contexte, attentes et effets », 9–28.
3 W. Andreff (ed.), *Les effets d'entraînement des Jeux olympiques d'Albertville*, Rapport au CNRS, PPSH 15, 1993; T. Terret (2008). The Albertville Winter Olympics: unexpected legacies-failed expectations for regional economic development, in *The International Journal of the History of Sport*, 25(14), 2079–2097.
4 International Olympic Committee, *Olympic Charter. In force as from 4 July 2003*, Lausanne, IOC, 2003.
5 International Olympic Committee, *Olympic Legacy*, Lausanne, IOC, 2013.
6 International Olympic Committee, *Olympic Legacy*, Lausanne, IOC, 2013, p. 6.
7 Since 2013 other long-term benefits were added relating especially to networks and innovation and to culture and creative development.

8 IOC, *Legacy Strategic Approach. Moving Forward*, Lausanne, IOC, December 2017.
9 In October 2008 the French national Olympic committee already used a national selection process for the French candidate cities, which explicitly included a part on "the legacy for sport and the promotion of Olympic values".
10 Ministère de la Ville, de la Jeunesse et des Sports, *Le sport au service de la société*, Paris, March 2017.

Acknowledgements

The editors wish to thank Université Paris-Est Marne-la-Vallée, the Urban Futures LabEx (laboratory of excellence) and I-SITE FUTURE (Université Paris-Est) for funding the conference that gave rise to these selected papers.

Introduction

Lessons from the past to understand the future of the Games

Marie Delaplace and Pierre-Olaf Schut

Seven, then five, and then one. This is the number of cities that applied to host the Summer Olympics during the latest allocations between 2016 and 2028. Today, some authors are wondering about the unpopularity of the Games (Scheu & Preuss, 2018) and the resulting candidacy crisis. Why is that so? The first cause mentioned is the gigantism of the Olympic Games. The specifications of the most-watched international event – the opening ceremonies of the Beijing and Sochi Games both exceeded one billion viewers – are very demanding. In addition to world-class sports facilities for the 34 disciplines (the number of events selected for Tokyo 2020), the organizers must be able to offer an international airport and several thousand hotel rooms. They are also directly responsible for hosting the 11,000 athletes (Rio 2016 figures), officials and journalists. Accepting this impressive set of criteria is already an important commitment. But gigantism goes further. The audience brought by the event encourages communities to further extend the expense to demonstrate to the whole world the modernity of their territory and generate more attractiveness at an international level. At this point, the investment turns out to be extremely high.

The application phase itself is already a large-scale project. Cities invest several tens of millions of euros (36 million for Paris 2024) to meet their goals, accepting the risk that their application may not succeed. As a result, today most of the submissions come from the world's largest cities: Sydney, London, Beijing, Rio, Paris, Los Angeles – the only ones capable of making such a commitment.

Some geopolitical factors have contributed to bring the Games to the level they have reached. Indeed, the BRIC countries (Brazil, Russia, India, China), driven by strong economic growth and seeking international recognition, have been candidates in the organization of many major international sporting events including the Olympic Games (Hiller, 2000). Between 2008 and 2022, four editions of the Olympic Games were or will be held in these countries. The economic situation that changed abruptly after the financial crisis of 2008 has considerably slowed down these initiatives.

Today, the host cities are weighing the relevance of this commitment (Guala, 2009). The economic context is not always favourable. Revisions of public policies are reducing the investment of communities and/or the state, and public debts are weighing heavily on taxation. Few cities can afford to embark on the Olympic adventure or want to go down that road given the financial weight of the commitment.

Public investment inevitably means an almost direct cost to the population (Zimbalist, 2016). Currently, local people are likely to follow one of three scenarios: most of them will watch the show via television or streaming services; many of them are not interested in the event; and only a small minority will go to the stadiums to attend the live events. For most of the population, there is no added value when the competitions take place a few kilometres from their home because they will follow them on their screen anyway, as if the event were being held on the other side of the world. However, these same people will have to participate in the financial effort of their country and suffer the nuisance caused by the organization of the event such as the restricted use of the Olympic avenues due to the mobility of athletes, media and officials. The discontent of the population is understandable, so the commitment to a candidacy represents a significant risk to which politicians expose themselves at the expense of their careers.

The purpose of this book is to illuminate these complex situations through various contributions concerned with the many issues underlying the hosting of the Olympic and Paralympic Games. In a resolutely multidisciplinary approach, the authors shed light on the controversies that take place from the very first stage: the application phase. Why apply? Is the initiative supported by the local population, and will the citizens actually benefit from it? Many cities seize the opportunity of hosting the Olympic and Paralympic Games to develop an urban project or boost their tourist activity. Here again, the impact of the event is questioned. Would the urban project not have taken place without the Games? And what benefits can be expected from a touristic point of view when the host city is already an attractive tourist destination? Lastly, this book underlines the fact that nowadays, hosting the Olympic and Paralympic Games is contingent upon sustainability and an environmentally friendly strategy. Henceforth, host cities are challenging themselves to take a further step in their environmental policy despite the difficulties that may arise as a result of climatic factors.

Based on critical examination, the authors highlight the issues, controversies and risks facing cities that host the Olympic and Paralympic Games. This reflection is steadfastly oriented towards the next Olympics and seeks to elicit the vigilance and caution of organizers of the Games. It also opens up research topics that are likely to arouse the interest of the academic world.

In the first part of this book, three papers deal with the issue of hosting Olympic Games and the debates the bidding process has induced in cities in recent years.

The first chapter, written by Nathalie Fabry and Sylvain Zeghni of Paris-Est-Marne-la-Vallée University, tries to explain the reasons why cities withdraw from hosting Olympic Games. By adopting a stakeholder's point of view, and using extensive literature surveys and a media corpus concerning host cities, the authors underline that the main reason for this is linked to local stakeholders' (politicians' and inhabitants') fears of increases in cost and the lack of certainty surrounding the benefits, and more broadly, the legacy of hosting the Games. They argue that long-term projects and a more inclusive urban policy are required to foster the sustainable development of host cities.

Chapter 2 written by Harry H. Hiller of the University of Calgary, also seeks to explain why the Olympics are under attack and, more specifically why there is a battle for public opinion in host cities. By producing a sociological analysis of the battleground for public opinion resulting from conflicts between different actors – and emerging ones in particular – at the local level, the author underlines the differences that can exist between expectations, experiences and outcomes of the Games. Based on a literature review and on his numerous articles and books on Olympic Games, Hiller identifies eight factors that impact local public opinion regarding the hosting of the Olympics, before, during and after the Games.

In Chapter 3, Anna Kobierecka and Michał Marcin Kobierecki of the University of Łódź, argue that, like state actors, the International Olympic Committee (IOC) is an actor that conducts its own public diplomacy in a context where the size of the event and the huge associated costs, induce various debates in host cities. By promoting sustainable development and the positive legacy of Olympic Games in these cities, the IOC is perceived as a driving force for these "good changes". But in doing so, it can also satisfy its own interests linked to the positive values of Olympism (such as respect, tolerance, integration and human rights).

In the second part of the book, four chapters raise the issue of Olympic Games as a tool for urban and territorial development.

In Chapter 4, José Chaboche and Alain Schoeny of the University of Orléans, France, conduct an explorative analysis of geographical, planning-related and managerial research concerning the Summer Olympics. In analysing 434 articles published in scientific journals from 1984 to September 2018, they have produced an invaluable database on this topic, organized around four research axes concerning first, the attraction, production and evaluation of the Summer Olympic Games; second, the urban project linked to these Games; third, the sports tourism dimension and the Games; and last, their territorial legacies. This database, if regularly updated by the scientific community, will serve as a form of legacy concerning Olympic research in these fields.

In Chapter 5, Pierre-Olaf Schut of Paris-Est-Marne-la-Vallée University, specifically stresses the challenges of candidacy, in particular when submission fails. Taking as an example the city of Paris, which went through two rejections in 2008 and 2012 before being accepted for the 2024 Olympics, he shows what strategies are implemented to develop world-class sports facilities. Examples of implementation reveal that the realization of a project relies on contingencies and political support. The completion of the constructions envisaged during the application phase only succeeds if these particular conditions are met. Indeed, the process provides important political support which can be of great help, but is not sufficient if this support is not carried on during and especially beyond the candidacy period by the contracting authorities directly concerned. Hence, this chapter underlines the limitations of the application system which should be part of a coherent territorial project to be continued independent of the IOC decision.

In Chapter 6, Geneviève Zembri and Cécile Doustaly of Cergy-Pontoise University present the role of heritagization in managing the uncertainties linked to major events and urban megaprojects by comparing the cases of London (2012) and Athens (2004). They argue that, from the conception of an Olympic site project to its legacy, there are numerous uncertainties that can be managed by heritagization which may be tangible or intangible, heritagization being a process of classification, preservation and enhancement of environmental, urban, historical or archaeological heritage.

In the last chapter of this second part, focusing on tourism, Marie Delaplace, of Paris-Est-Marne-la-Vallée University, underlines the heterogeneity of the relationship between Olympic Games and tourism, by suggesting a place-based approach. Through a review of the literature, she highlights the fact that, contrary to expectations in host cities, both leisure tourism and business tourism can decrease during the Games owing to a crowding out effect. Moreover, there is sometimes a substitution effect concerning spending. But both these effects are not systematic: they vary according to place. With this in mind, and following on from recent literature in regional science, she argues that the interactions between Olympic Games and tourism are likely to be place-based, however she asserts that this place-based approach must be analysed not just on a city-by-city basis but also at different scales and in particular at a micro-local scale.

The third part of the book raises a number of questions concerning risk, security and environmental issues.

In Chapter 8, Paul-Henri Richard, Patrick Laclémence and Guillaume Delatour of the University of Technology of Troyes, develop an analysis that aims to show that integrating public behaviours into operational responses to crisis situations is a way to improve the security of major events. Indeed, sporting mega-events like other types of mega-events can be targets for terrorists owing to the massive publicity such events provide. The authors show that the populations present are the first links in chains of assistance and solidarity, even though they are not professional. They show how important the integration of different populations can be not just in emergency preparedness but also during operational action in crisis situations.

In Chapter 9 written by Françoise Lucas, Bernard de Gouvello, Jean-Marie Mouchel, Laurent Moulin, Pierre Servais, Sébastien Wurtzer, the issue of a river's microbiological quality is raised, specifically the case of the River Seine. The question here is whether it is compatible with Olympic competitions in open waters as the triathlon and marathon swims are due to take place in the Seine during the Paris 2024 Olympics. The problem is that the microbiological quality of urban waters can quickly deteriorate, thus raising the issue of its safety for athletes. This study seeks to estimate the Seine's water upstream of Paris and within central Paris, by bringing together all current data on this subject. It shows that, for the moment, the microbial quality of the Seine does not conform to the required standards.

In Chapter 10, Gilles Foret, Matthias Beekmann, Olivier Ramalho, Martin Koning, Martial Haeffelin, Étienne de Vanssay, Rachel Nadif, Isabella Annesi-Maesano, Pietro Bernardara and Jean-David Bernard, who work for the Qi² research network on air quality in the Paris–Île-de-France region (officially recognized as an emerging key research sector, or *domaine d'intérêt majeur,* since 2016) present the main issues surrounding the Olympic Games and air quality. For the last 25 years, sustainability has been part of the debate concerning the Olympic and Paralympic Games. Host cities are often megalopolises with sometimes important air quality issues, as was the case in Beijing in 2008. This is also the case, to some extent, for Paris where pollution due to the high level of ozone and particulate matter is problematic. After addressing the question of air quality at certain previous Games and in the specific case of Paris, the authors present the Air Quality Research Action Plan for Paris 2024 by analysing different aspects of this issue such as mobility and traffic, air quality in Olympic arenas and facilities, the impact of air quality and how it affects city-dwellers.

Finally, Jean-Loup Chappelet concludes the book by demonstrating that the Olympic Games cannot be considered public–private partnerships (PPPs) between the different public (the host city, state authorities, etc.) and private bodies (the Organising Committee of the Olympic Games, the International Olympic Committee, etc.). Specifically, he shows that only the public partners take on the financial risks associated with the Olympic facilities that need to be built in the host city.

References

Guala, C. (2009). *To bid or not to bid: Public opinion before and after the Games. The case of the Turin 2006 Olympic Winter Games.* In J. Kenell, C. Bladen, E. Booth (eds.). *The Olympic Legacy People, Place, Enterprise.* Proceedings of the first annual conference on Olympic Legacy, University of Greenwich, 21–30.

Hiller, H. H. (2000). Mega-events, urban boosterism and growth strategies: An analysis of the objectives and legitimations of the Cape Town 2004 Olympic bid. *International Journal of Urban and Regional Research,* 24: 449–458. doi:10.1111/1468-2427.00256

Scheu, A. & Preuss, H. (2018). Residents' perceptions of mega sport event legacies and impacts. The case of the Hamburg 2024 Olympic bid. *German Journal of Exercise Sport Research,* 48: 376. doi:10.1007/s12662-018-0499-y

Zimbalist, A. (2016). *Circus Maximus: The Economic Gamble behind Hosting the Olympics and the World Cup.* Washington: Brookings Institution.

Part I

Some debates concerning hosting Olympic Games

1 Why do cities withdraw from hosting the Olympic Games?

Nathalie Fabry and Sylvain Zeghni

Introduction

The Olympic Games are events planned with long lead times, which belong to the category of *occasional mega-events* (Getz and Page, 2015) with high international visibility and high expectations about value creation. According to Persson (2002, p. 27) the Olympic Games are *big business*.

Academic literature is paying increasing attention to the Olympic Games because they are the subject of considerable social issues and tensions in the metropolises that organize and host them. Indeed, the political, economic and financial interests of both public authorities and private investors often strongly oppose those of local communities.

The authorities, keen to promote urban renewal projects, stress the positive repercussions rather than the considerable pressure on resources (workforce, land, infrastructure) that these mega-events can generate. Until recently, they decided and acted without prior consultation with residents.

The Olympic Games illustrate in an exemplary and empirical way the theory of *Right to the City*, developed by authors such as David Harvey (2008) or Manuel Castells (1983). According to these authors, the old industrial districts of most of the metropolis have undergone significant post-Fordist and post-modern transformations based on projects and events that are highly publicized, spectacular and ephemeral. These allow capital surpluses to rearrange urban environments by operating large amounts of expropriations and displacements of local populations. From Budapest to Rome, via Hamburg, Boston, Innsbruck, Oslo, and Munich, we have recently observed the rise of opposition movements against the Olympics, mostly because the Games are expected to confiscate space.

Because the official arguments in favour of the Olympic Games have received significant media coverage and very often the support of the citizens, anti-Olympic mobilizations have remained, until recently, unknown. This raises some interesting questions about the shaping of these mobilizations, the degree of the challenge, the actors involved, and the actions at stake.

The literature on the urban and geostrategic issues of the Olympic Games as a competitive mega-event reveals a lot of important controversies. Indeed, behind the apparent nobility of high-level sporting performance, which can pacify people and inspire the young, a considerable number of interests crystallize around the Olympic Games; thus, academic attention focuses on the dynamics of collaboration/protestation at various scales. The host city strengthens its image of a *world city* able to capture new global flows and, consequently, its territorial attractiveness in the context of exacerbated global competition.

Moreover, its ability to generate international consensus is fundamental. Also, some of the literature has focused on the political boycott of the Games and the Games' impact on diplomatic relations (Feizabadi et al., 2015; Monnin and Maillard, 2015). Others have shown how corruption and over-sponsoring by multinationals, using the Games to assert their commercial interests, might distort the Olympic ideal. One simply has to remember the famous Salt Lake City scandal in 1998 when the local organizing committee bribed the International Olympic Committee, and Atlanta, where the 1996 Olympics were nicknamed the *Coca-Cola Games* (Magdalinski et al., 2005) to be convinced that such a distortion is possible.

In other studies, authors stress the local aspect and, in particular, sub-urban relations. For example, Gursoy and Kendall (2006) have pointed out how consultation and prior buy-in of communities affect the success of the application. With regard to this same local dimension, other more critical views have emerged on the issues of social justice and the *right to the city* by showing that urban renewal projects, such as the Olympic Games, are essentially vehicles of property speculation and dispossession (Harvey, 2008; Soja, 1989). Local people may experience transgression of their most basic rights such as housing, or they can be subject to the exploitation and alienation of local labour.

In recent decades, some big cities have experienced rising and various urban social protests defending local population rights and making precise claims as a reaction against the processes of rehabilitation and gentrification of former industrial districts. David Harvey (2008) uses the concept of *militant particularisms* to refer to campaigns and struggles emanating from a particular urban area and likely to be expanded to other places, which ultimately gives them a much more global reach.

From a governance point of view, the primary challenge for the government is to defuse criticism of and resistance to the merits of this global sports event. Thus, the notion of legacy occupies a preponderant place in the construction of the discourse related to the Olympic imperative. It is not only a matter of the renovation of socio-economically disadvantaged neighbourhoods, but also a matter of the sustainability of the facilities to generate economic benefits in the medium or long term. This 'sustainable regeneration' is a relatively traditional perspective of legitimation based on local economic development.

The omnipresence of the concept of *legacy* should be emphasized in the debates, because the stakeholders are far from reaching a consensus on the idea. For example, a report from the London Assembly (2007) on the

Olympic legacies of Barcelona, Atlanta, Sydney, and Athens points out that actual costs and benefits are out of step with ex ante calculations. In terms of impact on employment in particular, the unemployed living near the Olympic Parks in the four cities studied did not experience an improvement in their situation after the Games.

Boston, Budapest, Hamburg, Rome, Innsbruck, Oslo, Munich, Krakow, Davos, and Calgary cancelled their Olympic bids recently for financial reasons, but also because of local protests and referenda. Politicians, inhabitants and, more generally, local stakeholders fear an increase in costs and doubt the benefits of hosting the mega-event. This raises interesting research questions: why do Olympic boosters not work and why is there no positive feedback relating to general claims about return on investment (ROI), impacts, and effects of mega-events in public opinion?

To answer this question, we first need to focus on the relevance of mega-events on local economic development. To understand the link between city and mega-events and to avoid simple balance accountancy, we will adopt a stakeholder's point of view and consider the place hosting a mega-event to be an ecosystem. Secondly, we will analyse some of the cities that withdrew from Olympic bids and analyse their motivations to do so. As history tells us, cities hosting Olympic Games never make money, because this event represents a significant financial risk. Among the reasons why these cities abandoned their Olympic commitments, we observed increased local protest, a deficit of a legacy of the Olympic Games; the demands of local stakeholders for more transparency; and a lack of involvement by local stakeholders. We will use extensive literature surveys and a media corpus (interviews, blogs, etc.) to deepen our understanding of the cities' withdrawals from the Olympics.

Olympic Games as a booster for the host city

First, we will focus on the way mega-events impact a host city. We will present, from a location point of view, the expected local benefits of hosting a mega-event. In a second point, we will adopt a stakeholder's point of view and consider the place hosting to be an ecosystem.

The expected local benefits of hosting mega-events

As Porter and Fletcher (2008) have noted, there is a gap between *ex ante predictions* of the economic impacts of the Olympic Games and the *ex post reality*. According to the OECD Local Employment and Economic Development Programme (OECD–LEED, 2010), the local benefits of hosting global events that 'might reasonably be expected but, of course, are not guaranteed' (OECD–LEED, 2010, p. 12), can be split into primary (short-term) and secondary (long-term) benefits.

The primary benefits of hosting global events

ALIGNMENT OF THE EVENT WITH SECTOR AND BUSINESS GROWTH STRATEGIES IN THE CITY OR NATION

The requirements of the event can be used to catalyse existing development and growth strategies, either at sector, business or city level. Effective management of the event in this manner yields significant benefits for cities looking to prioritize and accelerate their development goals.

PRIVATE–PUBLIC INVESTMENT PARTNERSHIPS

Increased co-operation, in the form of partnerships, between the private and public sector are increasingly seen as a key means by which to achieve development goals. The costs and benefits often associated with global events present ideal opportunities for public–private investment partnerships that can serve wider urban development goals.

IMAGE AND IDENTITY IMPACTS ATTRACTING INCREASED POPULATION, INVESTMENT, OR TRADE

The media exposure associated with a global event provides an ideal opportunity for the promotion of a city brand or identity. In an increasingly urban world, the need to differentiate is ever-greater and opportunities to embed a city's unique assets in the 'International imagination' are valuable.

STRUCTURAL EXPANSION OF VISITOR ECONOMY AND SUPPLY CHAIN DEVELOPMENT AND EXPANSION

Visitors coming to the city for the event will contribute to a more buoyant visitor economy with money they spend causing a multiplier effect on incomes throughout related supply chains. Well-managed events can attempt to focus this multiplier effect on local businesses and supply chains can therefore develop and expand to take advantage of increased business.

ENVIRONMENTAL IMPACTS, BOTH IN BUILT AND NATURAL ENVIRONMENTS

Both the built and the natural environment can greatly benefit from the investment and strategic planning involved in hosting a global event. With global attention turning on a city with the arrival of the event, city authorities can justify using funds to carry out much-needed, but perhaps not previously top-priority work on the built environment to give it a good facelift. Increasingly, ensuring the event is managed in an environmentally conscious manner is becoming a higher priority in terms of city branding as well. Not only can this reduce the environmental impact of the event itself, but it can have wider benefits in changing business and social practices throughout the city and its region which last far beyond the event itself.

The secondary benefits of hosting global events

POST-EVENT USAGES OF IMPROVED LAND AND BUILDINGS

Events may require land and buildings for specific purposes, but their use after the event is only restricted by practicalities and the imagination of the designers and planners. New buildings or land reclamations that subsequently serve local communities and contribute to urban development strategies can transform cityscapes.

CONNECTIVITY AND INFRASTRUCTURE LEGACIES

Transport links and other infrastructures constructed for the event are one of the most visible lasting legacies for a host city and can have real impacts on social inclusion if targeted at previously excluded groups.

LABOUR MARKET IMPACTS AND SOCIAL/ECONOMIC INCLUSION

Hosting a global event stimulates significant temporary employment to prepare for such a large undertaking, but can also generate long-term employment if the event is used to expand business sectors and implement structural change in the local economy. Specific efforts can be made to use the temporary employment created to provide qualifications for low-skilled workers who can then go on to find better employment, thus contributing to social and economic inclusion through processes of cyclical uplift.

SECONDARY IMPACT IN THE PROPERTY MARKET

Property prices are very likely to be affected in parts of a city where construction is focussed for a particular event. While this can lead to the gentrification of a district, attracting further investment and leading to the development of an area, it can also force existing, lower-income communities out. A strategic balance must be sought to optimize the local benefits.

GLOBAL POSITIONING, EVENT STRATEGY GOING FORWARD, AND PROJECT MANAGEMENT CAPABILITY

Hosting, or even bidding for an event dramatically increases the capabilities of the city authorities to manage similar projects in the future and makes vital steps towards furthering an events strategy and achieving development goals. Improvements in collaborative governance and co-ordination are fundamental elements of this process. A city with experience of hosting events is naturally held in higher esteem if there are any doubts about a competing candidate city. In an increasingly competitive urban world, having such experience can make all the difference.

Source: OECD–LEED (2010, pp. 12–13)

An Olympic bid may be a catalyst for urban development, as the *Barcelona Model* has shown. Even in the case of failed bids, the catalyst effect may be important, as was the case of Paris 2012. This failed bid permitted the development of the *Grand Paris Project* by a new government, which saw the metropolis develop an efficient transport network and an urban renovation program. A bid is also an occasion to imagine a new form of governance for the public authorities by developing a PPP (Public–Private Partnership), and a new dialogue with the local community. Finally, bids may be policy experiments in various domains such as green development, smart technology, pro-poor development, and industrial renewal, by financing micro projects and developing social unity. Except for an increase in notoriety and improved international image, results are never guaranteed in the short term nor in the long run (Chappelet, 2016).

Complex balance: The stakeholder's ecosystem

As Freeman (1984, p. 46) writes 'Stakeholders are all those individuals, groups, and/or organizations that influence or are influenced by the actions of the focal organization'. In the case of the Olympic Games, we may distinguish between internal stakeholders (International Olympic Committee, local organizing committee) and external stakeholders (government, community, sponsors, media, sports federation, international delegations).

All these stakeholder groups are essential in the planning and hosting of the Olympic Games. However, the relative importance of the different stakeholder groups depends on the exact issue at hand and managerial perspectives (Mitchell and Fergusson, 2015; Parent, 2008, 2010). These stakeholders expect a tangible or intangible return on investment (Levy and Berger, 2013; Matheson, 2008, 2009). Organizing the Olympic Games is context-dependent and also stakeholder-dependent (Burton, 2003). The number of stakeholders and their expectations may be different in each phase of the project (Kassens-Noor and Lauermann, 2017). According to Parent (2013, p. 33), the local organizing committee 'should not only understand the needs and wants of the stakeholders when dealing with them, but also how to create value for the stakeholder'.

Why not host the Olympic Games? Two emerging challenges

As Oliver and Lauerman (2017) suggest, the anti-bid contest has dramatically changed in the last few years. Before the 2022 and 2024 host cities' election campaign, protests took place during the Games and were organized by pre-existing activist groups mainly dealing with political and human rights causes

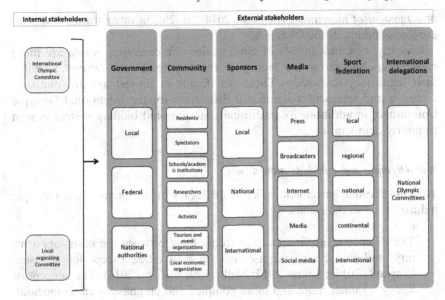

Figure 1.1 The main stakeholders of an Olympic bid

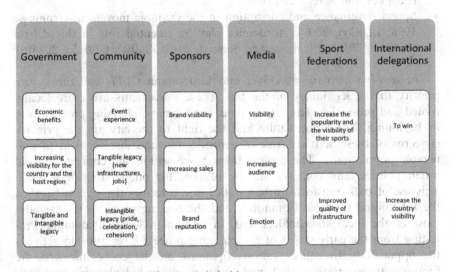

Figure 1.2 Example of ROI for the stakeholders

('black power' salutes at the 1968 Games, boycotts – Cold War, anti-apartheid movement, Tibetan nationalist protests during Beijing 2008 – or over-sponsoring at London 2012). The huge media interest was leveraged not to protest against the Olympics, but to protest another concern. The Games were seen as a temporary *platform for protesting other issues* (Oliver and Lauermann, 2017, p. 131) or a *moment of movements* (Boykoff, 2014a, p. 26). In other words, it was an exogenous protest of the Olympics.

Recently, new movements of contestation are emerging, which are more endogenous and stress the legacy of the Olympics (*anti-Olympic*) and/or their legitimacy (*anti-bids*). These two forms of protest are not mutually exclusive and represent a significant disruption for the Intentional Olympic Committee; in addition, its traditional international bidding system is seen as poorly democratic.

Anti-Olympic and anti-bids movements

The *anti-Olympic* movement criticizes the legacy of the international Olympic industry for two main reasons:

- The absence of explicit and rewarding links between the costs, opportunity, and impacts of mega-events on host cities, except for sponsors (Boykoff, 2014a; Louw, 2012; Müller, 2015; Zirin, 2014). The concept of legacy becomes more and more complex and emphasizes environmental, informational, educational, sustainable or regional planning benefits (Leopkey and Parent, 2012).
- Sports governance and corruption in the Olympic movement (Jennings, 1996; Lenskyj, 2008). Academics play an essential role in this debate (Boykoff, 2014b; Flyvbjerg and Stewart, 2012; Zimbalist, 2015a, 2015b).

The *anti-bid activists*, as Oliver and Lauermann (2017) call them, give priority to the legitimacy of the bid. These movements are more locally rooted and pro-active. They try to deter the Olympic planning process from its beginning. The urban future and the right to the city are the primary concerns of these activists (risk of gentrification and displacement of vulnerable populations). The protest takes place within the context of local urban politics, and contests the use of bids for public decision-making. This use of bids transforms urban policy into a technical program between the Intentional Olympic Committee and the hosting place, which excludes most of the local stakeholders and, in particular, local inhabitants. Protesting from the early stages of the planning process gives anti-bid activists the opportunity to collect various opinions on the costs, infrastructure (housing, transportation, etc.), and transparency in bid planning and budgeting; fears about cost overruns and the use of public funds; and the risk of tax increases (Billing and Holladay, 2012).

The *anti-bid* movement has experienced bid cancellations and political victories. The activists are not against the Olympic Games organization, but they are against wasting public funds and cost overruns. They are a counter-power asking for adjustments from bid planners, such as realistic cost projections and impact assessments to avoid cost overruns and optimize the future Olympic venues.

Application: Winter 2022 and Summer 2024 Olympic bids

Sample

Eight towns withdrew from their Olympic bids recently, either for Winter 2022 or Summer 2024. With the exception of Boston (USA), the cities (Budapest, Davos, Krakow, Hamburg, Munich, Oslo, Rome) are located in Europe.

Methodology

Using a second-hand data analysis research method, we did an extensive but not exhaustive compilation of resources based on academic journals, international institution reports, press releases, and the Internet, to collect examples of withdrawal, opinions, and results of referenda. The keywords we used to collect papers were '*Olympic bids* for the period 2003–2018'; we only selected papers in English with full content access. Reports freely available on the Internet came from international institutions such as the OECD. We also explored some activist movement websites, such as No Boston 2024.[1]

Results

The results we present here are derived from the aforementioned material and helped us, through data analysis, to put forward the following main results which need to be explored further. Eight towns withdrew from Olympic bids recently, either for Winter 2022 or Summer 2024, after referenda (Krakow, Davos, Munich, Hamburg), political concerns (Oslo and Roma), or local protests (Boston and Budapest) as Table 1.1 shows.

The main criticisms are linked to the financial dimension of the Olympic Games' organization. Table 1.2 presents the main Olympic bid criticisms from local stakeholders for each city.

The candidature process to host the Olympic Games is a long procedure divided into three steps: application, candidature, and final selections.

- *The application period.* Cities first declare their initial interest in hosting the Olympic Games. Each National Olympic Committee selects one national applicant city. The applicant city submits an application form (mini bid book) to the International Olympic Committee board and, finally, the committee selects a panel of candidate cities in the world.
- *The candidature period.* The candidate cities submit an application form (bid book) to the International Olympic Committee.
- *The final selection.* International Olympic Committee members elect the host city from the candidate cities.

Table 1.1 Withdrawals from Olympic bids

	Towns	Country	Year of withdrawing	As a result of	Leading movement
Winter 2022	Krakow	Poland	2014	Referendum	Krakow against the Games – anti-bids
	Davos	Switzerland	2013	Referendum	–
	Munich	Germany	2013	Referendum	No Olympia Munich – anti-bids
	Oslo	Norway	2014	Political concern	–
Summer 2024	Boston	USA	2015	Local protest (parallel protests)	No Boston Olympics
					No Boston 2024 – anti-bids
	Budapest	Hungary	2017	Local protest & political concern	Momentum – anti-bid group transformed into political party
	Hamburg	Germany	2015	Referendum	No Olympia Hamburg – anti-bids
	Roma	Italia	2016	Political concern	Five Star movement, mayoral campaign

Source: Authors

Table 1.2 Main Olympic bid criticisms by country

(X) Olympic bid criticism from local stakeholders	Boston	Budapest	Davos	Hamburg	Krakow	Munich	Oslo	Rome	Stockholm
Lack of transparency	X			X	X				
Use of public funds/opportunity cost of hosting	X	X	X		X	X		X	X
Lack of government guarantees on project risks	X		X	X		X	X		
Fear of cost overrun/increasing debt	X		X	X	X				
A democratic choice by local stakeholders		X							
Environmental concerns			X	X		X			
Unsuitable infrastructures	X	X		X	X				

Sources: Bakkenbüll and Dilger (2016), Dempsey and Zimbalist (2017), Hippke and Krieger (2015), Könecke and de Nooij (2017), and Oliver and Lauermann (2017), but also English language newspapers, mega-event industry trade journals, press releases from cities, bid corporations, and activist groups (web pages, blogs, books, etc.).

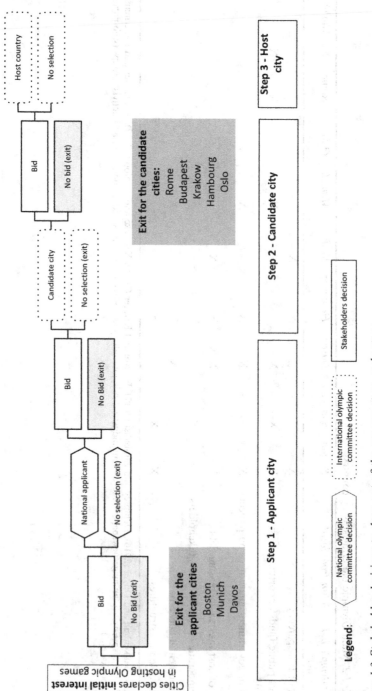

Figure 1.3 Stakeholder decisions to drop out of the process at an early stage

Stakeholders may decide to drop out of the process at an early stage of the candidature process, often at the first step before being nominated as applicant city or during the second stage, once nominated as a candidate city (Figure 1.3).

Conclusion

Olympic boosters do not automatically work and general claims about return on investment, impacts, and effects of mega-events have less and less positive impact on public opinion. Politicians, inhabitants, and, more generally, local stakeholders, fear an increase in costs and doubt the benefits of hosting a mega-event such as the Olympic Games. Hosting the Olympic Games is no longer a priority for most cities, even the richest and wealthiest. Recent referenda about the 2026 Winter Olympic Games seem to confirm this trend. After Graz (Austria), Sapporo (Japan), and Sion (Switzerland), Calgary (Canada) withdrew in December 2018 despite the project's plan to re-use the 1988 Olympic Games infrastructures to reduce costs.

If the International Olympic Committee wants to avoid a shortage of candidate cities able to host the Olympic Games in the future, it will need to take into account the new expectations of local stakeholders (Müller, 2015). Could this be the end of the traditional policy (one shot) and the beginning of a more inclusive urban policy? Without a long-term vision, the Olympic Games rely on solutions from the past. Olympic Games wisely based on realistic long-term projects which are useful for the sustainable development of cities may be a solution.

Note

1 https://www.noboston2024.org

References

Bakkenbüll, L-B. and Dilger, A. (2016). Willingness to pay and accept for hosting Olympic Games in Germany. Discussion Paper n°11/2016, Institute for Organisational Economics, Westfälische Wilhelms-Universität, Munster.

Billing, S. and Holladay, J-S. (2012). Should cities go for the gold? The long-term impacts of hosting the Olympics. *Economic Inquiry*, 50(3), 754–772.

Boykoff, J. (2014a). *Activism and the Olympics: Dissent at the Games in Vancouver and London*. New Brunswick, NJ: Rutgers University Press.

Boykoff, J. (2014b). *Celebration Capitalism and the Olympic Games*. London: Routledge.

Burton, R. (2003). Olympic Games host city marketing: An exploration of expectations and outcomes. *Sports Marketing Quarterly*, 12(1), 37–47.

Castells, M. (1983). *The City and the Grassroots: A Cross-cultural Theory of Urban Social Movements*. Berkeley: University of California Press.

Chappelet, J-L. (2016). *Jeux Olympiques, Raviver la Flamme*, Lausanne: Presses Polytechniques et Universtaires Romandes, Collection Opinion, p. 139.

Dempsey, C. and Zimbalist, A. (2017). *No Boston Olympics: How and Why Smart Cities Are Passing on the Torch*. ForeEdge Publisher: University Press of New England, p. 232.

Feizabadi, M-S., Delgado, F., Khabiri, M., Sajjadi, N. and Alidosut, E. (2015). Olympic Movement or Diplomatic Movement? The role of Olympic Games on development of international relations, *Journal of Sport Science*, 3(4), 186–194.

Flyvbjerg, B. and Stewart, A. (2012). Olympic proportions: Cost and cost overrun at the Olympics 1960–2012, Saïd Business School Working Papers, University of Oxford, June, https://papers.ssrn.com/sol3/papers.cfm?abstract_id=2238053.

Freeman, R.E. (1984). *Strategic Management: A Stakeholder Approach*. Boston, MA: Pitman.

Getz, D. and Page, S.J. (2015). Progress and prospects for event tourism research. *Tourism Management*, doi:10.1016/j.tourman.2015.03.007

Gursoy, D. and Kendall, W. (2006). Hosting mega events: Modeling locals' support. *Annals of Tourism Research*, 33(3), 603–623.

Harvey, D. (2008). The right to the city, *New Left Review*, 53, 23–40.

Hippke, A. and Krieger, J. (2015). Public opposition against the Olympic Games: Challenges and considerations in light of Hamburg's 2024 Olympic bid. *Journal of Qualitative Research in Sports Studies*, 9(1), 163–176.

Jennings, A. (1996). *The Lords of the Rings: Power, Money and Drugs in the Modern Olympics*. New York, NY: Simon & Schuster.

Kassens-Noor, E. and Lauermann, J. (2017). How to bid better for the Olympics: A participatory mega-event planning strategy for local legacies. *Journal of the American Planning Association*, 83(4), 335–345.

Könecke, T. and de Nooij, M. (2017). The IOC and Olympic bids from democracies and authoritarian regimes – A socioeconomic analysis and strategic insights. *Current Issues in Sport Science*, 2(9), 1–10. doi:10.15203/CISS_2017.009

Lenskyj, H. (2008). *Olympic Industry Resistance: Challenging Olympic Power and Propaganda*. Albany, NY: State University of New York Press.

Leopkey, B. and Parent, M. (2012). Olympic Games legacy: From general benefits to sustainable long-term legacy. *The International Journal of the History of Sport*, 29 (6), 924–943. doi:10.1080/09523367.2011.623006

Levy, B. and Berger, P. (2013). On the financial advantage of hosting the Olympics, *International Journal of Humanities and Social Science*, 3(1), 11–20.

London Assembly (2007). *A Lasting Legacy for London? Assessing the Legacy of the Olympic Games and Paralympic Games*, Greater London Authority. https://www.london.gov.uk/sites/default/files/gla_migrate_files_destination/archives/assembly-reports-econsd-lasting-legacy-uel-research.pdf

Louw, A. (2012). *Ambush Marketing and the Mega-Event Monopoly: How Laws are Abused to Protect Commercial Rights to Sporting Events*. The Hague: TMC Asser Press, 11–20.

Magdalinski, T., Shimmel, K.S. and Chandler, T.J.L. (2005). Recapturing Olympic mystique: The corporate invasion of the classroom. In Nauright, J. and Schimmel, K. S. (eds.) *The Political Economy of Sport*. Palgrave Macmillan, 38–54.

Matheson, V. (2008). Mega-events: The effect of the world's biggest sporting events on local, regional, and national economies. In Howard, D. and Humphreys, B. (eds.) *The Business of Sports*, vol. 1, Westport, CT: Praeger Publishers, 81–99.

Matheson, V. (2009). Economic multipliers and mega-event analysis. *International Journal of Sports Finance*, 4(1), 63–70, https://ideas.repec.org/p/hcx/wpaper/0402.html

Mitchell, H. and Fergusson Stewart, M. (2015). What should you pay to host a party? An economic analysis of hosting sports mega-events. *Applied Economics*, 47(15), 1550–1561.

Monnin, E. and Maillard, C. (2015). Pour une typologie du boycottage aux Jeux Olympiques. *Relations Internationales*, 2015/2(162), 173–198.

Müller, M. (2015). The mega-event syndrome: Why so much goes wrong in mega-event planning and what to do about it. *Journal of the American Planning Association*, 81, May, 6–17.

OECD – LEED (2010). Local development benefits from staging global events: Achieving the local development legacy from 2012. https://www.oecd.org/cfe/leed/46207013.pdf

Oliver, R. and Lauermann, J. (2017). *Failed Olympic Bids and the Transformation of Urban Space, Lasting Legacies?*Palgrave Macmillan Publishing.

Parent, M.M. (2008). Evolution and issue patterns for major-sport-event organizing committees and their stakeholders. *Journal of Sport Management*, 22(2), 135–164.

Parent, M.M. (2010). Decision making in major sport events over time: Parameters, drivers, and strategies. *Journal of Sport Management*, 24(3), 291–318.

Parent, M.M. (2013). Olympic Games stakeholder governance and management. In Frawley, S. and Adair, D. (eds.) *Managing the Olympic Games*. London: Palgrave Macmillan, 15–32.

Porter, P. and Fletcher, D. (2008). The economic impact of the Olympic Games: *Ex ante* predictions and *ex poste* reality. *Journal of Sports Management*, 22(4), 470–486.

Persson, C. (2002). The Olympic Games site decision. *Tourism Management*, 23, 27–36.

Soja, E. (1989). *Postmodern Geographies: the reassertion of Space in Critical Social Theory*. London: Verso Press.

Zimbalist, A. (2015a). *Circus Maximus: The Economic Gamble behind Hosting the Olympics and the World Cup*. Washington, DC: Brookings Institution Press.

Zimbalist, A. (2015b). Olympics numbers don't add up. *Boston Globe*, March 20. https://www.bostonglobe.com/opinion/2015/03/20/olympics-numbers-don-add/BqrAaenp4tKK3Q7ASU5OrJ/story.html

Zirin, D. (2014). *Brazil's Dance with the Devil: The World Cup, the Olympics, and the Fight for Democracy*. Chicago, IL: Haymarket Books.

2 The battle for public opinion in host cities

The paradox of the Olympics as a troubled brand

Harry H. Hiller

Introduction

Perhaps never before has the Olympics been under attack on so many fronts at once. The fallout from the Salt Lake City scandals and criticisms of the IOC in the 1990s (Jennings, 1996) was at least somewhat diffused by IOC reforms, but new controversies have emerged that add a different level of challenges to the Olympic movement. From doping and the integrity of competitions to the divergent attitudes about how to handle the Russian scandal, to charges of corruption and suspicions about the IOC, as well as the breakdown of the host city bidding process, the Olympic movement is in a battle for the shaping of public opinion about the Games (Giesen and Hall-mann, 2018). Many of the controversies which the Olympics are facing have tarnished the Olympic brand with specific impact on how the Games are viewed by residents of potential host cities, bid cities, and even cities that have been awarded the Games. While the Olympic brand may be troubled when viewed from a global perspective, the implications of this decline has had its strongest impact on residents of cities who encounter the Games' project from their own local perspectives.

In spite of these concerns, the business model of the IOC does not suggest that the brand is troubled because it has quite successfully turned sport into a profitable venture. The Games continue to generate immense global interest now spread to more than 220 countries (IOC, 2018b). The sale of broadcast rights has been the largest source of income for the IOC as roughly half the world watches the Games on TV as well as other social media platforms (Boudway and Panja, 2017). The TOP sponsor program (which increasingly includes Asian corporations) enables corporations with a global reach to use their Olympic affiliation to enhance brand awareness, and remains a significant source of revenue to the IOC (Grohmann and Baker, 2018). In addition to the commercial value, there is no question that multiple sports carried out in a globally competitive but festival atmosphere are attractive to spectators and viewers, making the Olympics a compelling brand.

The paradox then is that if the IOC has been highly successful in promoting sport as a marketable commodity generating huge global public interest, it must also deal with controversies that are not easily resolved and have tarnished the Olympic brand. One of the most critical matters which has raised the profile of the Olympics as problematic is the issue of finding cities willing to host the Games, given the global rotation system which the IOC has preferred, and the costs associated with doing so. Whereas once it was elites who made decisions about hosting the Games, it is now public opinion at the local level that is playing an increasing role in such decisions. Reputational issues about the Olympics and above all negative reports and experiences from previous host cities, particularly pertaining to costs, have created a new level of uncertainty for the IOC as it searches for host cities. Not only is the competitive bid model that creates cities as winners and losers viewed as problematic, but the idea of bidding at all has become controversial. In spite of Agenda 2020 and the New Norm (IOC, 2018a; Schnitzer and Haizinger, 2019) which have aimed to reduce the costs of bidding for and hosting the Games, the value of hosting the Olympics is being questioned by city administrators/politicians and especially by inhabitants whose goals and preferences do not necessarily align with high performance sport. In fact, the test of public opinion in hosting decisions has the potential of changing the current single host city model that mobilizes such a vast array of resources.

The host city perspective

From a host city's perspective, and especially that of local residents, the Olympics represents an intrusive project controlled by an external entity (the IOC) with myriad requirements and expectations over which they have little control. However, coloring these observations are general perceptions and observations which inhabitants have about the Olympic movement as a whole contained in media reports that impact their assessments about the Olympics and the wisdom of hosting the Games at all. Reports of corruption, doping, extravagance within the IOC, elitism, and the democratic deficit are some of the main issues that have emerged as critical to public opinion (McGillivray and Turner, 2017). The Olympic brand has been built on its world-wide reach with athletes competing from around the world in a type of global championship which then is thought to enhance the host city's reputation and provide it with an unusual marketing opportunity. But host city residents are now less likely to accept the prestige value of hosting the Games as an acceptable rationale on the grounds that the Games' image has been tarnished and the conviction that the interests of their own city needs to take priority. All of this means that there is a contrast between the brand identity that the franchise holder (the IOC) wants to project about the Olympics and the image that people at the grass-roots have of the Games and about what will remain in their city after the '16 days of glory' are over. When these observations are added to the struggle between external requirements and expectations and internal priorities and impact, hosting the Olympics has become increasingly problematic for host city residents in recent years.

Historically, bidding and hosting was primarily a decision and action taken by elites (specifically business and government leaders) who announced this initiative to the local citizens, which may or may not have aroused much public response (Kassens-Noor and Lauermann, 2017, 2018). Citizen participation was reserved for preparation and hosting the Games as an already established fact. What has changed is that local residents have been drawn into discussions about the Games at a much earlier point, especially to debate whether the value of hosting the Games is even self-evident. In many ways, then, especially in western democracies, even the decision about whether to host the Olympics is being taken out of the hands of elites and has become increasingly dependent on public support. Governments may be forced to allow citizens to have a say in this decision or may even choose to hold a referendum in order to place the responsibility for the decision on taxpayers, thereby reducing their own accountability.

The end result of these democratizing pressures is that there has been some serious questioning about whether the traditional model for choosing host cities can survive. Headlines such as 'Hosting the Olympics: the competition no one wants to win' (*The Guardian*, November 30, 2015), 'Why hosting the Olympic Games is viewed as problematic, not prestigious, for most western cities' (*Washington Post*, July 31, 2015), or, 'The Olympics aren't good for cities, so can the magic of the Games survive?' (*Bloomberg*, July 13, 2017) reflect a growing unease about hosting the Games, much of which emerges from opposition among city residents. Since the idea of hosting the Games usually begins with elites, it is public opinion that shifts as a result of controversies discussed in the media and the actions of protest groups that contribute to growing opposition to the idea of hosting the Games.

Contesting the decision to host

Public opinion in host cities is usually managed by bid boosters who attempt to define and control the narrative about the importance and benefits of hosting the Games, or what Kassens-Noor (2016) describes as the mega-event utopian vision. Depending on the local politics of the bid, opposition may be reflected in apathy and/or be muted or may be vocal through entities such as 'No Olympics' or 'Games Monitor'. While bid cities are required to report the level of public support as measured through polls in their bid books (Hiller and Wanner, 2017), the clearest expression of the Olympics as controversial is represented in the decision to put the idea of hosting the Games to a referendum. In his study of public referendums, Maennig (2017) has noted that more referendums have taken place in Central European locations than anywhere else and that negative results regarding hosting the Olympics have been more typical in recent years than positive results. There is considerable doubt over whether a referendum question adequately taps the issues involved but in most cases the result of the referendum is either considered binding by authorities or plays a major role in ultimate decisions about the Games.

The existence of an opposition movement to the Olympic project does not mean that it will have a decisive and conclusive impact. For example, the recent selections of Paris and Los Angeles are cases where opposition or the desire for public input was minimal. *NOlympics LA* was a coalition of over 25 community organizations started by the Democratic Socialists of America Los Angeles chapter and its housing and homelessness committee (nolymp icsla.com) who used the problem of homelessness as an example of a preferred priority in contrast to the Olympic agenda. Dozens of protesters shouted anti-Games slogans during the decision meeting at City Council, and yet the council voted 12–0 in support of hosting the Olympics (August 2017). One independent opinion poll in metro Los Angeles found support for hosting the Games in the 83–88% range (Guerra, Gilbert, and Solis, 2017). In Paris, only one of the 20 districts (*arrondissements*) that make up Paris refused to support the bid in 2015 and only one city councillor from one district argued for the need for a referendum. A small group called 'NO to the 2024 Paris Olympics' (*NON aux JO 2024 à Paris*) opposed the Olympics in which there was some demand for citizen input in the Olympic decision (Daldorph, 2017) but, in general, dissent was not significant. In neither of these host cities was a referendum held and there were limited expressions of dissent.

On the other hand, numerous potential host cities in recent years have decided against hosting the Olympics. In contrast to activist movements which have used the Games as an opportunity for protest about other issues (Boykoff, 2014), more recent activist action has begun much earlier in the Olympic cycle to challenge the Olympic industry (Lenskyj, 2008) and the rationale for bidding at all (Oliver and Lauermann, 2017). Budapest experienced a massive grassroots *NOlimpia* campaign led by young Hungarians in a movement called *Momentum Mozgalom* that collected over 260,000 signatures in opposition to bidding. Boston experienced multiple protest groups to the bid proposal including 'No Boston Olympics' and 'No Boston 2024' as well as opposition parties in local government which ultimately led to the mayor cancelling the bid (Lauermann, 2016). Numerous cities in recent years have held referendums such as Krakow (70% No), Hamburg (52% No), Munich (52% No), Vienna (72% No), St. Moritz/Davos (53% No), and Calgary (56% No). Even Oslo with a referendum result of 54% Yes eventually withdrew its bid due to public pressure. As further evidence of how public input has almost become normative, the city of Denver that is considering a bid for 2032, has proposed holding a referendum already in 2020 far in advance of the actual bid in order to obtain public endorsement early in the process.

In spite of the conclusions by some that no one wants to host the Olympics anymore or that the Olympics are bad for cities, new cities are repeatedly popping up as candidates or potential candidates to host the games (Oliver and Lauermann, 2017, pp. 74–81). The irony of a potential populist revolt about hosting the Games seems to be receiving uneven traction and the fact that not all cities have experienced significant opposition suggests that we need to understand more fully under what conditions critical public opinion evolves about hosting the Games. It is important to acknowledge that different political systems and different socio-political contexts make it difficult to develop one set of factors impacting public opinion anywhere in the world so there may be a western bias in what is to follow. The intriguing question is what factors play a role in framing public opinion about hosting the Games. In order to accommodate the fluidity of the relationship between the Olympic Games and host city residents in different contexts, eight factors are discussed but are represented as propositions.

Factors impacting local public opinion about hosting the Olympics

Propositions

1 The decision to host the Olympics is ultimately a public policy issue

This means that discussions about the Olympics always take place in a political context of policy priorities and preferences and reflects existing political dynamics and conflicts within a political entity (Andranovich, Burbank, and Heying, 2001; Trubina, 2014). In other words, support for the Olympic agenda is subject to the same political forces as any other policy issue in which there are advocates and adversaries and in which a united front may be difficult to obtain.

a   Political states with strong autocratic governments that announce hosting the Games as their public policy initiative are less likely to encounter opposition whereas western states with strong democratic traditions are more likely to receive strong responses at the grass-roots.
b   If the Olympic initiative is driven by national government elites for whom the Games are a central part of their policy agenda, local opposition in itself is less likely to be successful.
c   If the Olympic initiative is driven primarily by local elites, opposition (if it arises) has a greater prospect of succeeding, especially if there is not strong support from national elites. The closer residents are to the event envisioned as a local initiative, the greater the likelihood their opposition will be motivated by fiscal concerns.
d   If the Olympic initiative is jointly sponsored and supported by both local and national elites, opposition is less likely to be successful.

2 The role of opinion leaders

Public acceptance of hosting the Games or opposition to such action is more likely to have a significant impact if it is coordinated by strong and determined local leaders who actively engage in highly visible public debate. The adoption or rejection of the Olympics as a public policy preference among local residents is highly dependent on who makes the case and how the case is made in a public format that arouses public attention (Bennett et al., 2013; Kassens-Noor and Lauermann, 2018; Lauermann and Vogelpohl, 2017).

a Political leaders who not only endorse hosting the Games but who actively campaign for them with a strong rationale are more likely to generate stronger public support.

b The existence of a mood of general public uncertainty or unease about hosting the Games is not sufficient to provoke active and concerted opposition. There must be opinion leaders in opposition who publicly commit to advocacy of their position and/or who develop a strategy to convince the general public. In short, the presence of articulate spokespersons in opposition greatly enhances public rejection to hosting the Games whereas the absence of such leadership will produce either a lukewarm citizenry or passive public support for the Games. Of critical importance as well is that opposition must have a means of communicating their rationale to the general public which thereby enhances the legitimacy of opposition as a viable option.

3 Referendums or plebiscites

A demand for a referendum is considered the most effective opposition strategy because it removes the power of elites and democratizes the decision to host the Games. Boosters for the Games often resist such public input because they lose control of the advocacy agenda in which negativity can take over (Streicher, Schmidt, and Schreyer, 2018).

a Holding a referendum in itself makes hosting the Olympics controversial and encourages residents to view the Games as problematic. Holding a referendum may in itself actually energize the opposition to become even more vocal.

b Referendums may actually create considerable confusion because of the typical simplistic dichotomous Yes/No terms of the vote (e.g. 'Do you support the initiative that this city host the Olympic Games?'). Arguments are made that do not allow for more nuanced considerations of a complex issue. For example, support may be conditional on the presence of particular elements of the bid or there may be rejection if those elements are absent. Conversely, opposition may be based on unclarified details, but if those details are more carefully verified, opposition might be reduced.

c The logic of a call for a referendum almost always comes from people in opposition who reframe the initiative as a choice between preferred spending on existing poorly funded public services (e.g. education, health care, housing) versus the high cost of Olympic requirements and the debt likely to result, in which it is assumed that citizens will make the obvious choice to reject the Games.

4 Ideological predispositions

Support or opposition to hosting the Olympics is often part of a worldview. For example, the anti-globalization movement which has been energized by issues such as the democratic deficit, international corporate power, concern for marginalized and indigenous people, and environmentalism has identified the IOC and the Olympics as critical symbols which need to be challenged (Field, 2016; McGillivray and Turner, 2017). In contrast, a neo-liberal view of globalization supportive of free market trade and capitalist expansion is more likely to lead to a more affirmative view of the Olympics.

a   Becoming a booster means accepting a set of presuppositions about the benefits to be received from hosting the Games whereas opposing the Games usually means rejecting those presuppositions about benefits and instead advocating counter presuppositions about liabilities, costs, and risks.
b   Evidence is selected that supports a point of view with little middle ground in order to capture the support of local citizens for that per-spective. Much of the debate is built from the experience of previous Olympic host cities where evidence is selected to support that point of view. The evidence is particularly effective if it is negative such as pointing out cost over-runs, debt, or displacement of marginalized people at the same time that benefits are ignored. The challenge for advocates is to present only the benefits and ignore the challenges or to show how the bid plans address the challenges. Often arguments from either side fall on deaf ears because of the ideological lens which is brought to the issue in the first place.

5 The quantitative–qualitative logic debate

The battle for public opinion leads to confusing countervailing evidence that is both quantitative and qualitative in nature (Müller, 2015; Barclay, 2009).

a   Support or opposition to hosting the Games is usually a quantitative debate over cost–benefit. Boosters often stress the figures provided by consultants about the positive contributions to the GDP, employment, and tourism growth etc. Opponents on the other hand appeal to the work of academics that demonstrates that such gains are at best overdrawn if not outright false truths (Dempsey and Zimbalist, 2017).
b   When boosters feel their economic arguments are being undermined, they often appeal to non-economic justifications (qualitative factors such as place marketing or feel-good factors such as civic or national pride) to support of the Games. Opponents on the other hand minimize intangible outcomes which they argue only mask the fiscal liabilities.
c   In any case, supporters of the Games tend to focus on benefits of hosting the Games whereas opponents tend to focus on the costs and risks (Scheu and Preuss, 2018). Another way to put it is that these two positions of support and opposition are countered by two different mental states about the Games and their impact: optimism vs. pessimism, ambition vs. aversion, acclaim vs. criticism, and advocacy vs. skepticism or obstructionism.

6 Global city comparisons

Large cities with a high developmental index as well as cities in the western world are more likely to be able to absorb the challenges of hosting the Games with less difficulty because they may have much of the required infrastructure already in place (Müller and Gaffney, 2018). Cities with lower levels of development are more likely to have political instability and fiscal problems as well as poorer infrastructure which strains the resources of the city and produces controversial outcomes.

a   Ironically, it is in cities lower on the developmental index where coordinated opposition to hosting the Games has been less likely to occur, at least partially because the decision to host came from a central government authority. Trickle-down economic arguments are often made as a rationale for the event improving conditions in these cities which often generates cautious support among the poor. For example, poor black residents of Cape Town were more likely to support the Olympic bid for the 2004 Games with such optimism whereas white residents were more likely to reject hosting the Games on the grounds that they would have to bear the costs (Hiller, 2000).

b   The more taxpayers view hosting the Games from the point of view of their own interests and maintaining their own standard of living such as in cities higher on the developmental index, the more likely they are to critically evaluate hosting the Games.

c   Cities that have people already engaged in active levels of participation in sports that are part of the Olympics are more likely to support the Games from a legacy point of view because of their lasting infrastructure contribution to the sports in which they are involved. Cities for whom specific Olympic sports are not part of the local culture are more likely to have Games venues that become white elephants that fall into disrepair or disuse post-Games. Such outcomes play a significant role in public opinion in both pre-Game and post-Game evaluations. Since Olympic sports are more likely to be prominent in cities and countries on the high development index, hosting the Olympics in these places is more likely to be viewed as having key positive sport infrastructural outcomes. The basic issue here is that some Olympic sports are not part of the local culture as sport preferences vary around the world.

7 The size, scale and intensity of hosting the Olympics is problematic

The size (sometimes referred to as gigantism) and complexity of the Olympics produces a significant challenge for hosting the Games because myriad requirements disrupt local priorities and change the urban agenda (Jennings, 2012).

a   The intensity of the Games over a short period of time but requiring a very lengthy period of preparation is a challenge that strains the resources of the host region and impacts public opinion. There is virtually no segment of the city's population that does not have to take the Olympics into consideration in planning from schools to hospitals, places of employment, and even traffic patterns that require an adjustment to the demands of the Olympics (e.g. one of the most provocative is the requirement for Olympic lanes on major city streets). Multiple planning sessions by virtually every urban entity are required that can never be accounted for in budgeting and costs. These requirements provoke a wide range of local emotion and reaction.

b   The significant number of world-class competition sites over multiple sports (such as swimming, equestrian, and cycling for the Summer Games) in a relatively proximate location often results in difficult decisions over which there is much local debate and often disagreement. Somewhat differently, the Winter Olympics which imposes large numbers of athletes, officials, sponsors, and spectators into much smaller communities and mountain villages is often viewed as an unwelcome disruption to normal life. For both the Summer and Winter Games, residents in potential host cities easily question the rationale for taking on this hosting task because of the scale of the impact and its disruptive effect for both the short-term (the event itself) and the long-term (event outcomes).

8 Pre-Games controversies vs. Games-time experiences and post-Games evaluations

Public opinion tends to undergo an important shift from the controversies of the pre-Games period to the experiences of the Games themselves which then impacts post-Games evaluations.

a   Pre-Games. The multiple decisions that must be made in the pre-Games period almost always are filled with controversy that relate to siting, consultation processes, and financing. Where these venues are to be located and who is benefitting or being harmed (displaced) from these locations, and how original budgeting has to be revised due to cost overruns and possible corruption are issues that create considerable debate and conflict in the preparation phase for the Games. Deviations from what had appeared in the bid books sometimes even creates a sense of betrayal or being misled. In any case, the public often despairs of the controversy in which the project seems overwhelming.

b   Games-time. The Games themselves shift the mood from internal conflict to an external focus on 'welcoming the world' in which hospitality and civic pride can predominate. If one of the purposes of hosting the Games is place marketing, meaning the desire to project a positive global image of the host city, then every effort is normally made to ensure that an affirmative and confident representation of the city is projected. Urban residents themselves are also eager that their city is cast in a favorable light to outsiders but sometimes there is criticism of the false image that is projected that is the result of actions such as urban cleansing (e.g. the removal of homeless people or covering up poverty) that is often only temporary. Furthermore, the strategy adopted by Games organizers to create a Games-time festival experience for local residents (sometimes likened to a circus atmosphere) as well as non-athletic activities in a Cultural Olympiad normally plays a major role in changing the mood in the city. The end result is that opposition is likely to be suppressed and/or overwhelmed. One of the major outcomes from hosting the Games is that the dynamics of the event as they are available to local residents (such as in pedestrian corridors, pavilions, and live sites) encourage residents to experience their city in a more celebrious manner than exists in normal urban routines (Hiller, 2012).

c   Post-Games. To the extent that the Games are able to enlist local residents in participation in both paid (tickets to events) and non-paid (street corridors, live sites, community-based) Games activities, and to the extent that there are few or no disruptions or disasters related to the Games as they experienced them, local residents come to evaluate having hosted the Games more positively in post-Games years. The controversies may have lingering effects but there is a tendency by both supporting governments, Games organizers, and even local residents to want to view having hosted the Games in a more positive light (Vetitnev and Bobina, 2018). This outcome is enhanced by the fact that governments put out positive reports of the Games' impact and the media which have often been more critical in the pre-Games period have moved on to other issues.

The battleground for public opinion

Local residents encounter the Olympics in two ways: through their *perceptions of* the Games and through their *experiences with* the Games and they do so in two phases: the bid phase and the host phase. There are four groups of actors that play a role in shaping or framing public opinion: three of them are the boosters, the critics, and the media.

While boosters and critics may be found anywhere in the world in addition to the local city, it is the media that keep the Olympics and its controversies and issues alive from one Olympiad to another with reports about local issues as well as issues from other Olympic cities all over the world. The fourth channel of influence in developing perceptions about the Olympics comes from interaction with others with whom residents are networked (Hiller, 2012). This influence is important because public opinion is open to manipulation and people develop opinions, prejudices, and biases from learning what others think – and especially if those persons are people with whom they interact frequently.

Cell 1. When local residents think about hosting the Olympics, they do so through the filtered information flow that surrounds them. This includes evaluating the information they have been given but it could also be the result

	Perceptions Olympics as Perceived	Experience Olympics as Experienced
Bidding	(cell 1) Bidding as a possibility	(cell 2) Bidding as action
Hosting	(cell 3) Preparing to host	(cell 4) Hosting as action

Emergent actors in framing and agenda setting
Boosters
Opponents
Media
Friendship networks

Figure 2.1 The local public opinion battleground

of their own past history such as positive perceptions from having watched previous Games on TV or other media platforms that leads them to view hosting the Games as an exciting and perhaps honorific possibility. But it could also include knowing about problems and controversies about the IOC, the Olympics, or problems experienced by previous host cities. Local residents might lack significant knowledge and depend on rumor or even be apathetic about the Olympics. The point is that these *perceptions* present a starting point for the battle over public opinion about bidding for the Games (cell 1). It is the bid phase that has in recent years become a more intensive battleground for public opinion as the controversy over whether hosting the Olympics as even an appropriate course of action is debated given the frame or lens with which the public perceives this initiative.

Cell 2. The consideration of a bid and the discussion and action which that entails brings the boosters and the opponents in direct conflict. Both groups of people have their own constituencies which they attempt to mobilize. Boosters attempt to frame the Olympics in terms of its *benefits* and attempt to control the information flow from that perspective. Critics frame the Games in terms of its *risks and liabilities* and seek to attack and destabilize the booster position. Debates over costs, venue locations, leadership, and priorities cloud the public sphere and create division over the project. The extent to which the idea of bidding for the Olympics is controversial varies with location but the key thing is that while *perceptions* about the Games serve as the background for these debates, the struggle for public support for either side is something that local residents *experience* in a real way because of the awareness that this project will have real local consequences (cell 2). While referendums do not occur in all cities, in cities where they do occur, the battle for public opinion becomes most acute.

Cell 3. If a city's bid is successful, or as local residents anticipate hosting the Games (cell 3), the same dynamics are present in which *perceptions* about hosting the Games are fraught with similar conflicting images about what the Olympics will do to the city. Often rather than emphasize the positive contributions which the Games will make to the city, the emphasis is on the IOC/sport federation requirements, and anticipating all the problems which the Games will create: disruptions of normal traffic patterns, reprioritizing the urban agenda, shifts in original plans which create different or unexpected impacts, or announcements of cost-overruns – all of which lead residents to view hosting the Games as more of a problem than an opportunity. Announcements from OCOG's play a huge role in creating apprehensiveness or even fear about what the Games will do to the city. Needless to say, critics and boosters often conflict and the media eagerly reports these conflicts creating an atmosphere of trepidation about the Games rather than excitement. In other words, the *perception* of the Games about to take place among local residents is often one of confusion and uncertainty in the pre-Games period.

Cell 4. However, the shift to Games-time *experiences* has a significant impact on public evaluations of the Games (cell 4). Somehow the controversies are drowned out by the shift in mood caused by things like the arrival of international athletes, guests, and the intense media exposure, the erection of Olympic overlay in the city, the creation of pedestrian corridors, live sites, and a general celebrious mood which emerges giving the city the appearance of becoming a gigantic theater. There are hints that this outcome is rather unexpected by local residents given the problem-focused pre-Games period and there is considerable evidence that the conclusion about hosting the Games was that it was indeed a worthwhile experience (Hiller, 2017). The tone of the media also shifts, the city has been sanitized, and the projected global image of the city becomes particularly relevant to local residents. It is this Games-time experience that impacts post-Games evaluations to be more positive. Opposition groups lose their urgency once the Games are in progress and in the post-Games period, and the local media invariably paint a more positive picture about hosting the Olympics during the Games and normally move on to other issues when the Games are over.

Conclusion

The battle over public opinion about the Olympics at the local level thus begins with residents' perceptions about the Olympics as an event and its impact but changes as the result of how people experience the Games both in the bid phase as well as the event phase. Bidding and preparing to host the Games impacts public opinion in a very different way from interacting with or encountering the Games in real time. The public opinion battle over the Olympics, however, plays an important role for city residents in a number of ways. First of all, the conflicts force the city to confront its own challenges and problems in a direct manner even if these issues are not resolved. There is no better evidence of this than the fact that local social issues and local urban issues are now typically incorporated into OCOG planning for what otherwise could be considered purely a sports event. For example, low cost housing, employment for the marginalized, and better transportation options to enhance urban functioning are often part of the plan to justify public support. Whether of course the Olympics succeeds in addressing these objectives successfully remains an open question. But the public opinion battle raises the question of alternate priorities. Second, the unique nature of the Games-time experience allows residents to experience their city in a new way and in that sense can be an important consciousness-raising event or defining moment in a city's history. Typically, the Olympics provides a target date for lots of community organizations to accomplish all kinds of objectives (e.g. London organizations had physical activity goals, renovation plans, membership mobilization). In that sense, the public opinion battle can be a worthwhile experience because it can potentially serve as a catalyst for city-building. Third, the public opinion battle reminds us, however, that in spite of the fact that proposals continue to be made from cities who desire to host the Games, hosting the Olympics is indeed a contestable decision with outcomes that are indeed debateable and controversial and ensures that the Olympics as a mega-event and mega-project will continue to be a battleground for public opinion. Nowhere is this clearer than in the fact that outcomes seldom evolve as planned.

References

Andranovich, G., M. J. Burbank and C. H. Heying (2001). Olympic cities: Lessons learned from mega-event politics. *Journal of Urban Affairs*, 23(2), 113–131.

Barclay, J. (2009). Predicting the costs and benefits of mega-sporting events: Misjudgment of Olympic proportions. *Economic Affairs*, 29(2), 62–66.

Bennett, L., M. Bennett, S. Alexander, and J. Persky (2013). The political and civic implications of Chicago's unsuccessful bid to host the 2016 Olympic Games. *Journal of Sport and Social Issues*, 37(4), 364–383.

Boudway, I. and T. Panja (2017). The Olympics aren't good for cities, so can the magic of the Games survive? *Bloomberg*, July 13.

Boykoff, J. (2014). *Activism and the Olympics: Dissent at the Games in Vancouver and London*. New Brunswick, NJ: Rutgers University Press.

Daldorph, B. (2017). The quiet voices saying 'no' to Paris's Olympic bid. *France 24*, June 24.

Dempsey, C. and A. Zimbalist (2017). *No Boston Olympics: How and Why Smart Cities are Passing on the Torch*. University Press of New England.

Field, R. (2016). The new 'culture wars': The Vancouver 2010 Olympics, public protest, and the politics of resistance. In Field, R. (ed.). *Playing for Change: The Continuing Struggle for Sport and Recreation*. Toronto: University of Toronto Press, 67–93.

Giesen, N. and K. Hallmann (2018). *International Journal of Sport Policy and Politics*, 10(3), 509–523.

Grohmann, K. and L. B. Baker (2018). Tarnished? The Olympic brand still mints money like never before. *Japan Times*, February 19.

Guerra, F. J., Gilbert, B. and Solis, B. (2017). *LA Residents and the 2028 Olympics*. Thomas and Dorothy Leavey Center for the Study of Los Angeles, Loyola Marymount University, Los Angeles, California.

Hiller, H. H. (2000). Mega-events, urban boosterism and growth strategies: An analysis of the Cape Town 2004 Olympic bid. *International Journal of Urban and Regional Research*, 24, 457–476.

Hiller, H. H. (2012). *Host Cities and the Olympics: An Interactionist Approach*. London: Routledge.

Hiller, H. H. and R. A. Wanner (2017). Public opinion in Olympic cities: From bidding to retrospection . *Urban Affairs Review*, 54(5), 962–993.

International Olympic Committee (IOC) (2018a). *Olympic Agenda 2020 Olympic Games: The New Norm*. Report by the Executive Steering Committee for Olympic Games Delivery. PyeongChang.

International Olympic Committee (IOC) (2018b). *Olympic Marketing Fact File*. Lausanne.

Jennings, A. (1996). *The Lords of the Rings: Power, Money and Drugs in the Modern Olympics*. New York: Simon and Schuster.

Jennings, W. (2012). *Olympic Risks*. Basingstoke: Palgrave Macmillan.

Kassens-Noor, E. (2016). From ephemeral planning to permanent urbanism: An urban planning theory of mega-events. *Urban Planning*, 1(1), 41–54.

Kassens-Noor, E. and J. Lauermann (2017). How to bid better for the Olympics: A participatory mega-event planning strategy for local legacies. *Journal of the American Planning Association*, 83(4), 335–345.

Kassens-Noor, E. and J. Lauermann (2018). Mechanisms of policy failure: Boston's 2024 Olympic bid. *Urban Studies*, 55(15), 3369–3384.

Lauermann, J. (2016). Boston's Olympic bid and the evolving urban politics of event-led development. *Urban Geography*, 37(2), 313–321.

Lauermann, J. and A. Vogelpohl (2017). Fragile growth coalitions or powerful contestations? Cancelled Olympic bids in Boston and Hamburg. *Environment and Planning A*, 49(8), 1887–1904.

Lenskyj, H. (2008). *Olympic Industry Resistance: Challenging Olympic Power and Propaganda*. Albany, NY: State University of New York Press.

Maennig, W. (2017). *Public referenda and public opinion on Olympic Games*. Hamburg Contemporary Economic Discussions No. 57. University of Hamburg.

McGillivray, D. and D. Turner (2017). *Event Bidding: Politics, Persuasion and Resistance*. London: Routledge.

Müller, M. (2015). The Mega-Event Syndrome: Why So much goes wrong in mega-event planning and what to do about it. *Journal of the American Planning Association*, 81(1), 6–17.

Müller, M. and C. Gaffney (2018). Comparing the urban impacts of the FIFA World Cup and Olympic Games from 2010 to 2016. *Journal of Sport and Social Issues*, 42 (4), 247–269.

Oliver, R. and J. Lauermann (2017). *Failed Olympic Bids and the Transformation of Urban Space*. London: Palgrave Macmillan.

Scheu, A. and H. Preuss (2018). Residents' perceptions of mega sport legacies and impacts. *German Journal of Exercise and Sport Research*, 48(3), 376–386.

Schnitzer, M. and L. Haizinger (2019). Does the Olympic Agenda 2020 have the power to create a New Olympic Heritage? An analysis for the 2026 Winter Olympic Games bid. *Sustainability*, 11(2), 442; doi:10.3390/su11020442.

Streicher, T., Schmidt, S. L., and Schreyer, D. (2018). Referenda on hosting the Olympics: What drives voter turnout? *Journal of Sports Economics*. doi:10.1177/1527002518794777.

Trubina, E. (2014). Mega-events in the context of capitalist modernity: The Case of the 2014 Sochi Winter Olympics. *Eurasian Geography and Economics*, 55(6), 610–627.

Vetitnev, A. and N. Bobina (2018). Residents' perception of the 2014 Sochi Olympic Games: Comparison of pre-and post-impacts. *International Journal of Sport Management and Marketing*, 18(6), 453–477.

3 The International Olympic Committee's struggle against growing gigantism of the Olympic Games

Anna Kobierecka and Michał Marcin Kobierecki

Introduction

These days the Olympic Games, like other sports mega-events, have reached an enormous size and scope. The gigantism of the event has obviously led to a number of results, both positive and negative. For example, the Olympics became a great tool of communicating national identity and nation-branding, and many governments have attempted to employ hosting them as a focal point of their public diplomacy and nation-branding strategies. The negative effects refer to the enormous costs of hosting the event and often negative results for local communities. All this has led to a decreasing number of candidates wishing to host the Olympic Games. If the Summer Olympics are considered, there were 11 cities interested in hosting the 2004 Games. This number gradually decreased with nine bids for the 2012 Games, seven bids for the 2016 event and five for the Olympics in 2020 (Beacom, 2012). Concerning the Olympic Games in 2024, originally there were five candidate cities, but after three withdrawals (BBC, 2017) the International Olympic Committee (IOC) was left with just two bids and eventually decided on the double allocation of the Games in Paris in 2024 and Los Angeles in 2028 (IOC, 2007). There is a similar situation if Olympic Winter Games are considered. In 2015 when the IOC was selecting the host of the 2022 event, there were only two bids (Beijing and Almaty), both from countries with internationally criticized human rights records, after Munich (Germany), Stockholm (Sweden), Cracow (Poland) and Graubunden (Switzerland) withdrew their bids (Boykoff, 2015).

There are various reasons for the declining interest in hosting the Olympic Games, particularly among democratic nations. The most frequently mentioned are the growing awareness in the developed states of the rising costs of hosting the Olympic Games and other sports mega-events (Lenartowicz, 2015). Speaking of finances of the Olympic Games, between 1960 and 2016 there were average cost overruns of 176 per cent (Jackson and Dawson, 2017). This is obviously connected to the gigantism of the Olympic Games, a problem that the IOC has been trying to solve since the late 1950s. Reducing the size and scope of the Olympic Games has emerged as one of the greatest challenges for the Olympic Movement. The aim of this chapter is to review the attempts conducted by the IOC to counter the growing gigantism and costs of the Olympic Games and to analyse them from the perspective of the IOC's public diplomacy.

In this chapter we refer to the term public diplomacy. It might be understood in different ways, but it is usually referred to as the communication of international actors' policies to citizens of foreign countries (Pamment, 2013). Traditionally the term has been used to describe activity of states, but the considerations about the new public diplomacy in the twenty-first century claimed that it can also be pursued by non-state actors. Usually those actors work in cooperation and/or in favour of their country of origin, thus remaining in the area of states' foreign policy, but the scholarly literature on public diplomacy has also named transnational actors as the subjects of public diplomacy (Huijgh, 2016). It is therefore possible to speak of the public diplomacy of the International Olympic Committee. Nicolas Cull (2008) has referred to the public diplomacy of the IOC in reference to peacebuilding. The aim of this chapter is to present the IOC's public diplomacy in the context of its attempts to reduce the size and negative impact of the Olympic Games.

International Olympic Committee's attempts to reduce the gigantism of the Olympic Games

Limiting the Olympic programme

The problem of the gigantism of the Olympic Games might appear to be relatively new, but in fact the International Olympic Committee has been struggling with it since the 1950s. The first attempts to reduce the size of the Olympics were made already before the Games in Helsinki in 1952, when the number of officials accompanying the teams was growing (Hill, 1996). The first efforts that were made by the IOC in this field were associated with the Olympic programme, as limiting the number of athletes and sports present at the Games appeared to be a natural response to the growing challenge of too big and too costly Olympics. The IOC Session in Sofia in 1957 decided that since 1964 artificial team sports (team competitions based on results of individual participants) should be excluded from the Olympic programme (IOC, 1957). The decision led to protests by international federations for gymnastics, equestrian sports, modern pentathlon and wrestling, and eventually led to a partial withdrawal of the decision by the IOC one year later (IOC, 1958). Already this situation reveals the difficulties present in attempts to limit the size of the Olympic Games, as sports federations are generally interested in having their sports at the Olympic Games. From one side the right to define the Olympic programme is one of the reasons for the International Olympic Committee's superior position in the Olympic system, but at the same time it is under constant pressure from the International Federations (IFs) not to exclude sports already in the programme, and to include new ones.

The problem of gigantism of the Olympic Games from the beginning referred particularly to the Summer events. During the IOC Session in Athens in 1961 the IOC Members debated on the Olympic programme and the maximum number of sports. It was decided that during the Games in Tokyo in 1964 there would be 20 sports in the programme with handball and archery excluded (IOC, 1961). In the years that followed the Committee tried to exclude further sports, for example in 1963 volleyball and judo were also deleted from the programme (IOC, 1963), but the decision concerning volleyball was changed one year later after waterpolo was recognized as an event of swimming and a place for one more sport within the limit was spared (IOC, 1964a). The maximum number of sports in the Olympic programme was later adjusted, for example for the Munich 1972 Olympics it was set at 21 (IOC, 1964b). Before these Games the IOC Members had also discussed the issue of reducing the number of entries by country (IOC, 1972). According to J.-L. Chappelet (2014) it was the Munich Olympics when restrictions of the size of the Games was suggested for the first time by the organizers of the event. Such decisions understandably resulted in protests by IFs (IOC, 1973).

Further attempts to limit the programme of the Olympic Games followed. For example, it was decided that after 1992 Demonstration Sports could no longer be included in the programme (Hill, 1996). The International Olympic Committee became determined to reduce the size and cost of the Games in response to the problems experienced by the Olympics in Atlanta in 1996 (Chappelet, 2014). This is when the IOC imposed a maximum number of athletes of 10,500 and introduced minimum performance standards for each sport, excepting six participants from each National Olympic Committee that were allowed to compete in swimming and track and field despite not fulfilling these requirements. The maximum number of Olympic participants was amended before the Sydney 2000 Games after triathlon and taekwondo were included in the programme. The problem of rising size and costs was also one of the key elements of Jacques Rogge's programme while he was a candidate for the IOC Presidency (Chappelet, 2014).

The issue of the shape of the Olympic Games was analysed by the IOC's Olympic Games Study Commission. Its report from 2002 referred to the problem of the growing cost of hosting the Games, but there was no recommendation to expel sports from the Olympic programme. The IOC Session decided, however, that the Olympic programme should be reviewed occasionally on the basis of strictly defined criteria (IOC, 2002). In 2005 the IOC eventually decided that there could be 28 sports and 301 events at every Olympics, and there should be no more than 10,500 athletes competing. In reference to the London 2012 Olympics, baseball and softball were expelled, but the proposed karate and squash were not accepted so there were only 26 sports during these Games (IOC, 2005). Three years later in Copenhagen the IOC Session eventually decided that there would be 26 core sports and two additional ones which would be decided before the Games. At this time rugby sevens and golf were included in the programme (IOC, 2009).

In its efforts to limit the size of the Olympic Games the International Olympic Committee is constantly facing the same challenges. For example, when the programme of the Olympics in Athens was debated, it was claimed that on one hand there were pressures to reduce the number of athletes at the Games in order to address the effects of gigantism, while on the other there were equal pressures to add new sports and events and increase the athlete quotas (IOC, 2001). There was a vivid discussion worldwide after the IOC considered exclusion of wrestling from the programme, which is one of the traditional Olympic sports, present at the modern Olympics since their revival in 1896 (Chappelet, 2014).

Apart from attempts to limit the number of sports and events at the Olympics, the International Olympic Committee has also worked on other ideas. In 1965 the IOC Members discussed the initiative to transfer indoor sports such as boxing, basketball, fencing, weightlifting etc. from Summer to Winter events. The issue was later studied and discussed with sports federations. It was assessed that this could lead to a 900 to 1,000 reduction of Summer Games participants (IOC, 1966). However, the idea was not accepted and now only sports that are held on ice and snow can be included in the Winter Olympics programme.

Legacy and sustainability of the Olympic Games

Next to decreasing the cost of organising the Olympic Games, sustainability and providing positive impact on local communities are the most highlighted aspects of bringing back the glory of the Olympic Games. The topic of sustainability became popular in the 1990s. Since 1994 candidates to host the Olympic Games must be evaluated with regard to the environmental aspects of their bids. Additionally, in the Olympic Movement's Agenda 21 the IOC Members are obliged to play an active role in sustainable development, especially in counteracting poverty, and promoting integration and respect for wide diversity (IOC Sport and Environment Commission, 2003). Generally, the Olympic Games are associated with lack of respect for the environment since they cause increased traffic, and contribute to higher water consumption or waste production. However, together with popularization of the idea of sustainable development and increased environmental awareness, the IOC put a focus on 'being green'. Already in 1986 President of the IOC Juan Antonio Samaranch declared that the environment is the third pillar of Olympism next to sport and culture (Karamichas, 2013). In 1991 rule 2.10 – according to which the Olympics must be organized with regard to environmental issues – was added to the Olympic Charter (IOC, 1996). As a result of these and similar activities of the IOC, every organizing committee of the Olympic Games in the 21st century included its dedication to protecting the environment into the bid (IOC, 2008).

Together with environment and sustainable development, the case of Olympic legacy and influence on local society has been noticed. In 2000 the

IOC initiated an Olympic Games Global Impact programme that was generally aimed at improving the way hosting of the Olympic Games affects the host city, its environment and the people, with particular focus on the incoming tourism after the event (Gratton and Preuss, 2008). What is more, later during the international Olympic conference in Lausanne in 2002, the Olympic legacy was the main theme. Among others, urban, environmental, cultural, social and communication legacies were considered (Shipway, 2007). The IOC now expects cities applying to host the Olympics to describe the legacy of the proposed event (Grix, 2013; Holt and Ruta, 2015). Apart from having expectations of the future hosts of the Games to secure their legacy, the IOC has also attempted to support them, for example through Olympic Games Knowledge Management and Guide to Olympic Legacy (IOC, 2016; Leopkey and Parent, 2012). Focusing on substantial development and providing legacy and positive impact on local societies demonstrate a growing interest within IOC in redefining some of the Olympic Movement's priorities and areas of activity. Those adjustments seem to be related to accusations concerning the gigantism of Olympic Games and expecting host cities to utilize vast amounts of resources with no regard to the future of the city's residents. At the same time, they can be perceived as an answer to those challenges (Gold and Gold, 2017).

The topic of sustainability, legacy and positive impact on local societies remains significant within the Olympic Movement and the International Olympic Committee. These topics received a prominent place in the IOC's Agenda 2020 – an attempt to respond to contemporary problems of the Olympic Movement such as the lack of interest among most of the democratic and highly developed states in bidding for the Olympic Games. *Olympic Agenda 2020* was developed and agreed at the 127th IOC Session in Monaco on December 8 and 9, 2014. During one year of consultations with main stakeholders, experts and the public, a set of recommendations were made (IOC, 2014). Sustainability and positive impact are visible in many of the Agenda's recommendations. The fourth and fifth recommendations pertain to sustainability of the Olympic Games and everyday activities of the Olympic Movement. The positive impact of the Olympics on local societies is visible in the 11th (fostering gender equality), the 14th (strengthening the fundamental principle of Olympism concerning discrimination), and 23rd recommendations (concerning engaging local communities). All those recommendations referred to sustainability at the same time (*Olympic Agenda 2020*). Therefore, with the aim of providing sustainable Olympic Games which are beneficial for the local societies, the IOC engaged in, for example, promoting new technologies that are environmentally friendly, encouraging use of renewable energy sources, introducing new waste management systems and developing environmental education programmes (Furrer, 2002). Another initiative is 'The New Norm' which is deeply connected with *Agenda 2020*. It is a set of 118 reforms based on six recommendations of the *Agenda 2020* related to the organization of the Games. Its basic goal is to lead to maximum savings in hosting the Olympic Games (IOC, 2018a).

The IOC's emphasizing the aspects of the positive legacy of the Olympic Games has been observed for some time now. It can be related to the sustainability and impact on local societies to some extent. Especially the Olympic Games in Athens in 2004 showed negative consequences of hosting such a big sport event – many of the Olympic facilities have not been in use after Olympics, and only generate high costs in maintenance. Highlighting positive legacies of the Olympics helps to avoid social discontent in the first place, and also motivates potential future candidates for host cities. In terms of positive legacy, gaining knowledge and skills in event organizing, contributing to security systems, development of high-quality services, increasing hospitality and tolerance among local societies are highlighted (Gratton and Preuss, 2008). Providing positive development with a respect for the environment contributes positively to the host city and to the whole state as well. Therefore, the IOC can be perceived as a driving force for such positive change by undertaking actions that could be classified as public diplomacy activities, however in this case conducted not by a state but by a transnational organization.

Organizing the Olympic Games has a significant impact on the host city, mostly owing to wide investments in renovation and infrastructure, as well as concerning construction of sports venues. Such investments can improve mobility of people and goods, which is one of the key points of reaching sustainable development (Furrer, 2002). Generally speaking, IOC's public diplomacy aimed at promoting certain values, in this case contributing to the sustainable development, seems to be effective, at least to some extent. London's bid for the Summer Olympic Games in 2012 attracted IOC's attention among others owing to its environmental centrepiece. What is more, all five candidate cities to host the Olympics in 2012 included environmental standards in their bids. For example, Paris proposed building a solar stadium, which would have tripled the number of solar panels in France (Roper, 2006). Rio de Janeiro included ambitious environmental commitments and sustainability goals in its bid to organize the 2016 Summer Olympics as well (Tomlinson, 2014).

Public diplomacy of the IOC

As IOC's President Thomas Bach has stated, 'We need to change because sport today is too important in society to ignore the rest of society' (*Olympic Agenda 2020*, p. 2). Those words have significant meaning since sport nowadays is widely used by states within public diplomacy, but is also used by the IOC as a tool of influencing states interested in both organizing the Olympics and participating in them. Therefore, the IOC must be in line with its stakeholders, making sure that sport, and more precisely the Olympic Games, will not lose their attractiveness and popularity.

As has been shown, the IOC undertakes many efforts to combat potential risks and threats to the Olympic Movement. These can be seen as attempts to avoid the people in the host city or nation blaming the IOC for the burdens of the Olympic Games. IOC's efforts aim to provide evidence that the event was good for them as well, justify the high spending on hosting the event and encourage other cities to bid for the Games in the future (Beacom, 2012). Since the main problems of the IOC and the Olympic Movement are the growing gigantism and the decrease of interest in hosting the Olympic Games, major activities proposed for example within the *Olympic Agenda 2020* are related to the bidding process. The aim is to reduce the costs of organizing the Olympic Games, to provide a long lasting legacy of such an event and at the same time to secure the sustainability of the Olympic Games. In addition, for many years the IOC has been attempting to limit the size of the Olympics in terms of the numbers of sports and athletes, despite pressure from international sports federations.

Attempts to limit the gigantism of the Olympics have led to positive effects already. The Pyeongchang 2018 Organising Committee announced the hosting the event has achieved a surplus of at least 55 million USD (IOC, 2018d). The IOC has also claimed that owing to the *Olympic Agenda 2020* and its new norms, savings of the Tokyo 2020 Organizing Committee have reached 4.3 billion USD (IOC, 2018c). In the case of Tokyo we shall wait until the Games are finished for the final evaluation, but in general it is hard not to see the efforts. However, the bidding process for the 2026 Winter Olympics does not imply the end of the crisis yet. Calgary, Milan/Cortina d'Ampezzo and Stockholm were invited by the IOC to the Candidature Stage after the application of Turkish Erzurum was rejected (IOC, 2018b). However, Calgary withdrew its bid after a referendum, leaving IOC with only two candidates. Earlier in 2018 Japanese Sapporo, Swiss Sion and Austrian Graz also withdrew their applications (*The Guardian*, 2018). Therefore, as when selecting the host of the Winter Games in 2022 the IOC has been left with just two bids, although less controversial ones. The IOC's endeavours therefore have led to some positive change, but have not resulted in greater interest in organizing the Olympics.

All the IOC's attempts to limit the costly efforts of the host city and to recover the Olympics' status can be interpreted as strengthening the IOC itself and its soft power. According to Joseph S. Nye (2008) soft power is the ability to affect others through attraction rather than coercion or payment. Governments, in order to harvest soft power resources with the aim of communicating with the foreign publics, conduct public diplomacy. As has been noted, this activity generally refers to states, but in line with current trends in research on public diplomacy non-state actors such as International Non-Governmental Organizations (INGOs) are also seen as being able to pursue public diplomacy. The above-mentioned endeavours by the IOC might therefore be perceived through the perspective of its public diplomacy, since they aim at promotion of its interests (See: Beacom and Brittain, 2016) – in the context of making the Olympic Movement last and increasing its capacity to influence international affairs. Its other interests are promotion of fundamental values and principles. Those are, among others, harmonious development of humankind, blending

sport and culture, and respect for ethnic principles (IOC, 2017a). Such fundamental values promoted by the Olympic Movement seem to be closely related
to the concept of sustainable development as they can be equated with respect
in general.

In evidence that the IOC can be perceived as an actor conducting its own
public diplomacy, the role of National Olympic Committees (NOCs) can be
evoked. NOCs do not represent the national interests of their states but
instead represent IOC's interests in those states; they are tools in the hands of
the IOC to safeguard its interests worldwide (Walker et al., 2010). Such an
attitude is additional evidence that the IOC, similarly to states, has its own
interests as mentioned above. What is more, it is in possession of a significant
soft power resource – a sports mega-event, which can be perceived as yet
another tool of influencing states. In reaching its goals and interests, it pur-
sues public diplomacy activities aimed at further strengthening its soft power
and international image, as well as reaching its developmental goals. Those
are, among others, actions undertaken with the aim of promoting the sustainable development and positive legacy of the Olympic Games. The legacy
of the Olympic Games or the Olympic Movement in general can be related to
its public diplomacy as well since the host city is left after the Olympic Games
not only with a sporting infrastructure, but more importantly, with knowledge
and competences concerning urban and sustainable development or green
technologies (Kidd, 2013). Both ideas – sustainability and promoting a positive legacy of Olympic Games – are closely related to each other and at the
same time to the idea of IOC's public diplomacy in terms of achieving the
main goals of this organization, which are promotion of fundamental values
and principles – respect, tolerance, integration, and human rights. Both the
attempts to counter the gigantism of the Olympic Games and to provide them
with a positive legacy and sustainability have most of all economic significance, however at the same time they additionally strengthen IOC's soft
power and its image since they can be classified as public diplomacy activities.
They contribute to the IOC's external perception as being a driving force
towards positive changes and at the same time, they allow the IOC to achieve
its interests deriving from fundamental values included in the Olympic
Charter.

Conclusion

The International Olympic Committee has been struggling with the growing
size and gigantism of the Olympic Games since the 1950s. Initially its efforts
involved attempts to limit the Olympic programme, in order to decrease the
number of participants, although the IOC was faced with opposition from
international sports federations. Eventually the IOC imposed a limits on
sports (28), and athletes eligible to participate in the Olympics (10,500). This
also included introducing minimum standards for performance of athletes
except six participants from each NOC in swimming and track and field.

Apart from attempts to limit the size of the Olympic Games, the IOC has also made efforts to make the Olympics more sustainable, providing positive impact for local communities. This has included both expectations from candidates hosting the Olympic Games, and support for the future hosts by sharing knowledge. Most contemporary initiatives, such as *Agenda 2020* and the New Norm have responded to the challenge of diminishing interest in hosting the Olympic Games. Already they have led to savings being made by the Organizing Committees of the Olympic Games, although the interest in hosting the Olympic has not increased yet.

By promoting values related to sustainable development and tackling the challenge of gigantism of the Olympic Games, the IOC is able to potentially shape its positive image as a transnational actor contributing to the wide development of the world and counteracting social challenges such as lack of tolerance and respect, inequalities, discrimination and violations of human rights. Therefore, providing frames for promoting sustainable development, positive legacy and impact on local societies in the host cities, and conducting educational programmes or providing development aid might be compared to similar actions undertaken by states within their public diplomacy and aimed at strengthening those states' international perceptions. It therefore appears legitimate to speak of the public diplomacy of the International Olympic Committee.

This research was supported by the National Science Centre, Poland [grant number 2015/19/D/HS5/00513].

References

BBC (2017). 2024 Olympics: Budapest to drop bid to host Games, February 22. https://www.bbc.com/sport/olympics/39059452. Accessed May 3, 2018.

Beacom, A. (2012). *International Diplomacy and the Olympic Movement: The New Mediators*. Basingstoke: Palgrave Macmillan.

Beacom, A. and Brittain, I. (2016). Public diplomacy and the International Paralympic Committee: Reconciling the roles of disability advocate and sports regulator. *Diplomacy & Statecraft* 27(2), 273–294.

Boykoff, J. (2015). Beijing and Almaty contest Winter Olympics in human rights nightmare. *The Guardian*, July 30. https://www.theguardian.com/sport/2015/jul/30/china-kazakhstan-winter-olympics-2022. Accessed 6 May 2018.

Chappelet, J-L. (2014). Managing the size of the Olympic Games. *Sport in Society* 17 (5), 581–592.

Cull, N. (2008). The public diplomacy of the modern Olympic Games and China's soft power strategy. In M. Price and D. Dayan (eds.), *Owning the Olympics: Narratives of the New China*, 117–144. Ann Arbor: University of Michigan.

Furrer, P. (2002). Sustainable Olympic Games. A dream or reality? *Bollettino della Società Geografica Italiana: Serie XII* VII(4), 795–830.

Gold, J. R., and Gold, M. M. (2017). Introduction. In J. R., Gold, and M. M. Gold (eds.), *Olympic Cities: City Agendas, Planning, and the World's Games: 1896–2020*, 1–17. Abingdon: Routledge.

Gratton, C. and Preuss, H. (2008). Maximizing Olympic impacts by building up legacies. *The International Journal of the History of Sport* 25(14), 1922–1938. doi:10.1080/09523360802439023.

Grix, J. (2013). Sport politics and the Olympics. *Political Studies Review* 11, 15–25. doi:10.1111/1478-9302.12001.

Hill, C. (1996). *Olympic Politics: Athens to Atlanta, 1896–1996.* Manchester: Manchester University Press.

Holt, R. and Ruta, D. (2015). Introduction: Sport, legacy and leadership. In R. Holt and D. Ruta (eds.), *Routledge Handbook of Sport and Legacy: Meeting the Challenge of Major Sports Events*, 1–15. Abingdon: Routledge.

HuijghE. (2016). Public diplomacy. In C. Constantinou, P. Kerr and P. Sharp (eds.), *Sage Handbook of Diplomacy*, 437–450. London: Sage.

International Olympic Committee (IOC). (1957). *Minutes of the 53rd Session of the International Olympic Committee (The Sittings are held at the Hotel Balkan, Sofia 1957), September 23rd to September 28th 1957.* International Olympic Committee Historical Archives

International Olympic Committee (IOC). (1958). *Minutes of the 54th Session of the International Olympic Committee. Tokyo – Imperial Hotel – Sitting of Wednesday May 14th 1958.* International Olympic Committee Historical Archives

International Olympic Committee (IOC). (1961). *Minutes. 58th Session. International Olympic Committee. Athens – Senate House – June 19th, 20th and 21st 1961.* International Olympic Committee Historical Archives.

International Olympic Committee (IOC). (1963). *Minutes of the 60th Session. International Olympic Committee. Baden-Baden – Kurhaus from the 16th to the 20th of October 1963.* International Olympic Committee Historical Archives

International Olympic Committee (IOC). (1964a). *Minutes of the 61st Session of the International Olympic Committee. Innsbruck – Landeshaus. January 26th, 27th and 28th 1964.* International Olympic Committee Historical Archives.

International Olympic Committee (IOC). (1964b). *Minutes of the 63rd Session of the International Olympic Committee. Palace Hotel, Madrid, from Thursday 7 to Saturday, October 9, 1964, from 9.30 a.m. to 1.00 p.m. and from 3.30 p.m. to 7.00 p.m.* International Olympic Committee Historical Archives.

International Olympic Committee (IOC). (1966). *Minutes of the 64th Session of the International Olympic Committee. Hotel Excelsior, Rome, April 25, 26, 27 and 28, 1966.* International Olympic Committee Historical Archives.

International Olympic Committee (IOC). (1972). *Minutes of the 73rd Session of the International Olympic Committee. Munich: 21st – 24th August 1972.* International Olympic Committee Historical Archives.

International Olympic Committee (IOC). (1973). *Minutes: 74th Session of the International Olympic Committee. Varna – 1973.* International Olympic Committee Historical Archives.

International Olympic Committee (IOC). (1996). *The International Olympic Committee One Hundred Years: The Idea-The Presidents-The Achievements.* vol. III, IOC: Lausanne.

International Olympic Committee (IOC). (2001). *Minutes of the 112th IOC Session, Moscow 13, 14, 15 and 16 July 2001. Report by the Chairman of the Olympic Programme Working Group to the 112th IOC Session, Moscow July 2001.* International Olympic Committee Historical Archives.

International Olympic Committee (IOC). (2002). *Minutes of the 114th IOC Session. Mexico City, 28 and 29 November 2002*. International Olympic Committee Historical Archives.

International Olympic Committee (IOC). (2005). *Minutes of the 117th IOC Session. Singapore, 6, 7, 8 and 9 July 2005*. International Olympic Committee Historical Archives.

International Olympic Committee (IOC). (2007). IOC makes historic decision by simultaneously awarding Olympic Games 2024 to Paris and 2028 to Los Angeles, September 13. https://www.olympic.org/news/ioc-makes-historic-decision-by-simulta neously-awarding-olympic-games-2024-to-paris-and-2028-to-los-angeles. Accessed 3 May 2018.

International Olympic Committee (IOC). (2008). *Minutes of the 120th IOC Session. Beijing, 5, 6, 7 and 24 August 2008*. International Olympic Committee Historical Archives.

International Olympic Committee (IOC). (2009). *Minutes of the 121st IOC Session. Copenhagen, 2, 7, 8 and 9 October 2009*. International Olympic Committee Historical Archives.

International Olympic Committee (IOC). (2014).*Olympic Agenda 2020*. International Olympic Committee.

International Olympic Committee (IOC). (2016). *Factsheet. Legacies of the Games*, May. https://stillmed.olympic.org/media/Document%20Library/OlympicOrg/Fa ctsheets-Reference-Documents/Games/Legacies/Factsheet-Legacies-of-the-Gam es-May-2016.pdf#_ga=2.106999364.73645398.1512537312-977313445.1512537312, Accessed 6 December 2017.

International Olympic Committee (IOC). (2017).*Olympic Charter*. International Olympic Committee. In Force as from 15 September 2017.

International Olympic Committee (IOC). (2018a). The New Norm: It's a Games Changer, February 6. https://www.olympic.org/news/the-new-norm-it-s-a-games-cha nger. Accessed 25 May 2019.

International Olympic Committee (IOC). (2018b). Three cities recommended by IOC Executive Board as candidate cities for the Olympic Winter Games 2026, October 4. https://www.olympic.org/news/three-cities-recommended-by-ioc-executive-board-a s-candidate-cities-for-the-olympic-winter-games-2026. Accessed 25 May 2019.

International Olympic Committee (IOC). (2018c). *Olympic Agenda 2020* and its new norm saves Tokyo 2020 USD 4.3 billion, October 4. https://www.olympic.org/news/ olympic-agenda-2020-and-its-new-norm-saves-tokyo-2020-usd-4-3-billion. Accessed 25 May 2019.

International Olympic Committee (IOC). (2018d). Pyeongchang 2018 announces surplus of at least USD 55 million, October 8. https://www.olympic.org/news/pyeong chang-2018-announces-surplus-of-at-least-usd-55-million. Accessed 25 May 2019.

International Olympic Committee Sport and Environment Commission (IOC Sport and Environment Commission). (2003). *Olympic Movement's Agenda 21: Sport for Sustainable Development*. Lausanne: International Olympic Committee.

Jackson, S. and DawsonM. (2017). IOC–State–Corporate Nexus: Corporate diplomacy and the Olympic coup d'état. *South African Journal for Research in Sport, Physical Education and Recreation* 39(1:2), 101–111.

Karamichas, J. (2013). *The Olympic Games and the Environment*. Basingstoke: Palgrave Macmillan.

Kidd, B. (2013). The global sporting legacy of the Olympic Movement. *Sport in Society* 16(4), 491–502.

Lenartowicz, M. (2015). Polityczne uwarunkowania decyzji o organizacji największych imprez sportowych oraz ich społeczne i ekonomiczne konsekwencje [Political implications of decision to organize the biggest sports events and their social and economic consequences]. In Z. Dziubiński and K. Jankowski (eds.), *Kultura fizyczna a polityka* [*Physical culture and politics*], 45–53. Warsaw: AWF Warszawa.

Leopkey, B. and Parent, M. M. (2012). The (Neo) institutionalization of legacy and its sustainable governance within the Olympic Movement. *European Sport Management Quarterly* 12(5), 437–455. doi:10.1080/16184742.2012.693116.

NyeJr., J. S. (2008). Public diplomacy and soft power. *Annals of the American Academy of Political and Social Science*616, 94–109.

Pamment, J. (2013). *New Public Diplomacy in the 21st Century: A Comparative Study of Policy and Practice*. Abingdon: Routledge.

Roper, T. (2006). Producing environmentally sustainable Olympic Games and 'greening' major public events. *Global Urban Development Magazine* 2(1). http://www.globalurban.org/GUDMag06Vol2Iss1/Roper.htm. Accessed 11 May 2018.

Shipway, R. (2007). Sustainable legacies for the 2012 Olympic Games. *The Journal of The Royal Society for the Promotion of Health* 127(3), 119–124.

The Guardian (2018). Blow for IOC as Calgary set to be latest city to stop bid for 2026 Winter Olympics, November 14. https://www.theguardian.com/sport/2018/nov/14/blow-for-ioc-as-calgary-set-to-be-latest-city-to-stop-bid-for-2026-winter-olympics. Accessed 25 May 2019.

Tomlinson, A. (2014). Olympic legacies: Recurrent rhetoric and harsh realities. *Contemporary Social Science* 9(2), 137–158.

Walker, M., Heere, B., Parent, M. M. and Drane, D. (2010). Social responsibility and the Olympic Games: The mediating role of consumer attributions. *Journal of Business Ethics*95, 659–680.

Part II

Olympic Games as a tool for urban and territorial development?

4 The territorial and urban dimensions of the Summer Olympics

A review of publications (1984–2018)

José Chaboche and Alain Schoeny

Introduction

The Summer Olympic Games (SOG) are referred to as sport mega events (Roche, 2000) or sport giga events because of their tourist attractiveness, their media coverage, their costs and their urban impacts (Müller, 2015). Like the Football World Cup, they belong to the major level of the Downward et al. (2009) hierarchical classification of sports events. Since 1896, they have been held at a four-year rhythm in a candidate city selected by their owner, the International Olympic Committee (IOC). Described as "the quintessential spatial event" (Augustin, 2009), they give rise to abundant and multi-thematic scientific research. Thus, this chapter provides a critical review based on a corpus of 434 anglophone and francophone scientific articles on a specific topic: the territorial, reticular and multiscalar dimensions of the SOG. The objective is to identify the publishing journals, their impact on the scientific community, the frequency with which literature on the topic is published, the research fields concerned, the nature of the articles published, their research subject and main findings, in order to evaluate the general dynamic of this field of research, which is of particular interest to public and private decision-makers. It is therefore a matter of presenting successively the protocol followed, the materials collected, the analysis of the corpus constituted and the concluding remarks that this chapter calls for to gain insight into the territorial and urban dimensions of the SOG.

Methodological approach

Gathering 434 scientific articles published from 1984 to September 2018, this corpus is organized into four axes: SOG hosting strategies; urban project and SOG; sports tourism and SOG; territorial and urban legacies of the SOG. "Drawing from their personal experiences" (Chevrier, 2004: 71) and guided by their initial knowledge of the field (Paillé et Mucchielli, 2005), the authors of this article defined these axes *a priori* to circumscribe the scope of study in the framework of a qualitative and constructivist epistemology. Of course, choosing one axis over another for an article with cross-sectional content is difficult. Identification of the dominant theme, after thorough reading(s), then allows to link it to one of the four axes according to the subjectivity (Glaser, 1978; Strauss and Corbin, 1990) of the authors.

Indeed, the approach followed here is "analytical induction" (Paillé, 2002: 101) to reveal the information (Lamizet and Silem, 1997) contained in these articles and order them to establish a first state of the question. Induction occurs during the exploration of the original question, and throughout the "process of problematization [(Chevrier, op. cit.), then] in the context of the analysis and interpretation of the data [(Paillé, 1994)]", as Villemagne (2006: 134) points out in an epistemological essay on qualitative research. He also says that this "methodological choice [of analytic induction] for a set of data collected and analysed without necessarily relying on theories or theoretical framework solidly defined and pre-existing [requires] to give itself a structure [i.e. the four predefined axes] to carry out [this inductive process] regarding the diversity and the possible abundance of data" (*ibid.*).

In this context, this chapter provides a review of the papers that examine the territorial and urban dimensions of the SOG. It presents the first results of ongoing broader research work in the form of a systematic review, whose methodological approach we follow here to study simultaneously the four axes of a corpus of unprecedented size. The originality and significance of this work lies in the interdisciplinary and integrated approach to the Olympic cycle, from the hosting of the event to its legacies, whereas the literature reviews provided by the collected articles are characterized by a mono-disciplinary approach to a particular theme (e.g. sociology, about the interactions between urban policy and sport mega-events: Roche, 1994) or a sub-theme (e.g. resident perceptions of SOG: Ritchie et al., 2009) within this continuum.

This chapter presents the first elements of formalization of a systematic review of literature still in progress. Rather rare but usually highly consulted (Berland et al., 2013), this kind of work requires the implementation of a reliable methodology to prevent the risk of a simple descriptive listing, being too linear and failing to link the articles between them. The present work is based on the methodology of Arksey and O'Malley (2005), taken up by Roult, et al. (2018) for their analysis of the 35 articles published in the academic journal *Society and Leisure* from 1978 to 2018 concerning the relationship between sport and city. This methodology recommends five steps to design a systematic literature review.

Firstly, the research question guiding this work is formulated according to the triple objective of clarity, conciseness and univocity that qualitative research requires (Campenhoudt et al., 2017): what are the studied topics and the arguments defended about the scientific study of the territorial and urban dimensions of the SOG? Within the framework of this exploratory article, this question leads to several objectives, common to some with those pursued by Roult et al. (op cit): collect, analyse and discuss the relevant scientific literature; identify the journals supporting the articles studied and measure the overall pace of publication; inventory and order the subjects treated;

determine the nature of the work (ex ante, ex post or general); identify the editions of the SOG studied; deliver the main results and lessons of this corpus.

The next step is to determine a study period and collect the data from keywords. The study period spans 34 years from September 2018 to 1984, date of the Los Angeles edition, from which the IOC implemented the principles of its current global marketing strategy for the SOG. Based on the keyword "Olympic Games" and its French translation *"Jeux Olympiques"* in the databases of scientific publishers, specialized platforms and, finally, Google Scholar (Table 4.1) – one of the four most effective search engines of the world according to Lewandowski and Höchstötter (2008) – the queries revealed thousands of bibliographic references. We sorted the articles out and classified them accordingly in one of the four areas. We proceeded from the titles, summaries and key words, which made it possible to keep 935 references, recorded in the form of a computer matrix in a spreadsheet.

As indicated by the method, criteria for inclusion of these references to the final corpus must be established. Thus, we have chosen to use those published in English or in French (the two languages we have a good enough command of to conduct an in-depth qualitative analysis of the data) by researchers in scientific journals (paper-based or electronic) and reviewed by peers, i.e. a total of 352 articles. The bibliography of each of them was then explored in order to reach data saturation. The corpus thus constituted includes 434 articles (93.5% Anglophone, 6.5% Francophone). In line with international academic standards, almost all articles published in French-language have English-language bibliographic references, which justifies our use of a bilingual corpus. Performed for harmonization, reliability and scientific purpose of the corpus, this choice rules out book reviews and research notes. It also excludes theses and dissertations but their main results are generally published in the forms chosen here should they deserve to be. Texts, published in – sometimes high profile –journals of less scientific than institutional or promotional essence, signed by leaders of sports institutions or large companies, and which offer neither research question nor bibliography have been ruled out. This method also counters the financial impossibility of accessing a large number of books or book chapters. Thus, it does not urge us to select them within such a systematic literature review project (Lucarelli and Berg, 2011). Finally, articles are filtered whose title, summary or keywords announce a study of the territorial and urban stakes of the SOG. This

Table 4.1 Databases asked with the keywords *"Jeux Olympiques"* and "Olympic Games"

Scientific publishers	Cognizant Communication Corporation; Elsevier; Emerald; Routledge; Sage; Springer; Taylor and Francis; Wiley
Specialized platforms	CAIRN; PERSEE
Free search engine	Google Scholar

Design and production: J. Chaboche and A. Schoeny

objective of uniqueness, quality and accessibility of the corpus thus guaran-
tees its scientificity at the expense, unfortunately, of the exclusion of some
works that have become classics, such as Gold and Gold's *Olympic Cities.
City Agendas, Planning, and the Word's Games, 1896–2012* (2007) or Roche's
*Mega-events and Modernity: Olympics and Expos in the Growth of Global
Culture* (2000). Journals such as *Town and Country Planning* or *Geography
Review* did not post articles prior to the mid-1990s, thus depriving the corpus
of a dozen potential references for want of accessibility to the texts. However,
the effort of triangulation to obtain data by different techniques, by different
researchers, and from different sources ensures reliability, coherence and con-
sistency to the corpus (Jodelet, 2003: 160).

After this filtering, the step of extracting and grouping the relevant data
takes place from the previously exposed research objectives. For this purpose,
we adapted the methodological model of Lucarelli and Berg (op. cit.). The
latter offers a coding of the relevant indicators of the categories and sub-
categories identified for each article of the corpus: bibliographical data, object
of study, main results. Finally, using basic sorting and crossed sorting, the
results are interpreted at first in a descriptive manner then analytically in
order to highlight the information contained in the corpus and to match these
preliminary results to the three essential characteristics of any literature
review (Berland, op. cit.: 6): review of "(almost) exhaustive" work, at least in
the category of scientific journal articles for this area; "Real contribution
(concept of added value)" thanks to the four initial axes of analysis first
defined *a priori* and then divided into sub-axes by ordering the corpus of
articles to form the intellectual framework of this study; "presence of summary tables" (place of publication on the subject, nature of the work carried
out, etc.) for more conciseness.

Configuration and dynamics of scientific production

The scientific literature relating to the territorial and urban stakes of the SOG
appears dual. On the one hand, there is a high concentration in terms of
publishing media, 46.8% of the 434 articles collected from only 13.3% of the
195 journals, i.e. those having published at least four articles (Figure 4.1).
Among these 26 journals, seven have published at least ten articles and make
up 21.5% of the corpus. Ten others, which contributed six to nine articles
each, account for 16.1% of this corpus and nine others (four to five articles
each) for 9.2%. On the other hand, the second half of the publications is dis-
persed. Indeed 53.2% of articles come from journals that published only one
to three articles on the subject between 1984 and 2018. From the start, the
territorial and urban dimension of the SOG thus appears as a multi-thematic
and rich but marginal research object, even within the most popular journal
on the subject: the 22 articles listed in *The International Journal of the History
of Sport* represent less than half a thousandth of the 4,000 articles published
since 1984.

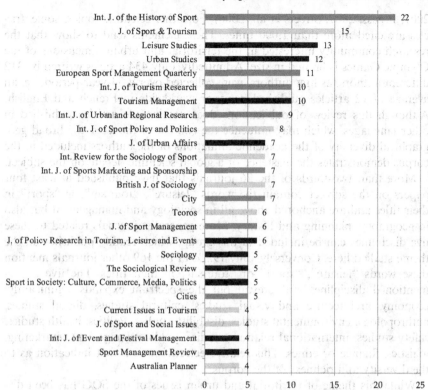

Figure 4.1 Journals that have published at least four articles on the territorial and urban dimension of the Summer Olympic Games and the period of creation of the journal

The SCImago ranking of scientific journals' global visibility indicates that, in 2017, 42.6% of the journals included in our corpus were among the 25% most visible journals in their respective subject areas. Among the 26 journals that have published the most articles on our topic of study, some occupy excellent ranking positions: *Tourism Management* and *Annals of Tourism Research* are first and third out of 101 in the subject area of "Tourism, Leisure and Hospitality Management"; *The International Journal of Urban and Regional Research* and *Urban Studies* are third and fifth out of 173 in the subject area of "Urban Studies". More than half (55.6%) of the 434 articles collected were published in journals positioned in the top quartile of their respective fields, reflecting an editorial interest in the territorial and urban dimensions of the Olympic Games. On the other hand, citations per article do not seem to match this potential visibility; indeed, according to Google Scholar, a quarter of the articles included in our corpus are only cited by zero to nine other articles. Only five articles are thought to have more than 500 citations (Waitt, 2003; Roche, 1994; Andranovich, Burbank and Heying,

2001; Preuss, 2007; Streets et al., 2006). For other scientific topics, some articles are cited more than 1,000 times. These elements tend to show that the research community interested in the territorial and urban dimensions of the Olympic Games is limited in size. Admittedly, only 434 articles written by 312 different authors, as first authors, were collected over a 34-year period, i.e. an average of 12 articles published per year worldwide in French and English. Although this review of publications does not include articles published in other languages, which may influence the content of the axes, the broad geographical diversity of the academic affiliations of the authors included in the corpus demonstrates the existence of a global scientific debate on the subject.

More than two-thirds of the 26 journals that have published at least four papers on the subject contain the words "leisure", "tourism" or "sport" in their titles and are anchored above all in sociology and management but also in geography, planning and history. More generalist journals related to these five disciplines can be included in this group, which readily publishes on the theme studied here. Conversely, only 19.5% of the 169 other journals mention these words "leisure", "sport" or "tourism" in their titles. The five above-mentioned disciplines still prevail but the spectrum expands significantly: economy, architecture and visual studies, cultural studies, digital studies, anthropology, environmental studies, disability studies, Politics, health studies, safety studies, international relations studies, public management, marketing, logistics, finance or ethics. This relative eclecticism is a first indication as to the diversity and richness of the corpus.

While this theme of territorial and urban issues of the SOG has been discussed in a number of publications since 1984, it was really placed on the scientific agenda during the process of urban planning for the 2000 Olympics in Sydney. Previously, the concept of disposable facilities of the SOG Atlanta (1996) seemed to have limited the literature on this theme; The Barcelona Games gave rise to a more consistent production but often published in books – which our chosen methodology excludes. The increase in volume and frequency of publications since 2006 is probably due to the awarding, the previous year, of the 2012 SOG to London; indeed the geographical, cultural and linguistic proximity of many authors to the future SOG sites enabled them to conduct extensive work on the subject. Since then, we have observed a circumstantial effect in favour of opportunistic editorial strategies. Indeed 30.9% of the articles in the corpus date back to 2008 (Beijing), 2011 and 2012 (London), with a decrease by one-third to almost one-half in the post-Olympic years (2009: 23, 2013: 36). This growth (82.2% of the corpus was published between 2006 and 2018) can be seen more generally as part of the scientific and institutional maturation of research in the social sciences of sport as indicated by the recent dates of creation of these journals (period studied: circa 1984–2018) (Figure 4.2).

Research in this field has intensified through the development of more solid theoretical foundations and of empirical and applied approaches that often meet the need for problem-solving knowledge expressed by public and private

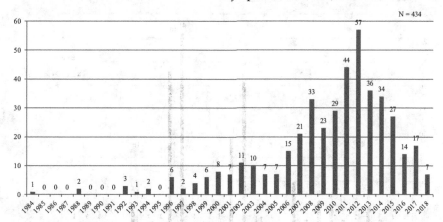

Figure 4.2 Scientific articles published from 1984 to 2018 on the theme of territorial and urban issues of the Summer Olympic Games

stakeholders in the Olympic system. Moreover, 61.8% of the corpus consists of studies based on the case of one of the SOGs editions in the period 1964–2020. While the pioneering studies were almost exclusively published *ex post*, the Beijing SOG gave rise to pre-event research aimed at producing predictive analyses, early-effects assessments and recommendations (Figure 4.3). The remaining part of the corpus (38.2%) includes comparative studies between two or more SOGs, or longitudinal studies on various objects.

Owing to their thematic syncretism or their high degree of generalization, 7.1% of the 434 articles in the corpus have contributed to the contextual and conceptual framework of the discussion below (see p. 60) but could not be linked to any one of our four analytical axes (Figure 4.4), even though they are undeniably relevant to the topic studied. Axis 1 concentrates 32.7% articles of the corpus without overly dominating the other three (25.3% for axis 2, 12% for axis 3 and 22.8% for axis 4 respectively), which tends to validate the definition of the four axes chosen before the collection. It is now necessary to analyse each one of them in order to pin-point elements of synthesis, discussion and conclusion.

Exploitation of the corpus

The territorial and urban dimension of the SOG gives rise to a bourgeoning scientific literature whose frame and object of study we wish to specify. Thus, some works synthesize the historical (e.g. Földesi, 1992) and contemporary (e. g. Augustin, 2011) spatial dynamics of the SOG, seen as catalysts of urban development (Essex and Chalkley, 1999), elements of soft power (Grix and Houlihan, 2014) and operators of globalization (e.g. Roche, 2006) according to political(e.g. Grix, 2013), sociological (e.g. Silk, 2011) or managerial (e.g. Burton, 2003) approaches. It highlights an expensive spectacularization of the

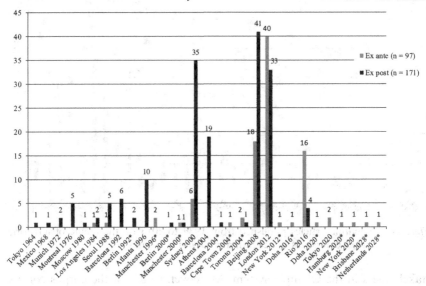

Figure 4.3 Articles based on an *ex ante* and/or *ex post* case study by Summer Olympic
        Games

Olympic space (e.g. Guthman, 2008) due to an entrepreneurial urbanism
intertwining public and private interest (Hall, 2006) and within which the
polysemic and protean character of the SOG would generate multiple leverage effects (Chalip et al., 2000). This prevailing urbanistic model dictates
public strategies for hosting sporting events (Chappelet and Pinson, 2015)
combining exaltation of territorial pride or even nationalism (e.g. Falcous and
Silk, 2010), a quest for urban competitiveness (e.g. Searle and Bounds, 1999)
and a promise of positive lasting legacies (e.g. Atkinson et al., 2008). These
hosting strategies – combining attraction, production and evaluation of the
SOG – are discussed in the next section. Three others sub-sections tackle
issues related to the urban project (p.003.2.), tourism strategies (p.003.3.) and
the creation of legacies (p.003.4.), respectively, involved in the analysis of the
territorial and urban dimensions of the SOG.

SOG hosting strategies

The attraction strategies of the SOG are linked first of all to the motives for
candidacy of host cities (e.g. Shoval, 2002), associated cities (Dussier and
Machemehl, 2014) and host countries (e.g. Zhou et al., 2012). As a counter-
point, understanding the logic underlying the choices made by the IOC (e.g.
Poast, 2007) facilitates the identification of key success factors (e.g. Maennig
and Vierhaus, 2017). Among them, the perceptions of populations (e.g.
Heslop et al., 2010) before or after the SOG (e.g. Lee et al., 2013) are studied,
even in non-host cities (op. cit., Ritchie et al., 2009). Some works therefore

Conceptual framework and theoretical contextualization (articles, n = 31 [7.1 %])

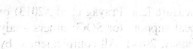

N = 434

Summer Olympic Games hosting strategies (n = 142 [32.7 %])
- General elements
- Perception of populations
- Production of the event by and with the host cities
- Costs and impacts

Urban Project and Summer Olympic Games (n = 110 [25.3 %])
- General elements
- Urban regeneration
- Image of the city or country
- Urban planning

TERRITORIAL AND URBAN ISSUES OF THE SUMMER OLYMPIC GAMES (n = 403)

Territorial and urban legacies of the Summer Olympic Games (n = 99 [22.8 %])
- General elements
- Sports equipment or Olympic Village
- Valorization of the Olympic legacy

Sports Tourism and Summer Olympic Games (n = 52 [12 %])
- Strategies of host cities and host countries
- Impacts

Figure 4.4 Distribution of articles between the conceptual framework and the four predefined research axes

measure (e.g. Prayag et al., 2013) or model (e.g. Gursoy and Kendall, 2006) local support for SOG; others analyse the conflicts created (e.g. Boykoff and Fussey, 2014). All complemented by those relating to media influence strategies (e.g. Ritchie et al., 2010) aimed at improving the social acceptance of the SOG through several leverage effects: individual and collective well-being (e.g. Hiller and Wanner, 2014); civic engagement and citizenship (e.g. Waitt, 2001); democratization (e.g. Black and Bezanson, 2004) and human rights (e.g. Brownell, 2012); national (e.g. Elder et al., 2006) or transnational (e.g. Giulianotti and Brownell, 2012) identity.

The related urban production to host SOG gives rise to other studies often at the intersection of planning and management. They relate to the overall management of the Olympic project (e.g. Davies and Mackenzie, 2014) or to one of its elements: communication (e.g. Theodoraki, 2009), organizational knowledge (e.g. Singh and Hu, 2008), logistics (e.g. Arnold et al., 2015), partnerships (e.g. Chalip and McGuirty, 2004), transport (e.g. Browne et al., 2014) and mobility (e.g. Giulianotti et al., 2015), safety (e.g. Tsoukala, 2006), environmental sustainability (e.g. Brajer and Mead, 2003), corporate social responsibility (e.g. Drucker and White, 2013), and so on.

The costs and impacts involved by hosting the SOG are mainly evaluated according to economic objectives: employment (e.g. Feddersen and Maennig, 2009) or wages (e.g. Hotchkiss et al., 2003); investments made (e.g. Li and Blake, 2009); regional impact calculations (e.g. Preuss, 2004); *ex ante* cost/benefit analyses of the SOG hosting project (e.g. Owen, 2005); *ex post* evaluations of the results of the preliminary studies of economic impacts (e.g. Kirkup and Major, 2006) including those conducted by a consulting firm (Madden, 2002). Non-economic evaluations are rarer such as those assessing the effects on the practice of sports in the host cities (e.g. Reis et al., 2013) and countries (e.g. Charlton, 2010) or those on the environmental footprint of the SOG (e.g. Huijuan et al., 2013) and its perception by the residents (e.g. Jin et al., 2011).

Urban project and SOG

The second axis of the studies included in the corpus of articles articulates the urban project and SOG through three sub-axes: urban planning; urban regeneration; place branding. The first sub-axis involves a chronological approach for synthesizing the effects of the SOG on urban development (e.g. Chalkley and Essex, 1999), a diachronic approach for modeling the development of sports facilities (e.g. Pitts and Liao, 2006) or the Olympic Village (Muñoz, 2006), a contemporary approach for remedying the gigantism "syndrome" of the SOG (e.g. Müller and Stewart, 2016) and a prospective approach for ensuring that bids for the 2028 SOG conform to the principles of IOC Olympic legacy planning (Hartigan, 2012 with the example of Brisbane) or local authorities (Hartmann and Zandberg, 2015 with the example of Amsterdam). Those studies contribute, on the one hand, to the analyses of the risks posed by the SOG, such as the difficulties related to their multi-sta-keholder governance (Liu et al., 2010) or, on the other hand, to the studies of the leverage effects the SOG are claimed to have (e.g. Karadakis et al., 2010) as regards, for example, their environmental sustainability perceived as a "global attractor" of capital flows for host cities (Mol, 2010). The gap between expected and observed effects (e.g. Davis and Thornley, 2010) then negatively impacts the poorest populations (e.g. Armstrong et al., 2011). It is thus argued that unsuccessful bidding cities ultimately gain in terms of quality of local democracy (Lenskyj, 1996), urban development programming (Lauermann, 2015) or rationalization of sports facilities development (Alberts, 2009). Some authors criticize SOG planning as it is sometimes undertaken and implemented under a state of emergency, as was the case in Rio (Sánchez and Broudehoux, 2013), and always under a state of exception (e.g. Richmond and Garmany, 2016). The latter is thought to remain in place over time due to the influence of the emerging smart city model, whose pur-pose of optimizing urban public space (security, mobility, etc.) tends to justify the continued control of the populations by the authorities and private operators (Gaffney and Robertson, 2016).

Within this framework, the link between the SOG and urban regeneration gives rise to critical analyses. The marketing strategies of host cities (e.g. Gold and Gold, 2008) are known to be the result of an entrepreneurial governance model (e.g. Owen, 2002) that leads cities to compete against one another to attract the mega events produced by the sports entertainment industry (e.g. Searle and Bounds, 1999). However, it is believed that, locally, the SOG would result in congested networks of transport routes and venues within areas that would draw little or no benefit from the SOG (Poncet, 2001); on a sub-metropolitan scale, attempts to take advantage of the SOG (Smith, 2009) would be rather ineffective (Bell and Gallimore, 2015). Barcelona, though the most praised case, would be less a model of post-industrial regeneration (Balibrea, 2001) than an example that could not be reproduced and which, as in all SOG cases, would not be flawless (e.g. Garcia-Ramon and Albet, 2000). This is why, for example, the evolution of land costs in the host cities is observed minutely (e.g. Kontokosta, 2011). The increase, in the pre-Olympic stage, of these costs in areas close to Olympic facilities (e.g. Lu and Yang, 2015), would negatively impact small-scale local commerce (Kennelly and Watt, 2012) and micro-enterprises (Raco and Tunney, 2010); it can lead to the accelerated eviction of vulnerable populations (e.g. Ninnin, 2014), since this phenomenon is sometimes part of a more general urban management policy, as in Seoul in 1988 (Davis, 2011); and finally it can promote gentrification (e. g. Watt, 2013). This overall privatization of space and urban development benefits large private developers eager to optimize their partnerships with the local organizing committee (e.g. Raco, 2012) in the production of the SOG and their legacies (Smith, 2014a). Glocalized urban spaces would then emerge, combining landscapes closely associated with local tradition and others spaces earmarked for the development of standardized and globalized urbanistic and architectural projects (Beriatos and Gospodini, 2004). Wherever the SOG take place – whether in Barcelona with the redevelopment of the waterfront (Roca i Albert and Faigenbaum, 2002) or in Sydney with the development of a large-scale marina and a waterfront on the site where nautical competitions were to be held (McManus, 2004), these spaces not only contribute to urban regeneration but also place branding.

According to Kavaratzis (2004: 70), the three place branding methods used to draw attention to an area, to make it recognizable and, especially, to associate it with attributes considered beneficial are event branding, flagship construction and personality branding. In the first case (event branding), studies show how the bids are an opportunity for the cities to create a seductive image in the process of globalization, whether they are ultimately awarded the SOG (Sydney: Waitt, 1999), or not (Manchester: e.g. Cochrane et al., 1996). This also applies to the host countries (e.g. Preuss and Alfs, 2011) through, for example, their influence on the media coverage of the event, as in the case of Greece and China (Panagiotopoulou, 2012). In a more critical perspective, other studies emphasize the counterintuitive effects of the SOG. Assimilated to a "mass distraction campaign" (Brady, 2009) aimed at diverting the local population from crucial issues (housing, pollution, democracy), at displaying a façade of social harmony (Shin, 2012), at letting national identification come close to chauvinism (Pamment, 2015) as well as at maintaining generalized security (Toohey and Taylor, 2012) and surveillance (Manley and Silk, 2014) measures even after the SOG have ended, the latter can then appear as elements of counter branding (Maiello and Pasquinelli, 2015). Thus, the London Legacy Development Corporation has promoted, with some success, the re-appropriation of their living place by the populations impacted by the development of the Olympic Park through a participatory mapping exercise. This one has contributed to replacing the previously negative narrative about the Olympic park with a more positive one (Froome-Lewis, 2014).

In London, photographic art has helped to counter the process of flagship construction linked to the gigantism of the SOG (Marrero-Guillamon, 2012). This monumentalization of urban space in a territorial marketing perspective is observed at the scale of the Olympic stadium, sometimes long after the SOG have ended as in Montreal for instance (Roult et al., 2016), and that of the metropolis, as in the controversial case of Beijing (Broudehoux, 2007) where images of power were conveyed through the local architectural forms of the globalized sports spectacle (Broudehoux, 2010).

We touch, here, on personality branding, through, on the one hand, the study of the general characteristics that a territorial brand – as that of a host city like Beijing (e.g. Xu and Cao, 2018), a host country like England (e.g. Bodet and Lacassagne, 2012) or a non-host country like Israel (e.g. Dubinsky and Dzikus, 2018) – endorses and, on the other hand, the specifically touristic dimension attributed to it. In particular, the impact of the image of the host city on the intentions to visit (Bilei and Kim, 2009) is then discussed, as well as the image of the Olympic event on the image of the destination (Lai, 2018) city (e.g. Kenyon and Bodet, 2018) and/or country (Li and Kaplanidou, 2013) or both (Hahm et al., 2018). It is then a question of shaping an image of the city in connection with key contemporary societal trends of free-market developed countries, for example by projecting a "LGBT friendly" image – as London did in 2012 (Hubbard and Wilkinson, 2014) – in order to optimize hospitality toward all participants, considered as guests (Bulley and Lisle, 2012). This set of studies related to place branding lie at the frontier of the field of tourism.

Sports tourism and SOG

The essential role of tourism in the territorialized Olympic strategies gives rise to studies whose number and richness places them in a third axis of research. Authors examine the logic behind the tourism policies – aimed, for example, at increasing centrality (Turner and Rosenstrau, 2002) – or host countries: England used extensive communication toward niche markets about the supposed quality and sustainability of the 2012 SOG (Weed et al., 2011). However, more papers examine the impacts of these policies. Their aims are conceptual (e.g. Roult and Lefebvre, 2014), methodological (e.g. Faulkner et al., 2003) or applied to specific objects such as expenditures and revenues (e.g. De Groote, 2005), flows of people (e.g. Fourie and Santana-Gallego, 2011), intentions to visit (e.g. Pratt and Chan, 2016) and revisit (e.g. Rocha and Fink, 2017) or to more general themes: medium-term urban post-Olympic tourist developments (e.g. Singh and Zhou, 2016); long-term effects of the SOG on the urban economy (e.g. Solberg and Preuss, 2007), etc. In a more psycho-sociological perspective, the links between Olympic territory and tourists are discussed in many studies focusing on their perceptions (e.g. security of the host city: George and Swart, 2015), their motivations (e.g. to travel: Funk et al., 2009), their behaviour (e.g. intention to participate in events and to practice a sport according to whether or not one attended the SOG: Brown and Cresciani, 2017) or on their experiences (e.g. self-ethnography of urban walks: Huang, 2010). Finally, some discuss tourism legacies: did the volunteer ambassador programs in 2012 succeed in creating this type of legacy in London? It seems they did not (Nichols and Ralston, 2011). More generally, is the tourism legacy not, in fact, often neglected by stakeholders? It seems it is (Ziakas and Boukas, 2012). Even if, in the particular case of the 2012 London SOG, the organizers would have been justified in claiming that the Games had provided a significant legacy (Weed, 2014), the general results of the post-Olympic tests of the short-term tourism impact of the SOG on the host cities remain unconvincing (Moss et al., 2018).

Territorial and urban legacies of the SOG

This concept of legacy nonetheless structures a fourth and last interesting axis of analysis of territorial and urban dynamics of the SOG. In practical terms the institutionalization of this concept of legacy within the IOC (Leopkey and

Parent, 2012), its state activation strategies (e.g. Grix et al., 2017) and its often chaotic local governance – as was the case in London (e.g. Girginov, 2011) – are well documented. Whether planned and tangible or not (Gratton and Preuss, 2008), the territorial legacies of the SOG are modelled for operational and evaluative purposes (e.g. Preuss, 2015). They also generate managerial frameworks to better assess them prior to the event (Dickson et al., 2011), or legal frameworks concerning their legal warranties (Stuart and Scassa, 2011), or even economic frameworks regarding their minimal effects on the metropolitan development (Li and McCabe, 2012) or, finally, a geo-historical frameworks with the emergence of the concept at the 1960 Rome SOG (Gold and Gold, 2009) and the obligation to take this concept of legacy into account imposed by the IOC since the 2016 SOG (Andranovich and Burbank, 2013). Aspirations to positive legacies are often difficult to fulfil (Kissoudi, 2010). According to this example this is due, for example, to the gap between the initial reassuring discourses and unsatisfactory outcomes in Athens, Beijing and London (Tomlinson, 2014) or to the changes made to legacy projects under the pressure of commercial interests (Smith, 2014b).

A multidimensional (Agha et al., 2012) "advantageous or disadvantageous, planned or unforeseen" (Mangan, 2008: 1869) construct, the Olympic legacy is material or immaterial in nature. In the first case, some rare studies have focused on the Olympic Village built for each edition of the SOG (e.g. Scherer, 2011). On the other hand, a large number of studies have examined the question of sports equipment adaptability of specific Olympic infra-structures such as velodromes or aquatic centers (Brown and Cresciani, op. cit.); the advantages for the metropolis of converting them into tourism attractions, as in the case of whitewater stadiums (e.g. Marsac, 2014); the cultural (e.g. Kiuri and Teller, 2015) and memorial (Pfister, 2011) legacy of Olympic stadiums and the factors of successful conversion (Roult and Lefebvre, 2010); patterns of use (He et al., 2010) and redevelopment of Olympic parks (e.g. Davidson and McNeill, 2012). The intangible Olympic legacy arises through the emergence of a memory and an urban (Gammon et al., 2013) or metropolitan (Dyreson and Llewellyn, 2008) identity. It takes the form of positive urban planning effects such as those mentioned in Sydney's positive development outcome ten years after the SOG (Searle, 2012), or negative effects with the social violence associated with the obliteration of informal spaces caused by the London Olympic Park development (Edensor et al., 2008). Scientifically stimulating, these contrasting results are observed for each theme of the literature on urban Olympic legacies: governance; right to the city; transport and mobility; social cohesion and participation; cultural and socio-cultural development; quality of life and well-being; surveillance and militarization of urban space, and so on. The notion of legacy thus appears controversial and essentially contradictory (e.g. Brownill et al., 2013), if only because of its socio-anthropological assimilation, sometimes to a gift, sometimes to a commodity (Macrury and Poynter, 2008). According to MacAloon (2008), this notion produces a form of "managerial/magical", or in a word, incantatory discourse by the great decision-makers and influencers of the Olympic system (IOC, local candidacy committees, transnational consulting agencies, sponsors...) to local contributors and public opinion. In this context, one of the main contributions of this corpus of scientific papers is to show, finally, how despite its power (diplomatic, financial, institutional), the Olympic model is currently seeking means of renewing itself (only one application by edition for 2024 and 2028) or even of surviving.

Concluding remarks

As an event conceived in a global perspective and produced in line with local specificities, each edition of the SOG faces a sum of paradoxical injunctions. It is a question of reconciling the expectations of the global (in particular those of the IOC and its sponsors) and those of the local, to articulate very long temporalities (the IOC estimates the lifetime of each edition to at least 13 years from the selection of the applicant cities to the valorization of heritages) or much shorter (the trials last two weeks) or to perpetuate "the Olympic ideal" to counter the image of "global circus" (Whitson and Macintosh, 1996) to which many assimilate the "cash cow" product of the IOC. On the whole, the literature on the SOG has been rather critical of them, judging by the distribution of the articles between the four approaches observed in the corpus, which is itself divided into four thematic axes (Table 4.2).

The so-called critical approach is adopted in 36.7% of the 433 articles studied. By contrast, the laudatory approach – called so because it highlights the expected or actual benefits of the Olympic Games – represents 22.6% of the articles. Lying between these two approaches, the mixed approach represents 14.4% of the corpus. Finally, the so-called general approach, primarily conceptual or methodological, accounts for 26.3% of the publications. About 40% of the publications in axes 1, 2 and 4 are characterized by a critical approach. Many of them take the form of qualitative case studies, often underpinned by an engaged or even activist stance. This is especially the case for axis 2 concerning urban planning, urban regeneration and place branding issues. The laudatory approach concerns 40.4% of the publications in axes 3 – which tend to use quantitative methods more than the studies in axes 2 or 4 – which is almost double the average score for the laudatory approach. However, at this stage of our exploratory review of the geographical, urban planning and management literature relating to the territorial and urban dimensions of the Olympic Games, we find that the research is characterized less by methodological convergence or divergence than by a variety of analyses that sometimes give rise to controversies, thus attesting to the vitality of a scientific field that still needs structuring and managing.

By another way, scientific literature generally highlights the disconnection of the SOG from local historical and socio-economic trajectories, despite the great efforts made by cities and countries to obtain the IOC's right to organize them against the commitment to comply with its demanding specifications.

Table 4.2 Articles distribution between the conceptual framework, the four predefined research axes and the four approaches observed in the corpus

	General approach	Critical approach	Mixed approach	Laudatory approach	Total number of articles per thematic axis
Conceptual framework	14 (45.2%)	8 (25.8%)	3 (9.7%)	6 (19.3%)	31 (100%)
Hosting SOG (axis 1)	32 (22.5%)	56 (39.4%)	20 (14.1%)	34 (24%)	142 (100%)
Urban project and SOG (axis 2)	27 (24.5%)	47 (42.7%)	19 (17.3%)	17 (15.5%)	110 (100%)
Sports tourism and SOG (axis 3)	17 (32.6%)	7 (13.5%)	7 (13.5%)	21 (40.4%)	52 (100%)
Territorial and urban legacies of the SOG (axis 4)	24 (24.2%)	41 (41.4%)	14 (14.1%)	20 (20.3%)	99 (100%)
Total number of articles per type of approach	114 (26.3%)	159 (36.7%)	63 (14.4%)	98 (22.6%)	434 (100%)

Design and production: J. Chaboche and A. Schoeny

Motivations to candidate exceed of course the simple sports considerations and relate globally to the will to count in the concert of the cities and nations. Each host city thus seeks to highlight a particular aspect in a more general context: the demonstration of the effectiveness of the American liberal economic model applied to Olympism from Los Angeles in 1984, the economic emergence of Southeast Asia in Seoul in 1988, the effervescence of Spanish society ("la movida") after the Franco dictatorship and the Barcelona urban regeneration in 1992, the celebration of entrepreneurship in Atlanta in 1996, the environmental concern in Sydney in 2000, the coupling between Olympic historicity and urban modernity in Athens in 2004, the greater acceptance of the Chinese "specificities" in Beijing in 2008, the happy communitarianism in the cosmopolitan and financialized city in London in 2012 or the affirmation of the now multipolar nature of the contemporary world in Rio in 2016. On the occasion of the upcoming 2024 edition, the Organizing Committee of the Olympic Games (OCOG) of Paris appears to take note that to welcome the world is no longer a sufficient justification to local public opinion in view of the costs and return on investment, at least questionable of mega-events as a whole.

Nevertheless, the SOG also remain vectors of a social construction which, even fleeting the time of competition, cannot be neglected in terms of pacification and unity between peoples. Extending and deepening the studies on the territorial and urban dimensions of the SOG therefore appears necessary in order to continuously update the knowledge about them and document the stakes and effects of these mega-events on the socio-economic living and well-being of the communities. Although qualitative studies often lack hindsight on the phenomena they observe and despite the methodological flaws that make it difficult to interpret the conclusions of any quantitative impact study, these studies still represent the majority of the corpus and are probably useful. But what private and public decision-makers need above all are medium- and long-term analyses of the conditions, methods, effects and scope of the maximization of the (territorial, economic, social, environmental, cultural, etc.) benefits derived from the Olympic Games, to transcend the observation that each "sport mega event is a flash in history" (Solberg and Preuss, op. cit.: 220).

In this respect it is noteworthy that, among the 38 articles published since 2016, only eight are in axis 1 ("Hosting SOG") – though the largest of the four axes. Indeed the more recent studies tend to focus more on the questions related to the articulation between the urban project and the SOG (axis 2) and to the Olympic legacies (axis 4) because there exists, to date, no sufficiently reliable predictive model for determining the selection criteria for host cities and evaluating the efficiency of the organization's project management. Many areas have been reviewed in this article and most probably deserve further study. The issues that have been discussed the most since 2016 are those related to the links between the SOG and tourism, urban regeneration and place branding. It would probably also be useful to explore other areas. These include the interactions between the smart city and the SOG, the spectacularization of unusual venues for Olympic events in the city (e.g. Château de Versailles for equestrian competitions in 2024) and the combinations between the IOC's mode of governance, which is meant to be universal, and that of the local SOG Organising Committees based on a hybrid form of management that must reconcile the often conflicting interests of public, associative and commercial actors. In any case, this is what ultimately the authors of this article wish to contribute to.

But as a preliminary, it will be necessary to develop further this first attempt at structuring and analysing this corpus – organized in a systemic way (four axes defined a priori) and analysed in a systematic way (434 articles collected and analysed). The ultimate objective is to propose a systematic review of the literature whose indicators are already known and partly identified. This includes bibliographic data (e.g. author(s); date; title; journal; DOI), indexing elements (keywords), object of study (e.g. field(s); scale of analysis), "paradigmatic set" of the research object and the main content elements of each article (e.g. summary; contributions and limitations; conclusion; main lessons). This course of action will have the advantage of being based on the methodological principles defined by Arksey and O'Malley (op.

cit.), Lucarelli and Berg (op. cit.) and Berland (op. cit.). This will make it possible to deliver a comprehensive, detailed and longitudinal systematic review which can be subsequently regularly updated, enabling the scientific community to enrich, develop and exploit the articles database in a collaborative way.

References

Agha, N., Fairley, S., and Gibson, H. (2012). Considering legacy as a multi-dimensional construct: The legacy of the Olympic Games. *Sport Management Review*, 15 (1), 125–139.

Alberts, H. C. (2009). Berlin's failed bid to host the 2000 Summer Olympic Games: Urban development and the improvement of sports facilities. *International Journal of Urban and Regional Research*, 33(2), 502–516.

Andranovich, G., Burbank, M.-J., and Heying, C. H. (2001). Olympic cities: Lessons learned from mega-event politics. *Journal of Urban Affairs*, 23(2), 113–131.

Andranovich, G., and Burbank, M.-J. (2013). Contextualizing Olympic legacies. *Urban Geography*, 32(6), 823–844.

Arksey, H., and O'Malley, L. (2005). Scoping studies: Towards a methodological framework. *International Journal of Social Research Methodology*, 8(1), 19–32.

Armstrong, G., Hobbs, D., and Lindsay, I. (2011). Calling the shots. *Urban Studies*, 48 (15), 3169–3184.

Arnold, R., Hewton, E., and Fletcher, D. (2015). Preparing our greatest team. *Sport, Business and Management: An International Journal*, 5(4), 386–407.

Atkinson, G., Mourato, S., and Szymanski, S. (2008). Are we willing to pay enough to "back the bid"?: Valuing the intangible impacts of London's bid to host the 2012 Summer Olympic Games. *Urban Studies*, 45(2), 419–444.

Augustin, J.-P. (2009). Les Jeux Olympiques, l'événement spatial par excellence [The Olympic Games, the quintessential spatial event]. *Bulletin de l'Association des Géographes Français*, 86(3), 303–311.

Augustin, J.-P. (2011). Introduction: le sport attracteur d'organisation sociale et intermédiaire de la mondialisation [Sport as an attractor of social organization and intermediary of globalization]. *Annales de géographie*, 680(4), 353–360.

Balibrea, M. P. (2001). Urbanism, culture and the postindustrial city: Challenging the "Barcelona model". *Journal of Spanish Cultural Studies*, 2(2), 187–210.

Bell, B., and Gallimore, K. (2015). Embracing the games? Leverage and legacy of London 2012 Olympics at the sub-regional level by means of strategic partnerships. *Leisure Studies*, 34(6), 720–741.

Beriatos, E., and Gospodini, A. (2004). "Glocalising" urban landscapes: Athens and the 2004 Olympics. *Cities*, 23(3), 187–202.

Berland, N., Piot, C., and Stolowy, H. (2013). La revue de littérature: état de l'état de l'art. *Comptabilité – Contrôle – Audit*, 3(19), 3–7.

Bilei, D., and Kim, C. (2009). Identifying impact of Olympic host city's image on intention to visit: Perspective of Beijing's image by Korean tourists. *International Journal of Tourism Sciences*, 9(3), 1–24.

Black, D., and Bezanson, S. (2004). The Olympic Games, human rights and democratization: Lessons from Seoul and implications for Beijing. *Third World Quarterly*, 25(7), 1245–1261.

Bodet, G., and Lacassagne, M. F. (2012). International place branding through sporting events: A British perspective of the 2008 Beijing Olympics. *European Sport Management Quarterly*, 12(4), 357–374.

Boykoff, J., and Fussey, P. (2014). London's shadow legacies: Security and activism at the 2012 Olympics. *Journal of the Academy of Social Sciences*, 9(2), 253–270.

Brady, A. M. (2009). The Beijing Olympics as a campaign of mass distraction. *The China Quarterly, 197*, 1–24.

Brajer, V., and Mead, R. W. (2003). Blue skies in Beijing? Looking at the Olympic effect. *Journal of Environment & Development, 12*(2), 239–263.

Broudehoux, A.-M. (2007). Pékin, ville spectacle: la construction controversée d'une métropole Olympique. *Journal of Global Cultural Studies, 3*, 5–25.

Broudehoux, A.-M. (2010). Images of power: Architectures of the integrated spectacle at the Beijing Olympics. *Journal of Architectural Education, 63*(2), 52–62.

Brown, L. A., and Cresciani, M. (2017). Adaptable design in Olympic construction. *International Journal of Building Pathology and Adaptation, 35*(4), 397–416.

Browne, M., Allen, J., Wainwright, I., Palmer, A., and Williams, A. (2014). London 2012: Changing delivery patterns in response to the impact of the Games on traffic flows. *International Journal of Urban Sciences, 18*, 244–261.

Brownell, S. (2012). Human rights and the Beijing Olympics: Imagined global community and the transnational public sphere. *The British Journal of Sociology, 63*, 306–327.

Brownill, S., Keivani, R., and Pereira, G. (2013). Olympic legacies and city development strategies in London and Rio: Beyond the carnival mask? *International Journal of Urban Sustainable Development*, 5(2), 11–131.

Bulley, D., and Lisle, D. (2012). Welcoming the world: Governing hospitality in London's 2012 Olympic Bid. *International Political Sociology*, 6(2), 186–204.

Burton, R. (2003). Olympic Games host city marketing: An exploration of expectations and outcomes. *Sport Marketing Quarterly, 12*(1), 37–46.

Campenhoudt, L., Marquet, J., and Quivy, R. (2017). *Manuel de recherche en sciences sociales* (éd. 5). Malakoff: Dunod.

Chalip, L., and McGuirty, J. (2004). Bundling sport events with the host destination. *Journal of Sport Tourism,* 9(3), 267–282.

Chalip, L., Green, B., and Vander Velden, L. (2000). The effects of polysemic structures on Olympic viewing. *International Journal of Sports Marketing and Sponsorship*, 2(1), 39–57.

Chalkley, B., and Essex, S. (1999). Sydney 2000: The "green games"? *Geography, 84* (4), 299–307.

Chappelet, J.-L., and Pinson, J. (2015). Évolutions des politiques publiques d'accueil d'événements sportifs. *Revue Européenne de Management du sport* (45), 8–16.

Charlton, T. (2010). "Grow and sustain": The role of community sports provision in promoting a participation legacy for the 2012 Olympic Games. *International Journal of Sport Policy and Politics*, 2(3), 347–366.

Chevrier, J. (2004). La spécification de la problématique. In B. Gauthier, *Recherche sociale: de la problématique à la collecte de données* (éd. 4, pp. 51–84). Ste Foy: Presses de l'Université du Québec.

Cochrane, A., Peck, J., and Tickell, A. (1996). Manchester plays Games: Exploring the local politics of globalisation. *Urban Studies, 33*(8), 1319–1336.

Davidson, M., and McNeill, D. (2012). The redevelopment of Olympic Sites: Examining the legacy of Sydney Olympic Park. *Urban Studies, 49*(8), 1625–1641.

Davies, A., and Mackenzie, I. (2014). Project complexity and systems integration: Constructing the London 2012 Olympics and Paralympics Games. *International Journal of Project Management, 32*(5), 773–790.

Davis, J., and Thornley, A. (2010). Urban regeneration for the London 2012 Olympics: Issues of Land Acquisition and Legacy. *City, Culture and Society,* 1(2), 89–98.

Davis, L. K. (2011). International events and mass evictions: A longer view. *International Journal of Urban and Regional Research, 35*(3), 582–599.

De Groote, P. (2005). Economic and tourism aspects of the Olympic Games. *Tourism Review, 60*(3), 20–28.

Dickson, T. J., Benson, A. M., and Blackman, D. A. (2011). Developing a framework for evaluating Olympic and Paralympic legacies. *Journal of Sport & Tourism, 16*(4), 285–302.

Downward, P., Dawson, A., and Dejonghe, T. (2009). *Sports Economics: Theory, Evidence and Policy.* London: Elsevier.

Drucker, J., and White, G. (2013). Employment relations on major construction projects: The London 2012 Olympic construction site. *Industrial Relations, 44*(5–6), 566–583.

Dubinsky, Y., and Dzikus, L. (2018). Israel's country image in the 2016 Olympic Games. *Place Branding and Public Diplomacy,* in press.

Dussier, M., and Machemehl, C. (2014). Devenir la capitale du nautisme: Aménagements portuaires, urbains et Jeux olympiques: le site de La Rochelle. *Teoros, 33*(1), 75–86.

Dyreson, M., and Llewellyn, M. (2008). Los Angeles is the Olympic city: Legacies of the 1932 and 1984 Olympic Games. *The International Journal of the History of Sport, 25*(14), 1991–2008.

Edensor, T., Christie, C., and Lloyd, B. (2008). Obliterating informal space: The London Olympics and the Lea Valley: A Photo Essay. *Space and Culture, 11*(3), 285–293.

Elder, C., Pratt, A., and Ellis, C. (2006). Running race: Reconciliation, nationalism and the Sydney 2000 Olympic Games. *International Review for the Sociology of Sport, 41*(2), 181–200.

Essex, S., and Chalkley, B. (1999). Urban development through hosting international events: A history of the Olympic Games. *Planning Perspectives,* 369–394.

Falcous, M., and Silk, M. (2010). Olympic bidding, multicultural nationalism, terror, and the epistemological violence of "making Britain proud". *Studies in Ethnicity and Nationalism, 10*(2), 167–186.

Faulkner, B., Chalip, L., Brown, G., Jago, L., March, R., and Woodside, A. (2003). Monitoring the tourism impacts of the Sydney 2000 Olympics. *Event Management,* 6(4), 231–246.

Feddersen, A., and Maennig, W. (2009). Wage and employment effects of the Olympic Games in Atlanta 1996 reconsidered. *Hamburg Contemporary Economic Discussions, 25.*

Földesi, G. S. (1992). Introduction to Olympism in sport sociology. *International Review for the Sociology of Sport, 27*(2), 103–106.

Fourie, J., and Santana-Gallego, M. (2011). The impact of mega-sport events on tourist arrivals. *Tourism Management, 32*(6), 1364–1370.

Froome-Lewis, O. (2014). Lea Valley drift: Paths, objects and the creation of urban narratives. *Architectural Research Quarterly, 18,* 377–388.

Funk, D. C., Alexandris, K., and Ping, Y. (2009). To go or stay home and watch: Exploring the balance between motives and perceived constraints for major events. A case study of the 2008 Beijing Olympic Games. *International Journal of Tourism Research, 11,* 41–53.

Gaffney, C., and Robertson, C. (2016). Smarter than smart: Rio de Janeiro's flawed emergence as a smart city. *Journal of Urban Technology, 23*(3), 47–64.

Gammon, S., Ramshaw, G., and Waterton, E. (2013). Examining the Olympics: Heritage, identity and performance. *International Journal of Heritage Studies, 19*(2), 119–124.

Garcia-Ramon, M. D., and Albet, A. (2000). Pre-Olympic and post-Olympic Barcelona, a model for urban regeneration today? *Environment and planning, 32*(8), 1331–1334.

George, R., and Swart, K. (2015). Tourists' perceptions of London, United Kingdom (UK), as a safe host city during the 2012 Olympic Games. *Journal of Travel & Tourism Marketing, 32*(8), 1117–1132.

Girginov, V. (2011). Governance of the London 2012 Olympic Games legacy. *International Review for the Sociology of Sport, 47*(5), 543–558.

Giulianotti, R., and Brownell, S. (2012). Olympic and world sport: Making transnational society? *The British Journal of Sociology, 63*(2), 199–215.

Giulianotti, R., Armstrong, G., Hales, G., and Hobbs, D. (2015). Global sport mega-events and the politics of mobility: The case of the London 2012 Olympics. *The British Journal of Sociology, 66*(1), 118–140.

Glaser, B. (1978). *Theoretical Sensitivity.* Mill Valley, California: University of California Press.

Gold, J. R., and Gold, M. M. (2007). *Olympic Cities. City Agendas, Planning, and the Word's Games, 1896–2012.* London: Routledge.

Gold, J. R., and Gold, M. M. (2008). Olympic cities: Regeneration, city rebranding and changing urban agendas. *Geography Compass, 2,* 300–318.

Gold, J. R., and Gold, M. M. (2009). Future indefinite? London 2012, the spectre of retrenchment and the challenge of Olympic sports legacy. *London Journal, 34,* 180–197.

Gratton, C., and Preuss, H. (2008). Maximizing Olympic impacts by building up legacies. *The International Journal of the History of Sport, 25*(14), 1922–1938.

Grix, J. (2013). Sport politics and the Olympics. *Political Studies Review, 11*(1), 15–25.

Grix, J., and Houlihan, B. (2014). Sports mega-events as part of a nation's soft power strategy: The cases of Germany (2006) and the UK (2012). *The British Journal of Politics and International Relations, 4,* 572–596.

Grix, J., Brannagan, P. M., Wood, H., and Wynne, C. (2017). State strategies for leveraging sports mega-events: unpacking the concept of "legacy". *International Journal of Sport Policy and Politics, 9*(2), 203–218.

Gursoy, D., and Kendall, K. W. (2006). Hosting mega events. Modeling locals' support. *Annals of Tourism Research, 33*(3), 603–623.

Guthman, J. (2008). Accumulation by spectacle and other teachable moments from the 2008 Beijing Olympics. *Geoforum, 39*(6), 1799–1801.

Hahm, J., Tasci, A. D., and Terry, D. B. (2018). Investigating the interplay among the Olympic Games image, destination image, and country image for four previous hosts. *Journal of Travel & Tourism Marketing, 35*(6), 755–771.

Hall, C. (2006). Urban entrepreneurship, corporate interests and sports mega-events: The thin policies of competitiveness within the hard outcomes of neoliberalism. *The Sociological Review, 54*(2), 59–70.

Hartigan, M. (2012). Applying Olympic planning principles to assess Brisbane's potential as a 2028 Olympic host city. *Australian Planner, 49*(3), 239–248.

Hartmann, S., and Zandberg, T. (2015). The future of mega sport events: Examining the "Dutch Approach" to legacy planning. *Journal of Tourism Futures, 1*(2), 108–116.

He, Y., Chen, T., and Zhang, M. (2010). Utilization pattern of Olympic Parks and its application in Beijing. *China Geographical Science, 20*(5), 414–422.

Heslop, L. A., Nadeau, J., and O'Reilly, N. (2010). China and the Olympics: Views of insiders and outsiders. *International Marketing Review, 27*(4), 404–433.

Hiller, H. H., and Wanner, R. A. (2014). The psycho-social impact of the Olympics as urban festival: A leisure perspective. *Leisure Studies, 34*(6), 672–688.

Hotchkiss, J. L., Moore, R. E., and Zobay, S. M. (2003). Impact of the 1996 Summer Olympic Games on employment and wages in Georgia. *Southern Economic Journal, 69*(3), 691–704.

Huang, S. (2010). Post-Olympic tourist experience: An autoethnographic perspective. *Journal of China Tourism Research, 6*(2), 104–122.

Hubbard, P., and Wilkinson, E. (2014). Welcoming the world? Hospitality, homo-nationalism, and the London 2012 Olympics. *Antipode, 47*, 598–615.

Huijuan, C., Fujii, H., and Managi, S. (2013). Environmental impact of the 2008 Beijing Olympic Games. *Economics Discussion Papers, Kiel Institute for the World Economy, 30*.

Jin, L., Zhang, J. J., Xingdong, M., and Connaughton, D. P. (2011). Residents' perceptions of environmental impacts of the 2008 Beijing green Olympic Games. *European Sport Management Quarterly, 11*(3), 275–300.

Jodelet, D. (2003). *Les représentations sociales.* Paris: Presses Universitaires de France.

Karadakis, K., Kaplanidou, K., and Karlis, G. (2010). Event leveraging of mega sport events: a SWOT analysis approach. *International Journal of Event and Festival Management, 1*(3), 170–185.

Kavaratzis, M. (2004). From city marketing to city branding: Towards a theoretical framework for developing city brands. *Place Branding, 1*(1), 58–73.

Kennelly, J., and Watt, P. (2012). Seeing Olympic effects through the eyes of marginally housed youth: Changing places and the gentrification of East London. *Visual Studies, 27*(2), 151–160.

Kenyon, J. A., and Bodet, G. (2018). Exploring the domestic relationship between mega-events and destination image: The image impact of hosting the 2012 Olympic Games for the city of London. *Sport Management Review, 21*(3), 232–249.

Kirkup, N., and Major, B. (2006). The reliability of economic impact studies of the Olympic Games: A post-Games study of Sydney 2000 and considerations for London 2012. *Journal of Sport & Tourism, 11*(3–4),275–296.

Kissoudi, P. (2010). Athens' post-Olympic aspirations and the extent of their realization. *The International Journal of the History of Sport, 27*(16–18),2780–2797.

Kiuri, M., and Teller, J. (2015). Olympic stadiums and cultural heritage: On the nature and status of heritage values in large sport facilities. *International Journal of the History of Sport, 32*(5), 1–24.

Kontokosta, V. (2011). The price of victory: The impact of the Olympic Games on residential real estate markets. *Urban Studies, 49*(5), 961–978.

Lai, K. (2018). Influence of event image on destination image: The case of the 2008 Beijing Olympic Games. *Journal of Destination Marketing & Management, 7*, 153–163.

Lamizet, B., and Silem, A. (1997). *Dictionnaire encyclopédique des sciences de l'information et de la communication*. Paris: Ellipses.

Lauermann, J. (2015). Temporary projects, durable outcomes: Urban development through failed Olympic bids? *Urban Studies, 53*(9), 1885–1901.

Lee, S. B., Lee, C.-K., Kang, J.-S., and Jeon, Y. (2013). Residents' perception of the 2008 Beijing Olympics: Comparison of pre- and post-impacts. *International Journal of Tourism Research, 15*(3), 209–225.

Lenskyj, H. J. (1996). When winners are losers: Toronto and Sydney bids for the Summer Olympics. *Journal of Sport & Social Issues, 20*(4), 392–410.

Leopkey, B., and Parent, M. M. (2012). The (neo) institutionalization of legacy and its sustainable governance within the Olympic Movement. *European Sport Management Quarterly, 12*(5), 437–455.

Lewandowski, D., and Höchstötter, N. (2008). Mesurer la qualité des moteurs de recherche Web. *Questions de communication, 14*, 75–93.

Li, S. N., and McCabe, S. (2012). Measuring the socio-economic legacies of mega-events: Concepts, propositions and indicators. *International Journal of Tourism Research, 15*(4), 388–402.

Li, S., and Blake, A. (2009). Estimating Olympic-related investment and expenditure. *International Journal of Tourism Research, 11*, 337–356.

Li, X., and Kaplanidou, K. (2013). The impact of the 2008 Beijing Olympic Games on China's destination brand: A U.S.-based examination. *Journal of Hospitality & Tourism Research, 37*(2), 237–261.

Liu, Y. W., Zhao, G. F., and Wang, S. Q. (2010). Many hands, much politics, multiple risks – The case of the 2008 Beijing Olympics Stadium. *Australian Journal of Public Aministration, 69*(1), 585–598.

Lu, Q., and Yang, Y. (2015). A longitudinal study of the impact of the Sydney Olympics on real estate markets. *International Journal of Event and Festival Management, 6*(1), 4–17.

Lucarelli, A., and Berg, P. O. (2011). City branding: A state-of-the-art review of the research domain. *Journal of Place Management and Development, 4*(1), 9–27.

MacAloon, J. J. (2008). "Legacy" as managerial/magical discourse in contemporary Olympic affairs. *The International Journal of the History of Sport, 25*(14), 2060–2071.

Macrury, I., and Poynter, G. (2008). The Regeneration Games: Commodities, gifts and the economics of London 2012. *The International Journal of the History of Sport, 25*(14), 272–290.

Madden, J. (2002). The economic consequences of the Sydney Olympics: The CREA/Arthur Andersen study. *Current Issues in Tourism, 5*(1), 7–21.

Maennig, W., and Vierhaus, C. (2017). Winning the Olympic host city election: Key success factors. *Applied Economics, 49*(31), 3086–3099.

Maiello, A., and Pasquinelli, C. (2015). Destruction or construction? A (counter) branding analysis of sport mega-events in Rio de Janeiro. *Cities, 48*, 116–124.

Mangan, J. A. (2008). Prologue: Guarantees of global goodwill. Post-Olympic legacies – too many limping white elephants? *The International Journal of the History of Sport, 25*(14), 1869–1883.

Manley, A., and Silk, M. (2014). Liquid London: Sporting spectacle, Britishness and ban-optic surveillance. *Surveillance & Society, 11*(4), 360–376.

Marrero-Guillamon, I. (2012). Photography against the Olympic spectacle. *Visual Studies, 27*(2), 132–139.

Marsac, A. (2014). Les stratégies de conversion touristique des stades d'eau vive olympiques: Une approche par l'avantage métropolitain. *Teoros, 33*(1), 67–74.

McManus, P. (2004). Writing the palimpest, Again; Rozelle Bay and the Sydney 2000 Olympic Games. *Urban Policy and Research, 22*(2), 157–167.

Mol, A. P. (2010). Sustainability as global attractor: The greening of the 2008 Beijing Olympics. *Global Networks, 10*(4), 510–528.

Moss, S. E., Gruben, K. H., and Moss, J. (2018). An empirical test of the Olympic tourism legacy. *Journal of Policy Research in Tourism, Leisure and Events*.

Müller, M. (2015). What makes an event a mega-event? Definitions and sizes. *Leisure Studies, 34*(6), 627–642.

Müller, M., and Stewart, A. (2016). Does temporary geographical proximity predict learning? Knowledge dynamics in the Olympic Games. *Regional Studies, 50*(3), 377–390.

Muñoz, F. (2006). Olympic urbanism and Olympic villages: planning strategies in Olympic host cities, London 1908 to London 2012. *The Sociological Review, 54*, 175–187.

Nichols, G., and Ralston, R. (2011). Social inclusion through volunteering: The legacy potential of the 2012 Olympic Games. *Sociology, 45*(5), 900–914.

Ninnin, J. (2014). Le rêve carioca: entre planification urbaine et déplacements forcés de population. *L'Espace Politique, 22*(1).

Owen, J. (2005). Estimating the cost and benefit of hosting Olympic Games: What can Beijing expect from its 2008 Games? *The Industrial Geographer, 3*(1), 1–18.

Owen, K. A. (2002). The Sydney 2000 Olympics and urban entrepreneurialism: Local variations in urban governance. *Australian Geographical Studies, 40*(3), 323–336.

Paillé, P. (1994). L'analyse par théorisation ancrée. *Cahiers de recherche sociologique*, 23, 146–181.

Paillé, P. (2002). Sensibilité théorique. In A. Mucchielli, *Dictionnaire des méthodes qualitatives en sciences humaines et sociales* (ed. 1996, p. 225). Paris: Armand Colin.

Paillé, P., and Mucchielli, A. (2005). *L'analyse qualitative en sciences humaine et sociales*. Paris: Armand Colin.

Pamment, J. (2015). Putting the GREAT back into Britain. *The British Journal of Politics & International Relations, 17*, 260–283.

Panagiotopoulou, R. (2012). Nation branding and the Olympic Games: New Media Images for Greece and China. *The International Journal of the History of Sport, 29* (16), 2337–2348.

Pfister, G. (2011). Lieux de mémoire/sites of memories and the Olympic Games: An introduction. *Sport in Society: Cultures, Commerce, Media, Politics, 14*(4), 412–429.

Pitts, A., and Liao, H. (2006). A brief historical review of Olympic urbanization. *The International Journal of History of Sport, 23*(7), 1232–1252.

Poast, P. D. (2007). Winning the bid: Analyzing the International Olympic Committee's host city selections. *International Interactions, 33*, 75–95.

Poncet, P. (2001). Sydney et les JO ou le complexe de Cendrillon. *Pouvoirs Locaux, 49*, 78–81.

Pratt, S., and Chan, W. S. (2016). Destination image and intention to visit the Tokyo 2020 Olympics among Hong Kong Generation Y. *Journal of China Tourism Research, 12*(3–4),355–373.

Prayag, G., Hosany, S., Nunkoo, R., and Alders, T. (2013). London residents' support for the 2012 Olympic Games: The mediating effect of overall attitude. *Tourism Management, 36*, 629–640.

Preuss, H. (2004). Calculating the regional economic impact of the Olympic Games. *European Sport Management Quarterly, 4*(4), 234–253.

Preuss, H. (2007). The conceptualisation and measurement of mega sport event legacies. *Journal of Sport & Tourism*, 12(3–4), 207–227.

Preuss, H. (2015). A framework for identifying the legacies of a mega sport event. *Leisure Studies, 34*(6), 643–664.

Preuss, H., and Alfs, C. (2011). Signaling through the 2008 Beijing Olympics—Using mega sport events to change the perception and image of the host. *European Sport Management Quarterly, 11*(1), 55–71.

Raco, M. (2012). The privatisation of urban development and the London Olympics 2012. *City, 16*(4), 452–460.

Raco, M., and Tunney, E. (2010). Visibilities and invisibilities in urban development: Small business communities and the London Olympics 2012. *Urban Studies, 47*(10), 2069–2091.

Reis, A. C., Rodrigues de Sousa-Mast, F., and Gurgel, L. A. (2013). Rio 2016 and the sport participation legacies. *Leisure Studies*, 33(5), 437–453.

Richmond, M. A., and Garmany, J. (2016). "Post-third-world city" or neoliberal "city of exception"? Rio de Janeiro in the Olympic era. *International Journal of Urban and Regional Research, 40*(3), 621–639.

Ritchie, B. W., Shipway, R., and Chien, P. M. (2010). The role of the media in influencing residents' support for the 2012 Olympic Games. *International Journal of Event and Festival Management, 1*(3), 202–219.

Ritchie, B. W., Shipway, R., and Cleeve, B. (2009). Resident perceptions of mega-sporting events: A non-host city perspective of the 2012 London Olympic Games. *Journal of Sport & Tourism, 14*(2–3),143–167.

Roca i Albert, J., and Faigenbaum, P. (2002). Le front de mer de Barcelone: chronique d'une transformation. *Cités, 11*(3), 49–62.

Rocha, C. M., and Fink, J. S. (2017). Attitudes toward attending the 2016 Olympic Games and visiting Brazil after the games. *Tourism Management Perspectives, 22*, 17–26.

Roche, M. (1994). Mega-events and urban policy. *Annals of Tourism Research*, 21, 1–19.

Roche, M. (2000). *Mega-events and Modernity: Olympics and Expos in the Growth of Global Culture.* London: Routledge.

Roche, M. (2006). Sports mega-events, modernity and capitalist economies: Mega-events and modernity revisited. Globalization and the case of the Olympics. *The Sociological Review, 54*(2), 25–40.

Roult, R., and Lefebvre, S. (2010). Planning and reconversion of Olympic heritages: The Montreal Olympic Stadium. *International Journal of the History of Sport, 27* (16), 2731–2747.

Roult, R., and Lefebvre, S. (2014). Tourisme événementiel et méga-événements sportifs. *Téoros, 33*(1), 3–7.

Roult, R., Adjizian, J. M., and Auger, D. (2016). Tourism conversion and place branding: The case of the Olympic Park in Montreal. *International Journal of Tourism Cities, 2*(1), 77–93.

Roult, R., Machemehl, C., and Gaudette, M. (2018). 40 ans de la revue *Loisir et Société*: revue systématique des articles publiés sur le sport et la ville. *Loisir et Société/Society and Leisure, 41*(1), 27–45.

Sánchez, F., and Broudehoux, A.-M. (2013). Mega-events and urban regeneration in Rio de Janeiro: Planning in a state of emergency. *International Journal of Urban Sustainable Development, 5*(2), 132–153.

Scherer, J. (2011). Olympic villages and large-scale urban development: crises of capitalism, deficits of democracy? *Sociology, 45*(5), 782–797.

Searle, G. (2012). The long-term urban impacts of the Sydney Olympic Games. *Australian Planner, 49*(3), 195–202.

Searle, G., and Bounds, M. (1999). State powers, state land and competition for global entertainment: The case of Sydney. *International Journal of Urban and Regional Research, 23*(1), 165–172.

Shin, H. B. (2012). Unequal cities of spectacle and mega-events in China. *City: Analysis of urban trends, culture, theory, policy, action, 16*(6), 728–744.

Shoval, N. (2002). A new phase in the competition for the Olympic Gold: The London and New York bids for the 2012 Games. *Journal of Urban Affairs, 24*(5), 583–599.

Silk, M. (2011). Towards a sociological analysis of London 2012. *Sociology, 45*(5), 733–748.

Singh, N., and Hu, C. (2008). Understanding strategic alignment for destination marketing and the 2004 Athens Olympic Games: Implications from extracted tacit knowledge. *Tourism Management, 29*, 929–939.

Singh, N., and Zhou, H. (2016). Transformation of tourism in Beijing after the 2008 Summer Olympics: An analysis of the impacts in 2014. *International Journal of Tourism Research, 18*, 277–285.

Smith, A. (2009). Spreading the positive effects of major events to peripheral areas. *Journal of Policy Research in Tourism, Leisure and Events, 1*(3), 231–246.

Smith, A. (2014a). "De-risking" East London: Olympic Regeneration Planning 2000–2012. *European Planning Studies, 22*(9), 1919–1939.

Smith, A. (2014b). From green park to theme park? Evolving legacy visions for London's Olympic Park. *Architectural Research Quarterly, 18*(4), 315–323.

Solberg, H. A., and Preuss, H. (2007). Major sport events and long term tourism impacts. *Journal of Sport Management, 21*, 213–234.

Strauss, A., and Corbin, J. (1990). *Basics of Qualitative Research: Grounded Theory Procedures and Techniques.* Newbury Park, CA: Sage Publications, Inc.

Streets, D. G., Fu, J. S., Jang, C. J., Hao, J., He, K., Tang, X., Zhang, Y., Wang, Z., Li, Z., Zhang, Q., Wang, L., Wang, B., and Yu, C. (2006). Air quality during the 2008 Beijing Olympic Games. *Atmospheric Environment, 41*(3), 480–492.

Stuart, S. A., and Scassa, T. (2011). Legal guarantees for Olympic legacy. *The Entertainment and Sports Law Journal, 9*(1), 1–21.

Theodoraki, E. (2009). Organisational communication on the impacts of the Athens 2004 Olympic Games. *Journal of Policy Research in Tourism, Leisure and Events, 1*(2), 141–155.

Tomlinson, A. (2014). Olympic legacies: Recurrent rhetoric and harsh realities. *Contemporary Social Science, 9*(2), 137–158.

Toohey, K., and Taylor, T. (2012). Surveillance and securitization: A forgotten Sydney Olympic legacy. *International Review for the Sociology of Sport, 47*(3), 324–337.

Tsoukala, A. (2006). The security issue at the 2004 Olympics. *European Journal for Sport and Society, 3*(1), 43–54.

Turner, R. S., and Rosenstrau, M. S. (2002). Tourism, sports and the centrality of cities. *Journal of Urban Affairs, 24*(5), 487–492. *Journal of Urban Affairs, 24*(5), 487–492.

Villemagne, C. (2006). Des choix méthodologiques favorisant une approche inductive: le cas d'une recherche en éducation relative à l'environnement. *Recherche Qualitative, 26*(2), 131–144.

Waitt, G. (1999). Playing Games with Sydney: Marketing Sydney for the 2000 Olympics. *Urban Studies, 36*(7), 1055–1077.

Waitt, G. (2001). The Olympic spirit and civic boosterism: The Sydney 2000 Olympics. *Tourism Geographies, 3*(3), 249–278.

Waitt, G. (2003). Social impacts of the Sydney Olympics. *Annals of Tourism Research, 30*(1), 194–215.

Watt, P. (2013). It's not for us. *City, 17*(1), 99–118.

Weed, M. (2014). Is tourism a legitimate legacy from the Olympic and Paralympic Games? An analysis of London 2012 legacy strategy using programme theory. *Journal of Sport and Tourism, 19*(2), 101–126.

Weed, M., Stephens, J., and Bull, C. (2011). An exogenous shock to the system? The London 2012 Olympic and Paralympic Games and British tourism policy. *Journal of Sport and Tourism, 16*(4), 345–377.

Whitson, D., and Macintosh, D. (1996). The Global Circus: International sport, tourism and the marketing of cities. *Journal of Sport and Social Issues, 20*(3), 278–295.

Xu, J., and Cao, Y. (2018). The image of Beijing in Europe: Findings from *The Times, Le Figaro, Der Spiegel* from 2000 to 2015. *Place Branding and Public Diplomacy*, in press.

Zhou, Y., Ap, J., and Bauer, T. (2012). Government motivations for hosting the Beijing 2008 Olympic Games. *Journal of Tourism and Cultural Change, 10*(2), 185–201.

Ziakas, V., and Boukas, N. (2012). A neglected legacy: Examining the challenges and potential for sport tourism development in post-Olympic Athens. *International Journal of Event and Festival Management, 3*(3), 292–316.

5   Bidding for the Olympic Games

A gearing effect?

Pierre-Olaf Schut

Introduction

Bids for the Olympic and Paralympic Games have evolved into a game of one-upmanship to a point where they are now only presented by major state-supported international cities. In effect, they have become huge communication campaigns, consistent with the challenges of the event. The Olympic and Paralympic Games call for a budget of nearly 12 billion euros (Rio 2016), excluding the indirect actions organized during the hosting of the event. As a result, the required investment of tens of millions of euros in a bid (60 million euros for Paris 2024) has become vital to win the International Olympic Committee (IOC) vote.

The international sports institution has taken these issues into account along with their devastating effects on public opinion. Although this investment in communication is widely supported by public funds, unsuccessful applicants are left with significant losses of public money while host cities commit to even greater debts. Taxpayers have increasingly questioned this risk, and decisions to withdraw from a bid have multiplied. As in Rome for the 2024 Games[1] or the referendums in Sion[2] and Calgary concerning the Winter Games in 2026.

The IOC has been conscious of this challenge for some years now and has requested that cities base their application on a long-term development project with positive potential, even in the case of unsuccessful bids. Local areas would benefit from a candidacy and avoid being subject to any risks involved. The question is in what way do the candidates follow this pious hope. In other words, it is a matter of weighing up the promises of a bid against the actual benefits for the area. Does the project continue to develop at the outcome of the bid? Does its implementation change if the city is not elected?

To structure our analysis, we will mobilize the sociology of public intervention and in particular the notions of ineffectiveness, inefficacy and inefficiency that allow, as specified by Lascoumes and Le Galès (2007), resistance, passivity and anomalies in public policies to be identified. In fact, ineffectiveness translates a policy that is defined but never implemented, for example a law for which the decrees are never published. Inefficacy reveals policies whose implementation prevents the expected results to be obtained. Finally, inefficiency translates a situation for which the means put in place are excessive in relation to the effects achieved. This modelling is particularly relevant to describing bids and their implications when applied to large-scale public issues, for example obtaining the Games or not, often criticized for the excessive investment involved.

The following analysis of the bids, both successful and unsuccessful, will identify the effects of the campaigns and examine the outcome of the projects planned for the hosting of the Olympics. For this study, Paris is the selected example. Although the analysis of one city only will limit the scope of our conclusions, it does present interesting factors: Paris has presented three bids for the Games since the beginning of the 2000s. The outcome in 2008 was unfavourable; Beijing received without a doubt the majority of votes. While Paris had a very good chance of gaining the bid in 2012, the project presented by London obtained the majority of the IOC votes. The margin was very close and was visible in the conviction that Paris would succeed in this second campaign right up to the announcement of the results. At last, the bid for the 2024 Olympic and Paralympic Games was a complete success. Albeit a relative one due to the withdrawal of all the other candidates except for Los Angeles, also selected as part of a dual attribution.

To support our demonstration, we will give a detailed account of the development plan described by each candidacy. The information is stored at the Olympic Studies Institute in Lausanne. Each proposal will be compared with the real changes in the Metropolis. An analysis of press coverage identifying the political commitments in support of or against the projects in particular will be a major factor in this study. Beyond words, we will also follow-up concrete achievements by including the analysis of aerial photography from the National Geographical Institute, which will reveal the progress of the actual groundwork.

Our unique focus will concentrate on infrastructures. We shall analyse successively the provision of sports amenities and the Olympic village. These two approaches address different rationales in the development plan: the Olympic village creates accommodation while the specialized amenities remain dedicated to sport and especially high performance sport.

The uncertain future of sports amenities

The Olympic project

Infrastructures really put sports amenities at the heart of an Olympic project. They are where sports events attracting media attention take place. The hosting of the Olympics is often synonymous with the creation of large-scale sports amenities, and stadiums are at the forefront. This was the case in 1936 to celebrate Olympism (Bolz, 2008), or in 1976 in Montreal at the expense of tax paying Quebecers (Roult & Lefebvre, 2010). This last example is a mark of failure to reuse the over-sized infrastructures of the Games and is not unique. Abandoned 'white elephants' (Alm, Solberg, Storm & Jakobsen, 2016) punctuate Olympic cities. If the memory of sport retains the achievements that took place there, people also remember the wastage of abandoned buildings.

The bids of Paris and Los Angeles for the 2024 and 2028 Games specifically highlighted the availability of sports amenities as strong points of their campaigns. Indeed, without the need for dedicated structures, the risk of excessive or uncontrolled public expenditures is removed. Before bidding for the 2024 Games, Paris developed projects in order to have nearly all the required sports amenities by 2017. These projects were often included in the previous biddings. Reading the successive presentations for Paris, it appears that the list of sports amenities to create diminished over time, and projects were completed in spite of failures to obtain the Games for 2008 and 2012.

For 2008,[3] the construction of sports amenities were planned as for:

- an Olympic pool in St Denis
- a velodrome in Aubervilliers
- an artificial river for white water events in Vaires-sur-Marne

For 2012,[4] the main amenities were practically identical with the exception of the velodrome that was then planned for Saint-Quentin-en-Yvelines.

Finally, during the bid for 2024,[5] the only sustainable construction planned was for the Olympic pool. But what was the outcome of the other amenities? Had some of them been built in spite of the unsuccessful bid?

The main difference can be found in the dossiers of Paris in 2012 and 2024. More precisely, the candidacy for the 2024 Games particularly highlights the fact that two major amenities were a legacy from the earlier 2012 bid: the velodrome in Saint-Quentin-en-Yvelines and the white water descent in Vaires-sur-Marne. The development project for sports infrastructures planned in the prospective of the 2012 Games was therefore partially carried out.

Effectiveness of the proposal

The first analysis consists in measuring the effectiveness of the proposal. The three dossiers put forward by the city of Paris reveal that only some of the amenities presented in the bid for 2012 were carried out. Hence, it appears that no action was taken following the project developed for the 2008 Games. The first question is thus to understand the reasons for the effectiveness of the Olympic project. Our hypothesis is that the political support gained during the bid phase contributes to ensure the promises are fulfilled. Even so this support is not sufficient to guarantee the actual outcome as not all the projects are carried out.

The Paris bids for 2008 and 2012 were not conducted under the same conditions. The first campaign took place in an extremely competitive context. An implicit selection factor of the host cities ensures a rotation between the continents, in particular for the Summer Games. Hence, since Helsinki in 1952, no Olympiad has taken place twice consecutively on the same continent. So it appeared difficult for Paris to host the Games after Athens in 2004.

Without going into all the details of each bid, Beijing's application very quickly took on a particular dimension. Certain internal factors are important: the city deployed considerable means to obtain the Olympic Games, and geopolitical factors also need to be taken into account. China's economy had rapidly and regularly grown since 1980 and the country had become the leading global economic power. This growth was linked to an opening market economy that, by extension, was also a cultural opening to the world. The challenge for the sports movement was to gain access to a population of 1.4 billion people until then hardly touched by the globalization of sport (Tan & Bairner, 2010). The other BRICS countries (Brazil, Russia, India, China and South Africa) have also had the same success in their partnerships with sports institutions in the organization of major international sports events over the last 20 years (Grix & Lee, 2013). In short, the Paris bid rapidly found itself up against a serious competitor that strongly reduced its chances of success. The final IOC vote was irrevocable: Paris received 15 votes against 44 for Beijing during the first round of votes then respectively 18 and 56 during the second. The weak chances of success for Paris moderated any implication, notably political, in favour of the Games.

The situation was quite different during the campaign in 2012 and European cities were in competition. Apart from New York, four capitals on the old continent were in the starting blocks: Madrid, London, Paris and Moscow. While competition was very strong, Paris had very good chances of winning the Games. Four rounds of votes took place with the successive elimination of Moscow, New York and Madrid. It was not until the final vote that a majority emerged: London won by just four votes. This campaign was thus conducted from start to finish with conviction and commitment.

In this context, political support for Paris was significant at all levels: the City had the support of the Île-de-France region and the State. This positive commitment was reflected in strong declarations, notably in the unlikely event of failure. Hence, J.-P. Huchon then president of the Île-de-France Regional Council, declared: 'We are very disappointed, very sad. But we must keep the energy of this positive adventure and strive, with the public authorities and with the state, to build the sports venues we need for the future.'[6] Therefore, the sanction of the vote was a great disappointment. So as not to be discredited after having been strongly implicated towards the population, the government confirmed its support for the completion of the town-planning project. Hence, D. de Villepin announced: 'We will build the planned infrastructures that our country badly needs'.[7] And in fact, certain projects soon emerged.

The first analysis that can be done is linked to political commitment. When it is very firm and extended till the end of the bid with good chances of success, the project may, as in Paris during the vote for 2012, be maintained and become a reality. This is the main difference between the bid for 2008 and that of 2012. The second constituted a more important political investment. Hence, the continued commitment, the conviction of implicated parties and the support of elected representatives were prerequisites to get the established project for 2012 off the ground... in part.

A local efficiency

If the project borne by the bid for 2012 was carried out, as the government hoped for, it is surprising to see that only part of it came to fruition and that areas with the most needs (Lessard, 2018) were those that benefitted the least. Here, we refer to the pool intended for Seine-Saint-Denis, an area marked by social difficulties and the subject of a development plan to restructure sports amenities. Unfortunately this plan did not suffice to reduce the backwardness of the municipalities in the department (Lessard & Schut, 2016). Henceforth, the conditions of its completion should be questioned and thus the efficacy in the implementation of this project.

All the amenities proposed during the Olympic bid are subject to legal and financial arrangements that lead to their implementation. The form may vary from one amenity to another, though the model is based on two consistent elements: 1. In the long run, local communities become the proprietors of sports infrastructures; 2. Funding results from the mutualization of the resources of stakeholders. In the case of a defeat, local authorities maintain strong power of decision for the completion or not of amenities in spite of the Prime Minister's position. This power is all the more important as financial support for the project will probably be less in the absence of the sports event.

Indeed, local communities play a major role in decision making for the construction of the infrastructure. For each amenity considered, the concerned stakeholders differ (Table 5.1). Hence, depending on the amount of support by the communities for the completion of the project, the amenities will be implemented or not.

Table 5.1 Principal sports amenities to build as proposed by the Paris 2012 bid committee

Amenities to create in the bid portfolio for the 2012 Games	Principal communities involved	Provisional cost
White water river for canoeing and kayaking	Île-de-France Regional Council	$44.6 million
Olympic pool	Plaine-Commune urban community	$83 million
Velodrome	Saint-Quentin-en-Yvelines urban community	$44.9 million

Source: Candidacy Committee Paris 2012 (2005)

The Regional Council for Île-de-France is proprietor of the outdoor and leisure centres and its president, at that time, Jean-Paul Huchon was particularly involved in the bid. The council was implicated in the projected construction work of the artificial river for the Vaires-Torcy site where international kayaking competitions could take place. The velodrome project at Saint-Quentin-en-Yvelines was also supported by the local urban community. While the swimming pool project in Seine-Saint-Denis never saw the light of day. The reason being that departmental policy was focused on a local approach and had as an aim to give all young people the opportunity to learn to swim.[8] A unique 50m Olympic pool represented considerable cost for lesser efficacy in the implementation of local politics.

This contrasted situation shows how the carrying through of a local project is at first dependant on the investment of local communities that, in France, are the main proprietors of sports amenities (Falcoz & Chifflet, 1998). Each area determines its priorities that more or less coincide with those of the Olympic bid project.

Efficiency of accomplishments

The hosting of the Olympic and Paralympic Games is frequently touted as a 'boost for public policies'.[9] To a certain extent, the gain in time can be seen as an improvement in public policy efficiency. Nevertheless, this promptness in execution can also be the source of inefficiency at two levels: 1. Inadequate amenities or those needing refitting in order to fulfil their role; 2. The need to accelerate building to meet delivery deadlines creates additional cost.

If we consider amenities that have actually been completed, we can take into account three indicators to estimate the efficiency of public policies by comparing the project and its fulfilment. To do this we can use as a base:

- actual delivery dates of the amenities;
- layout of the amenities and its possible reconfiguration;
- cost of the amenities.

Of course this comparison remains within the limit laid out by a theoretical project, one that would probably entail several modifications, for instance cost. For this reason the last indicator will be treated with caution.

The first consideration is linked to the layout of the amenities. Both the velodrome in Saint-Quentin-en-Yvelines and the nautical activities centre in Vaires-Torcy required a new definition of needs in relation to the purpose initially planned. If the prospect of hosting important international events remains the standard of amenities for high-level sport, other factors are to be taken into account and some characteristics redefined.

The project to host the 2012 Games planned the construction of a peninsula for the reception of judges and media. The completed project excluded this important expenditure which only made sense for the elite competition and which divided the nautical space at the expense of the variety of possible practices on the water. Building out of the Olympic context has reduced the oversizing effect of sports amenities; one of the main consequences for the abandonment or under-use of equipment post event.

Project reviewing entails an additional period of study and definition and amenity delivery dates entail longer delays than that of a simple complementary expertise. Infrastructures had to be ready for the events projected for the summer of 2012. Finally, the velodrome in Saint-Quentin-en-Yvelines officially opened January 30, 2014, 18 months after the London Games. At Vaires-Torcy, the first phase of work was delivered in July 2018. This date can be explained not only by a more significant transformation of the initial project but also building delays. It is quite obvious that the building of the venues took longer than expected and the delivery demands of the Games resulted in an effort to speed up procedures.

The difficulty is to estimate whether efficiency is only a matter of delivering the amenity within short time delays or delivering a more sustainable one where its future use is better planned.

The question of cost is a relevant indicator of efficiency. On-time delivery may incur extra cost in order to speed up the construction (night work, etc.). The initial budget for each amenity was significantly exceeded. In the context of a public–private partnership, the velodrome was estimated at 73 million euros. The final construction cost reached 101 million. For Vaires-Torcy, the Île-de-France Regional Council at first released 55 million euros, then an extra 20 million. An unscheduled additional 15 million followed to finalize the construction, bringing the total bill to 90 million euros. In both cases, the cost of the amenities significantly exceeded the initial scheduled budget. It is worth noting that the Vaires-Torcy project integrated office space for the Canoe-Kayak and Rowing Federations and accommodation with 140 beds. It is therefore difficult to compare the complex to the 50 million dollars invested for the Lee Valley waterway created for the 2012 London Games.

To complete the analysis, it is difficult to assume that the velodrome and nautical activity complex are symbols of efficient public involvement. In a sense, there was no need to invest in a significant and probably rarely used hosting capacity. Nevertheless, the projects remain ambitious: compliance with specific standards for sports when hosting international competitions, centres including accommodation, etc. In spite of delays to deliver amenities, financiers cannot avoid additional costs. To conclude, the Games do not guarantee the efficiency of public involvement.

The opportunity of an Olympic village

An urban project above all

Through the Olympic village, the effects of the Olympic and Paralympic Games leave a mark on the urban landscape. Accommodating over 10,000 athletes, the Olympic village can have the stature of a town. In the major cities that host the Games, it generally covers a district. In some cases, it has offered the opportunity to extend the town and in others to renovate an entire area. This is notably the case in major European cities that are constrained by lack of space and at the same time have under-used spaces that need significant funding to rejuvenate them. Stratford in London will probably long remain a case study (Davis & Thornley, 2010) even if criticism brought about by *gentrification* has arisen since the Games (Watt, 2013).

In Paris, the first point to note in each of the three projects is the systematic change of location for the Olympic village. In 2008, it was supposed to be built in Plaine-Commune. In 2012, the district of Batignolles inside Paris was targeted. Then, for 2024 the location returned to Seine-Saint-Denis, just slightly further to the east than the projected site for 2008. The question we can consider is to understand why these changes multiplied in such close vicinity.

Firstly, the choice of vicinity can be understood by looking at the overall project. The Paris applications have always prioritized, in accordance with the expectations of the IOC, the compactness of the event based on a geographical zone spreading from the north to the east of Paris. In other words, from the Stade de France to the amenities of Porte d'Auteuil: Roland-Garros, the Parc des Princes and the Jean Bouin stadium.

Secondly, it is important to measure the amount of land needed to establish the village. This problematic is one of the first considerations for the successive bid committees. The Olympic villages are projected in the different bids for 2008, 2012 and 2024. Identifying these areas of land in compliance with the relevant requirements for location and the creation of sports infrastructures is extremely limiting.

Finally, the intentions of the bid committees to construct new buildings that will be converted into housing after the event need consideration. If the requirement to build on existing infrastructures is a powerful argument in the sports world, the creation *ex nihilo* of the Olympic village is a strong commitment. While it may be possible to use existing property assets, for instance student accommodation available during a particular time of year, the creation of an Olympic village appears as a major legacy and not subject to the criticism often directed towards sports amenities as the need for housing in large cities remains constant.

On the other hand, it is also possible to reverse a standpoint and to question the link that exists between the urban project and the sports event. Does the sports event generate an urban project or rather does the urban project become implicitly attached to a sports event by means of the windfall effect? In fact, the Olympic dynamic represents many advantages: exceptional urban planning procedures,[10] a sustained effort by community stakeholders and above all, an image that enables to both reduce expenditure on publicity and increase market prices. From this viewpoint, our approach consists in analysing the synergy between the Olympic and Paralympic Games and the urban project for the Olympic village. Does hosting the event determine the implementation of an urban project? Does it modify the project? Does it accelerate it?

An unchallenged achievement

The first question to tackle concerns the effectiveness of an urban project. Was an Olympic bid at the origin of the urban project? Does the success or failure of the bid determine the beginning or the end of it?

During the bid for the 2012 Games, the city of Paris identified a new real estate opportunity for the establishment of an Olympic village inside Paris. The Société Nationale de Chemins de Fer (the French National Railway Society) had released a vast railway maintenance site, due to relocating to a new centre outside Paris. More than 50 hectares were proposed to planners for a comprehensive development. The bid committee saw an ideal opportunity here for the establishment of the Olympic village. The district had the advantage of being inside Paris and was ideally positioned at the north east of the city between two major hubs for sport.

First and foremost, it should be noted that the bid committee was not at the origin of the urban planning project. In fact, a first urban study was launched as early as 2001 with the ambition to create a park area of 10 ha.[11] The forming of a bid committee in 2003 was therefore later. Even so, at the time when it turned its attention on the potential of the district, further extensive studies were carried out to define the project and so transform the area into an exemplary urban setting. Extensive analysis of environmental challenges was carried out to echo the committee's campaign message: environmentally friendly, green Games.

This dynamic was not limited to project definition; the time to finalize urban development policies for local areas is at the bid phase. The first zone of concerted district planning took effect in June 2005, a month before the IOC vote. Consequently, it appears that the urban project was not initiated by the bid committee and indicates that it took place without the enthusiasm generated by the Olympics. Nevertheless, the significance of the application for this urban project prompted the bid committee to develop complementary means during the definition phase and provided particularly strong ambition with regard to environmental respect and also the social goals set out, for instance the redevelopment of the site.

A mutable form

The fact that Paris did not manage to host the 2012 Games had an impact on the development of the Clichy-Batignolles district even though the project was not cancelled. The limited available land in Paris, the city's commitment to create another large green space and the private interests of property developers all provided sufficient grounds to continue with the project – although not exactly according to the original plan, due to the sudden increase of the population in that area.

Even if the reconversion of the Olympic village amenities into housing was projected from the start, its completion was not. There was no longer a question of delivering an Olympic village with accommodation for athletes but for a mixed neighbourhood, integrating the main housing and offices. This change in purpose led to modifications in design. Indeed, the district offered generous hosting capacity for the athletes participating in the Games. While big, this would never correspond to the need for housing in Paris or indirectly slow down price inflation of real estate in the third most expensive city in the world for accommodation.

Consequently, the definition of the final project changed. As shown in Figure 5.1, density increased. The height of buildings was increased, in particular the office areas alongside the railway line. At the same time, the costly architectural elements that had their place in a high quality environmental initiative disappeared. This was the case in the covering of the railway line at the approach to Saint-Lazarre station. Finally, while the park remains in the centre of the neighbourhood, the stadium with its distinctive athletics track in the north has disappeared.

We have already mentioned the accelerating effect of the bid for the Games as regards preliminary studies or the establishment of the first concerted development area. However, the unsuccessful bid also led to a phase of redefinition that itself slowed down the development of the area. The delivery of work chronology was quite different from that originally presented. In 2015, the first phase was completed and the delivery of 1,500 homes enabled the first inhabitants to move into the neighbourhood. In 2018 the second phase was completed offering a great number of homes and also many office buildings. However, certain amenities, such as transport infrastructures, are still in progress. The project will finally be considered as complete at delivery of the third phase projected for 2020.

Figure 5.1 View of the Clichy-Batignolles district in the bid portfolio for the 2005 Games (left) and the project selected in 2009 (right)
Sources: Paris 2012, *Bid portfolio for Paris 2012*, Volume 2, 2005; *Clichy-Batignolles Project*. Retrieved from https://www.lemoniteur.fr/article/a-la-decouverte-de-l-opera tion-d-amenagement-clichy-batignolles.1912234 (visited March 25, 2019). Copyright © 2005 International Olympic Committee – all rights reserved

By comparison, in the Olympic village project for 2012 the delivery of housing for athletes and public transport links was scheduled for 2012. In fact, the duration of the works doubled! The organization of the Games in Paris would certainly have led to shorter delays. However, the bid did not appear, in retrospect, to have played such a decisive part. On the one hand, the project existed before the bid; on the other, the failure of the Games did not put in doubt the actual realization of the project. In this example, it appears that the bid committee seized the opportunity of using an urban project to affix the Olympic seal. The realization of the Games would have presumably triggered changes in its form although their pertinence and shorter completion date can be questioned.

To go further than supposition, Stratford may be referred to as counterfactual insofar as both districts, and both European capitals, present many structural similarities. Stratford was effectively transformed very rapidly to become an Olympic village consistent with a project: numerous new homes, connection to public transport networks and proximity to sports amenities. Nevertheless, major design flaws attributed to the hosting of the Games can be identified, for example, the absence of kitchens in the apartments. What may seem acceptable for an Olympic village with centralized catering services becomes ludicrous in the case of conversion into permanent homes.

The planning of an Olympic village is quite different from that linked to other sports infrastructures. If the fear of marking the landscape with a new 'white elephant' had completely orientated the project towards using existing sports amenities or installing dismountable temporary fixtures, the reasoning regarding the Olympic village was in total opposition. In an old city like Paris or London, the rejuvenation of a district would present an opportunity if not an obligation to leave behind a tangible legacy. Up until now, criticism regarding 'Olympic quarters' is marginal even if hindsight reveals a few mixed trends in the long run (Joly, 1978; Guibourdenche & Joly, 1979). The reusing of what already exists, although entirely sustainable, gives way to the creation of eco-districts where environmental standards are high.

Conclusion

Bringing this analysis to conclusion, it appears that the bids provide for limited investment in sports infrastructures and, systematically, a major urban project for the Olympic village. This situation arises from the idea that bidding is the moment to put forward a local project but also the moment to woo the IOC electors. The project is thus largely orientated towards this target. All too often there have been excesses in sports infrastructures created for the Games and which are underused after them. The examples we have chosen clearly illustrate that the amenities implemented in the absence of Games have all been reviewed downwards regarding the hosting capacity of spectators or enhanced with additional features. In the end, it is the bid that provides for the least investment in sports amenities that obtains the Games.

The reality will be even more rational as the Olympic pool, the only important construction maintained, will finally only be a dismountable, temporary amenity.[12]

As for the Olympic village, this represents an entirely different challenge. It is first of all an urban development project. It is then embellished with the Olympic label and upgraded to become an international showcase of urban know-how and therefore takes into consideration contemporary environmental challenges. It has however the power to meet a real local need even without the Games as the demand for housing in major cities is never entirely satisfied.

In any event, the bid projects for urban development seem to be implemented, if only in part. The proposal concerning the Olympic village is carried out almost systematically since it often forms an opportunity for a complete remodelling and is not entirely abandoned by the city. Funding depends of course on the financial viability of the project. That is how the new eco-quarter in Batignolles benefitted more from the revised planning than the buildings constructed following the incentive prompted by the bid for 2008.

For sports infrastructures, the role played by political commitment in the bid was considerable though not necessarily enough. The long-term backing of local authorities is essential as they are the guarantors of achievements concerning sports amenities.

To conclude, Olympic bids can effectively play a part in the defining of town planning. Nevertheless, the end of the bid procedure, even when successful, results in a re-examination of the project. This phase marks an end to a part of the project. Backing is thus capital to help re-launch the amenities. In this context political backing obtained during the bid can be beneficial but only the really cost-effective projects, regardless of the Games, are sure of being accomplished. Finally, the bid certainly has a positive effect in triggering a wave of support but retains the gigantic hallmark when it defines above all the projects dedicated to the Olympic Games, before considering rationally what is best for the local environment.

Notes

1 JO 2024: la candidature de Rome définitivement enterrée, *Le Monde*, October 11, 2016.
2 Sion 2026: le jour où les Valaisans ont éteint pour de bon la flamme olympique, *Le Nouvelliste*, June 10, 2018.
3 Paris 2008, *Dossier de candidature*, 2001.
4 Paris 2012, *Dossier de candidature*, 2005.
5 Paris 2024, *Dossier de candidature*, 2017.
6 'Les réactions', *L'Obs*, July, 2005. Retrieved from https://www.nouvelobs.com/sport/20050706.OBS2633/les-reactions.html (visited on March 2, 2019)
7 *Le Figaro*, July 11, 2005.
8 *Dossier de presse Plan Piscines 2016–2021*. Retrieved from https://seinesaintdenis.fr/IMG/pdf/dp_plan_piscines.pdf (visited on March 25, 2019)
9 *Les Jeux olympiques et paralympiques, accélérateurs des politiques publiques*, Mairie de Paris, 2016, 86p.

10 See the 'Olympic law' (March 26, 2018).
11 SEMAVIP, *Clichy-Batignolles Project*. Proposal bid for new urban districts, 2009.
12 Lefèvre S. 'Paris 2024: la piscine olympique sera bien semi-démontable', *Le Parisien*, June 7, 2018. Retrieved from http://www.leparisien.fr/sports/la-piscine-sera -bien-semi-demontable-05-06-2018-7753218.php (visited March 25, 2019).

References

Alm, J., Solberg, H., Storm, R. K. & JakobsenT. (2016). Hosting major sports events: the challenge of taming white elephants, *Leisure Studies*, 35(5), 564–582. doi:10.1080/02614367.2014.994550

Bolz, D. (2008). *Les arènes totalitaires. Hitler, Mussolini et les jeux du stade*. Paris: CNRS éditions.

Candidacy Committee Paris 2012 (2005). *Bid for Paris 2012* (vol. 2).

Davis, J. & Thornley, A. (2010). Urban regeneration for the London 2012 Olympics: Issues of land acquisition and legacy. *City, Culture and Society*, 1, 89–98.

Falcoz, M. & Chifflet, P. (1998). La construction publique des équipements sportifs. Aspects historique, politique et spatial. *Les Annales de la recherche urbaine*, 79, 14– 21

Grix, J. & Lee, D. (2013). Soft power, sports mega-events and emerging states: the lure of the politics of attraction, *Global Society*, 27(4), 521–536, doi:10.1080/ 13600826.2013.827632

Guibourdenche, H. & Joly, J. (1979). Changement social et structures spatiales dans l'agglomération et les quartiers de Grenoble (1968–1975). *Revue de Géographie Alpine*, 67(4), 391–406.

Joly, J. (1978). Structure sociale de l'agglomération et des quartiers de Grenoble. *Revue de Géographie Alpine*, 66(4), 385–407.

Lascoumes, P. & Le Galès, P. (2007). *Sociologie de l'action publique*. Paris: Armand Colin.

Lessard, C. (2018). Les politiques municipales de la jeunesse et des sports dans les quartiers. Espoirs et illusions de la mixité sociale et de la discrimination positive. University Paris-Est, unpublished PhD thesis.

Lessard, C. & Schut, P.-O. (2016). Les politiques publiques d'équipements sportifs vues à travers quatre villes françaises de 1960 à nos jours. *Loisir et Société/Society and Leisure*, 39(1), 61–86. doi:10.1080/07053436.2016.1151219

Roult, R. & Lefebvre, S. (2010). Planning and reconversion of Olympic heritages: The Montreal Olympic Stadium. *International Journal of the History of Sport*, 27(16– 18), 2731–2747, doi:10.1080/09523367.2010.508257

Tan, T-C. & Bairner, A. (2010). Globalization and Chinese sport policy: The case of elite football in the People's Republic of China. *The China Quarterly*, 203, 581–600. doi:10.1017/S0305741010000603

Watt, P. (2013). 'It's not for us' regeneration, the 2012 Olympics and the gentrification of East London. *City*, 17(1), 99–118.

6 The role of heritagization in managing uncertainties linked to major events and mega urban projects

Comparing the Olympic Games in London (2012) and Athens (2004)

Cécile Doustaly and Geneviève Zembri-Mary

Introduction

This chapter tackles the lack of comparative long-term analyses of the urban dimension of the Olympics. It introduces research planned from 2018 to 2028 to analyse the role of heritagization in reducing risks, detecting opportunities and ensuring a positive legacy for mega projects such as Olympiads, and reconciling local expectations with mega urban projects. The transversal study of these concepts and theories of risk and heritagization has never been explored by scientific literature.

There is a significant need for more contextualized, interdisciplinary and multi-scalar urban studies research on the Olympic Games (OG) as the literature tends to focus on each Olympiad, on short or medium-term impacts or media coverage of the Games as mega events (Chaboche & Schoeny, 2018). Publications attempting comparative and historical analysis necessary to study the urban dimension of Olympic projects remain rare (Gold & Gold, 2017).

Although built on ambitious Olympic ideals, Olympic urban projects are potentially very risky. Among the more frequent risks is the lack of reuse of permanent sports venues after the event that can create urban wastelands. The example of Athens with its long abandoned and now unusable venues is eloquent. The second main risk is that the final cost of the project will exceed forecasts. All host cities which have organized summer or winter games have met overcosts, but their proportion can vary greatly (up to 12 times the initial planned costs in the case of Peking) (Bellanger & Pouchard, 2018). These overcosts may be the consequence of other risks that can appear during the planning or the implementation of the project: public opposition, impacts on the natural and human environment, financing problems, inappropriate governance, construction delays etc. — all possibly requiring a project review.

This contribution focuses on the position that heritagization, in the form of the classification, preservation and enhancement of environmental, urban, historical or archaeological heritage, can be a response to uncertainties and risks which characterize Olympic projects. Heritagization is considered here as a long-term approach which can be encouraged by public policies to ensure sustainability. A typology discerning different forms of heritagization illustrates there are diverse values and references to the past. With the enlargement of the definition of heritage assets, heritagization has become a more inclusive process which can concern Olympic sites through tangible and intangible dynamics. Natural and cultural heritage integration allows limiting the risk for such projects to endanger assets, lead policies in relation with the Olympic project (such as urban regeneration, reuse of urban wastelands) and create opportunities for economic, urban and tourism development after the Games. Projects integrating heritagization may rely on participation processes which aim at encouraging inhabitants' acceptance of the Games and associated urban change, based on exchanges on the values and objectives they wish to associate with them, often including a better preservation of natural and cultural heritage assets. Depending on the countries, these participation processes may be less or more profound.

This chapter analyses how heritagization may be a solution to reduce the uncertainties and risks faced by Olympic projects, drawing on two contrasted examples: London 2012 and Athens 2004. The first part presents each of the Olympic projects, explains how they were integrated into larger urban projects, and which project governance was chosen by the host city. The second part details the theoretical and methodological framework allowing to cross risks and heritagization forms. The third part makes a cross analysis of risks, uncertainties and opportunities faced by the London 2012 and Athens 2004 projects. The fourth part shows how heritagization may be a solution to reduce risks and uncertainties. The conclusion underlines the assets and the limits of heritagization, particularly concerning project governance.

The urban projects of Athens 2004 and London 2012

Comparing the cases of Athens and London is enlightening as although the first is generally presented as a failure and the second as a success, analysis of the urban project from the cross perspective of risk and heritagization unveils a more nuanced picture. The cases also share relative similarities: their Games were organized quite closely timewise, they were both affected by the 2008 crisis and their final cost reached around 10 billion euros, both with an over-cost of about 100%. The United Kingdom GDP being 10 times higher than Greece's in 2004 and 11 times in 2012 (World Bank GDP Statistics, 2012), the drain on Greece's financial resources proved far more challenging.

The urban project and the Olympic project of Athens 2004

Athens' Olympic project led to the building of numerous sites scattered around the metropolis (ATHOC, 1996) (Map 6.1):

- the Olympic village was isolated in the northern part of the city (114 ha);

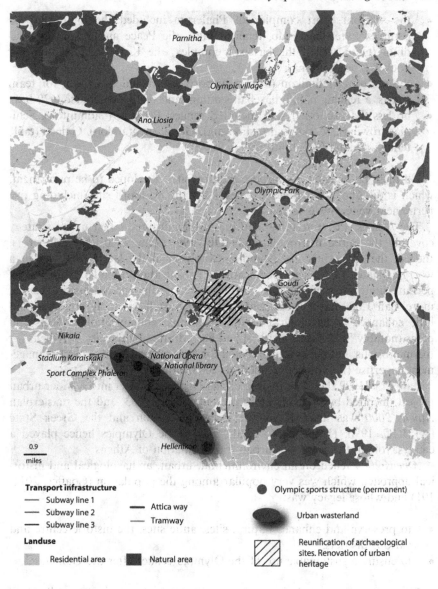

Map 6.1 The Olympic and urban project of Athens 2004 after the Games
Adapted from Henry, 2005 and field work

- the Olympic Park gathered the Olympic stadium, the tennis centre, the indoor hall for gymnastics and basket-ball, the nautical complex and the velodrome (96 ha);

- the seafront sport complex of Phalerum included the multi purpose complex (wrestling, judo, fencing, etc.), the Peace and Friendship stadium (team sport), the baseball complex, the Karaiskaki stadium for hockey (about 500 ha);
- the seafront Hellinikon (former airport) site included a room for team sports, a fencing hall, a baseball stadium and the canoe course (620 ha);
- no less than six other sites included venues: Peristeri (badminton), Schinias (rowing), Markopoulo (shooting), Goudi (pentathlon), Galasti (table tennis), Nikaïa (weightlifting).

All these buildings were purpose built on sites developed to be permanent, which is different from London where only the Stratford site (including five permanent venues) was to remain.

The Athens sites were integrated into a long awaited larger urban strategy covering the entire metropolis (ATHOC, 1996; Law 2730/1999; Map 6.1). Indeed, the city, when the candidacy was won in the late 1990s, was in a worrying state: its extensive and scattered urbanization often lacking building permits, high levels of pollution, a dilapidated and congested historic centre, more than 1,000 ha of urban and industrial wasteland, badly preserved and little enhanced archaeological heritage. Various reorganization projects and plans (notably SOS Attica in 1994) had been drafted by the city of Athens for the metropolis, but never implemented for lack of funds and project management expertise (Beriatos & Gospodini, 2004; Boukas et al., 2013).

Law 2730/1999 therefore integrated the Olympic project into a wider urban project, inspired by previous plans presented since 1983, and the masterplan *Athens 2000* was financed by the European Union and the Greek State (ATHOC, 1996; Henry, 2005; et al., 2004). The Olympics hence played a catalyst role in the project of urban transformation of Athens.

Athens 2004 relied on an environmental, urban, archaeological and historical approach which was very popular among the population (Coaffee, 2011: 191) and whose legacy was:

- to preserve and enhance natural sites, antic sites, the historic centre and various districts;
- to ensure a sustainable use of the Olympic venues after the Games.

The project promoted the universal character of culture (Papanikolaou, 2013) based on the ancient Olympic heritage and the humanist values of Antiquity (Garcia, 2008).

Athens' generally overlooked achievement was not only a great number of new Olympic venues and sites but also major infrastructure, such as three subway lines, the Attica Way (a highway) and a tramway line that were delivered on time for the Games. The historic centre also evolved greatly: the archaeological sites were connected to the metro and a pedestrian path, the National Museum of Archaeology of Athens was renovated, archaeological sites were enhanced, the nearby Syntagma Square and buildings were restored (Potsiou & Apostolatos, 2006). But the ambitious plan for renovating all degraded areas of the centre could not totally be achieved. In Phalerum and Hellinikon, the projects for enhancing 1,000 hectares of urban wastelands (Law 2730/1999) were abandoned after the Games, and only the National Library and the Opera were built in Phalerum. Currently, two private projects are planned for these areas.

The final cost of the Olympic project reached around 10 billion euros. This final cost was the same as that of the London Olympic project, but the labour cost per hour being around 20% lower in 2008 for instance[1], *Athens 2004* project benefitted from large funding.

The Olympic and urban project governance was similarly organized on two levels. The Organizing Committee for the Olympic Games (OCOG) was responsible for the delivery of sports venues and auxiliary facilities (public transport, etc.) for the beginning of the Games as well as for the organization of the Games. It included the Greek National Olympic Committee (NOC), the City of Athens and Greek State representatives, and worked very closely with the International Olympic Committee (IOC).

Working on a wider scale and longer term, the Organization of Planning and Environmental Protection of Athens (ORSA in Greek) was the competent authority to implement the *Athens 2004* project and law 2730/1999 project for the metropolis and its region, the Attica. In addition to the sport venues (ATHOC, 1996), the city wide strategy focused on:

- 'the development of contemporary infrastructure for sports, culture, tourism and social services' ;
- 'the rehabilitation, sustainable development and integrated management of the waterfront';
- 'the protection, conservation and development of the natural and cultural heritage of Attika';
- 'the promotion of the city's history, culture and aesthetics' (article 1, law 2730/1999).

The reconversion strategy for the sports venues had been anticipated in 1999, but little implemented afterwards as the Greek government hesitated on which forms of management and use strategy to adopt after the Games (Henry, 2005; Garcia, 2018). A Bill on the reuse of Olympic venues was voted in May 2005 to entrust their management and maintenance to the private sector, as well as the building of housing, commercial centres, congress centres, cultural facilities and parks foreseen in their vicinity. The bidding process dragged on and was eventually interrupted by the 2008 crisis, which strongly impacted the Greek economy (Garcia, 2018). The Hellenic Republic Asset Development Fund (Taiped) was set up at the request of the Troïka[2] in 2011 to sell public Greek assets and reimburse the creditors of the Greek State. It was tasked with selling the huge urban wastelands of Phalerum and Hellinikon to developers and to find a solution for their abandoned sports venues.

The urban project and the Olympic project of London 2012

To minimize spend, London's Olympic project included competitions in as many as 20 sites and 30 venues (22 in Greater London), a majority of which already existed and were to go back to their previous use after the Games (such as Earl's Court, Hyde Park, Wimbledon, O2, Wembley, Horse Guard's Parade, etc.). So, if London too seized the opportunity to "imagine and engineer" its city (Horne & Whannel, 2016), it focused the urban renewal dimension of its Olympic project on the site of the Olympic Park, situated in Stratford, East London and overlapping four boroughs.

London's Olympiads had four strategic objectives. One related to the sport legacy, the other to the organization of an "inspirational, safe and inclusive" event, while two focused on the long-term urban project in Stratford and were entrusted to the Olympic Delivery Authority (ODA):

- "deliver(ing) the Olympic Park and all venues on time, within agreed budget and to specification, minimising the call on public funds and providing for a sustainable legacy".
- "maximis(ing) the economic, social, health and environmental benefits of the Games for the UK, particularly through regeneration and sustainable development in East London." (LLDC, 2005)

As in Athens, a dedicated agency, the LOCOG (London Organising Committee of the OG), created in 2005, was initially responsible for the timely delivery of the Olympic Park and new venues and the organization of the event. A private limited liability company included the UK government, the Greater London Authority (GLA) and the UK Olympic National Committee (ONC). However, the 2006 Olympic Act established the Olympic Delivery Authority (ODA), a non-departmental public body (NDPB) under the responsibility of the Department for Culture, Media and Sport (DCMS) to focus on land acquisition, planning, new infrastructures and venues in Stratford. It was in charge of coordinating actions from bodies involved in the future park (LOCOG, London Development Agency, transport authorities, boroughs and its private construction delivery partner CLM), supervising clearance, depollution, transport, constructions and delivery of games venues within deadline and budget, but also planning ahead for the urban legacy (ODA, 2007).

The Games were used as a catalyst to rejuvenate initially 400 ha cut across by dilapidated railway and canal infrastructure, most of which were either loosely occupied and derelict or polluted and littered brownfield and marshes. A master plan for the Eastern part of the Stratford City Olympic site (old railway) had already gained planning permission in 2003 and was privately redeveloped (Westfield shopping centre opened in 2011). The Olympic park itself was built publicly on Stratford west industrial area for which the timeline and exceptional governance associated with the Games allowed compulsory purchase orders (for around 300 businesses and an estate) (Map 6.2). Focusing on the positive results, the ODA noted: "The ODA's planning application, one of Europe's largest, was scrutinised by an independent planning authority which actively sought the views of local

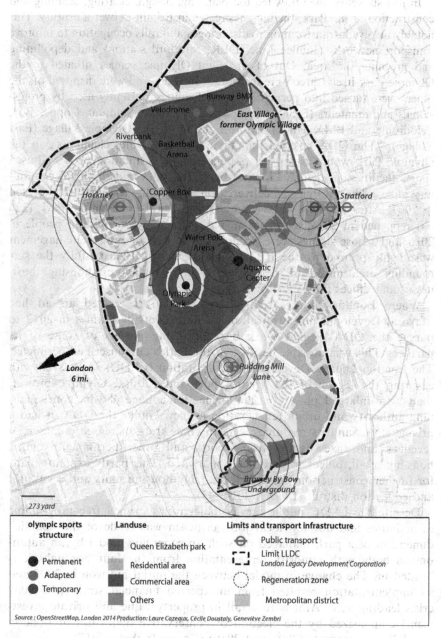

Map 6.2 London's Olympic urban park project after the Games (2014)

people. The ODA turned the vision laid out in the London 2012 master-plan into a reality, transforming a brownfield site into an urban green space" (ODA, 2015: 5).

In just six years, the ODA led the planning, design, clearing, cleaning and construction of the Park, the biggest created in Britain in over a century. This notably involved: transforming roads, bridges and rails occupation to improve transport networks (Jubilee Line, DLR, Stratford station) and depolluting and greening the area. Out of the eight Olympic venues situated in the Olympic Park itself, three were temporary facilities and were disposed of, the others were turned into permanent sport facilities, currently used by professionals and amateurs (Eton Manor, Aquatics Centre, Stadium, Copper Box, Velodrome and BMX Track) or into housing for the Olympic Village (East Village). "The ODA ensured that there were no 'white elephants', so the Olympic Park would become a popular visitor destination with well-used sports facilities, in demand for use by global stars and the local community alike." The project was delivered on time, below the budget allocated in 2007. After adaptations, the now Queen Elizabeth Olympic Park (226 ha) reopened in 2014, as an urban park visited by 9.3 million people in 2016 and whose homes were occupied. The overall project management was highly praised by the IOC as it also managed successfully the surrounding area mixed-use development project including housing, businesses and offices (ODA, 2015: 1–6).

Where London differs from Athens is that it created an ad hoc Mayoral Development Corporation at the end of the Games in 2012 to pursue the ODA's legacy work by centralizing powers of some of its partners. This was possible because of the Park's circumscribed perimeter. The London Legacy Development Corporation (LLDC) was tasked with ensuring the legacy of the urban, sport and cultural Olympic project, thanks to enlarged powers as landowner for a huge 480 ha zone, planning authority and urban regeneration agency. Unlike the ODA, it had a private status and its resources were to come from increased commercial revenues and taxes issued from sports and other permanent venues, housing, retail, offices to be quickly marketed. This partly explains plans for further constructions until 2030, notably housing units and a cultural and education district (LLDC, 2014: 33).

Despite the LLDC public service objectives to run a free programme of activities and develop local jobs, criticism was made of the "public" dimension of a park managed on such an economic model by an autonomous body with minority representation from the four boroughs it is located in. The change in model between the initial bid won in 2005 and its implementation resulted from unexpected financial strain (the 2008 crisis leading as in Athens to a fall in property value and private investment) emphasized by the election of conservative majorities in London and UK governments (2008 and 2010) (Cohen & Watt, 2017).

Table 6.1 Distribution of responsibilities according to the Olympic or urban project phase (ante et post-OG)

Responsibilities	Athens	London
Delivery of event, sports venues, transport and other infrastructure for the OG with the help of the IOC	Organising Committee of the OG (OCOG) including ONC, Athens municipality, Greek State	- 2005: LOCOG (event planning), includes ONC, Greater London Authority, UK State - 2006 (OG Act): Olympic Delivery Authority (ODA) (public body under DCMS ministerial responsibility) for venues and infrastructure
Planning and implementation of the associated urban project before and during the OG	Athens Development and Environmental Protection Organization (ORSA) (a metropolitan state body under the authority of the Ministry of Interior, Public Administration and Decentralization)	(ODA) (responsible for legacy), London Boroughs, Transport for London, London Development Agency (LDA 2000–2012)

Management of the sites and implementation of the urban project after the OG	ORSA
	    Law on private concession fails to attract private companies
	    Since 2011: intervention from the privatization of Greece Fund (Taïped)
		2012: Responsibilities gathered in the London Legacy Development Corporation (LLDC) (a private Mayoral Development Corporation answerable to Mayor of London)

Cross-analysis of uncertainties, risks, opportunities and heritagization forms: methodological and theoretical framework

This second part of the chapter demonstrates how forms of heritagization can provide a solution to reduce the risks and uncertainties faced by Olympic projects and associated urban projects. To do so, a theoretical framework of the notions of risk, opportunity and heritagization was created and a typology of risks, opportunities and heritagization forms is proposed. Then forms of heritagization are crossed with types of risks in a matrix, which is illustrated by examples of heritagization practices intended to sustain and limit risks in Olympic urban projects. This matrix is used as a methodological basis for the Heritrisk research project.

Risks, uncertainties, opportunities

Theoretical framework

Research on uncertainties and risks within the planning, design, building and use of mega projects was developed in Economics as a consequence of increased use of public–private partnership contracts. The allocation of risks between the private and public stakeholders and the monetarization of these has been the subject of scientific research since the 1990s (Ward et al., 1991; Forshaw, 1999; Faruqi, 1997; Arndt, 1998). Then researchers in Economics worked on typologies of risks impacting projects on optimization methods which identify, analyse, reduce, avoid or transfer risks (Grimsey & Lewis, 2002) and on assessment methods to analyse the planning strategies of players (Macharis & Nijkamp, 2013).

Research has focused on the study of unforeseen events, such as conflicts, during public–private partnerships contracts (Gould, 1998). A new research field also explored cooperation processes between stakeholders in the context of public–private partnerships contracts (Campbell & Harris, 1993; Siemiatycki, 2013).

Within this literature on mega projects, that researching risks specific to Olympic projects remains very focused on the event itself by addressing the risks that may impact the delivery of sports venues on time and that may occur during the event (crisis management) (Jennings, 2010, 2012a, b; Jennings & Lodge, 2010, 2011, 2012). The analysis of post-Olympic logics has been little analysed (Gold & Gold, 2017), except for a few articles on the reuse of infrastructure Roult, Lefebvre 2010; Stögerer, 2015). Potential risks and opportunities which may appear after the Games have rarely been addressed.

The 1990s also saw the development of research in Geography on perceived risks, in parallel with more classical approaches to the risk as assessed by experts, under the influence of Anglo-Saxon "constructivist" studies which consider risk as a representation, a "social, cultural, and technical construction" (Faugères & Vasarhelyi, 1988; Coanus, et al., 1999). This notion has not been used by literature on the Olympic Games yet.

Research on risk as a territorialized object of study was developed in the 2000s under the influence of works on conflict and consultation methods. It focused on risk negotiation (Gralepois, 2012; Osadtchy, 2014; Suraud et al., 2009) and acceptance thresholds (Bernier, 2007), but also on the negotiation of risk management practices, standards and compensations, especially in the case of technological or natural risk (Osadtchy, 2014). The use of risk (by elected representatives and associations of environment protection to defend their own interests) and the management of risk (by practitioners or lay people) and the power relations these can create have been studied in the case of transport projects and urban projects (Zembri-Mary 2019a, b; 2016). This research strand, however, cannot concern risks related to Olympic projects, but their formalization of negotiation, consultation and participation can draw light on this case study.

Types of risks, uncertainties and opportunities

Olympic projects and associated urban projects are very risky, because of their size, tight timeline, uniqueness and cost. Risk can be defined as follows:

Risk is the possibility that events, their resulting impacts and their dynamic interactions will turn out differently than anticipated. Risk is typically viewed as something that can be described in statistical terms, while uncertainty is viewed as something that applies to situations in which potential outcomes and causal forces are not fully understood.

(Miller & Lessard, 2008: 148)

Different categories of external risks, uncertainties and opportunities can be distinguished (Miller & Lessard, 2008; Zembri-Mary, 2014; 2019a, b).

There are also internal risks, such as the financial risk (the cost is higher than expected), the commercial risk (i.e. the sales of offices, housings or the commercial use of sports venues are lower than expected) and it is difficult to make long-term sales forecasts (Flyvbjerg et al., 2003). This contribution explores all types of risks and opportunities, except for institutional risks which will be studied drawing on legal sources later in the project.

Heritagization

Theoretical framework

This research analyses heritage as a dynamic construct where a generation selects objects to preserve for future generations. The European Faro Convention on the Value of Cultural Heritage defines cultural heritage as "a set of resources inherited from the past that people consider, beyond the property ownership regime, as a reflection and an expression of their values, beliefs,

Table 6.2 Typology of external uncertainties, risks and opportunities

	Examples of uncertainties and risks	*Examples of opportunities*
Social	Opposition of associations and citizens to the project Evictions, gentrification	New territorial issues (social, environmental, etc.) notably revealed by public consultation, social inclusion programmes
Political	Refusal of elected representatives to support/finance the project	Participation of elected representatives to the design and the financing of the project
Institutional	Regulatory changes impacting the project	Reinforcement of the Law to limit the impacts of the project on the natural and human environment
Environmental	Impact of the project on the natural and human environment	Preservation and enhancement of a natural site
Archaeological	Impact of the project on an archaeological site	Preservation and enhancement of an archaeological site

knowledge and traditions in continuous evolution. This includes all aspects of the environment resulting from the interaction over time between people and places" (Council of Europe, 2005). The 2003 UNESCO declaration on intangible heritage, the recognition of industrial or vernacular assets as heritage, the multiplication of value systems (local or international listings, expert or lay), mean that heritage has become a multifarious and global concept. Processes of heritagization have been criticized for being increasingly politically or commercially driven and interconnected with a maturing tourism industry (Hewison, 1987; Crivello, et al., 2006; Heinich, 2009; Harrison, 2013). In this context, the dedicated interdisciplinary field of Heritage Studies emerged (Harvey, 2015), with a critical strand focusing on questioning dominant value systems (Smith, 2006; Waterton & Winter, 2013).

Heritage, as a symbolic system, bears a strong identity-building function. From a conceptual point of view, heritagization within sustainable urban projects amounts to a fine balancing act between heritage and creation to ensure the protection of local identity, the respect of authenticity, while contributing to sometimes divergent political and economic development objectives. Heritage driven policies mediate between these and can involve:

- (i) the discarding or preservation of heritage assets (buildings, natural and public spaces) and cultural practices and memories,
- (ii) the creation of potential heritage assets (iconic buildings, new housing, natural and public spaces etc.), memorial legacies of collective events and associated urban project.(Doustaly, 2019a)

The link between direct/indirect cultural policies and planning in Athens and London has been little documented (Stevenson, 2012; Boukas et al., 2013; Garcia, 2015). A theoretical framework of Olympic heritagization can however draw from a number of arts and heritage governance practices: sustainable governance for listed heritage sites (UNESCO, 2011; UN, 2016; Doustaly, 2019a), culture-led urban regeneration programmes (Doustaly, 2008; Harvey, 2015) as well as participative budgeting or planning (Doustaly, 2019b; Doustaly & Peng, 2019). Acceptance of change and appropriation of the sites can be harnessed through various forms of heritagization. They are bound to stakeholders' power relations during projects extending over years, on different scales, with conflicting heritage, cultural, social and economic opportunities.

To limit risk and uncertainty and seize opportunities, joined-up methods allowing for participation and co-construction have been found more effective than models commodifying culture or relying on mere consultation (Doustaly, 2013, 2019c). The heritagization approach, if understood as a way to locally inscribe cultural governance to balance local identity preservation, urban change and place attractiveness, could therefore be one of the main answers to encourage communication and create consensus between stakeholders at all stages of the project.

Forms of heritagization

Guy Di Méo (2008) underlined that the heritagization process refers not only to the definition of heritage, but also to heritage preservation, conservation and enhancement procedures. There are different forms of heritagization depending on heritage types. Tangible heritagization concerns objects such as archaeological objects and sites, historical buildings, natural assets and the environment. The heritagization approach consists in identifying an object/site as heritage, preserving it notably by its inclusion in a collection, listing or protected area (Natura 2000) and enhancing it, respecting certain associated conditions. Heritagization may also refer to intangible cultural heritage such as social and cultural practices (ICH convention, UNESCO, 2003).

Cross-analysis of types of risks, opportunities and forms of heritagization: methodological framework

Heritagization in an urban context implies the sustainability and preservation of spaces integrating tangible or intangible assets. It is also associated with an enhancement approach, to expose them, generally also targeted at attracting investments (to create a museum, develop a tourist area). Depending on the context, this approach is often associated with the planning and building of attractive facilities generating commercial revenue (sport and leisure venues,

Table 6.3 Heritagization forms in the Olympic urban project context

Heritagization forms		Examples
Tangible heritagization	Architectural, urbanistic	Renovating ancient buildings and constructing new venues and transforming them into sustainable places
	Archaeological and historical	Preserving ancient objects (movable heritage), buildings and sites (immovable heritage) and making urbanistic choices allowing their enhancement
	Environmental	Considering the natural environment in the broad sense (natural space, wildlife, flora, air, water, etc.) as a common asset that must be preserved and enhanced
Intangible heritagization		Preserving and enhancing cultural or artistic practices, such as dance, music, theatre, food, festivals, oral traditions and expressions, professional skills, etc. notably through support to communities, cultural programming and cultural institutions

Table 6.4 Matrix associating heritagization forms to risks types in Olympic projects

Heritagization forms (Olympic venues and associated urban projects) Uncertainties and risks types	Tangible heritagization			Intangible heritagization
	Architectural and urbanistic heritagization - Building/ urban renovation - Symbolic and iconic constructions (venues, facilities, urban space)	**Archaeological and historical heritagization** Historic objects and sites preservation and enhancement	**Environmental heritagization** Natural environment preservation and enhancement	Preserving and enhancing cultural, artistic practices (dance, music, theatre, etc.)
	The heritage process includes a consultation with all players and inclusive governance that allows them to discuss heritage values and the objectives of the project, to appropriate the OG and associated urban project by identifying with it.			
Environmental risk *Impact of the project on the natural and human environment*	Industrial heritage reuse after depollution (buildings, canals, public space etc.)		Depollution, flood and air quality protection Creation of preservation areas, of urban parks	Agricultural practices conservation
Archaeological risk *Impact of the project on an archaeological site*	Onsite presentation and mediation Archiving, collecting Museums renovation	Creation of archaeological/ historical preservation zones Creation of museums space or building (for objects)		
Political risks *Opposition of elected representatives to the project*	Consultation with elected representatives Regulations/ policies to limit potential gentrification	Consultation on archaeological issues Creation of preservation areas	Consultation on environmental issues Creation of preservation areas	Participation of elected representatives to the definition of a cultural policy Memory of the event
Social risks *Opposition of associations and citizens to the project; evictions, gentrification*	Consultation with inhabitants	Consultation on archaeological issues Creation of preservation areas	Consultation on environmental issues Creation of preservation areas	Participation of inhabitants to the definition of a cultural policy Memory of the event

Heritagization forms	Tangible heritagization			Intangible heritagization
(Olympic venues and associated urban projects)	**Architectural and urbanistic heritagization**	**Archaeological and historical heritagization**	**Environmental heritagization** *Natural environment preservation and enhancement*	*Preserving and enhancing cultural, artistic practices (dance, music, theatre, etc.)*
Uncertainties and risks types	*- Building/ urban renovation - Symbolic and iconic constructions (venues, facilities, urban space)*	*Historic objects and sites preservation and enhancement*		
	The heritage process includes a consultation with all players and inclusive governance that allows them to discuss heritage values and the objectives of the project, to appropriate the OG and associated urban project by identifying with it.			
Regulatory risk Regulatory changes impacting the project	Urban planning in-depth studies	In-depth excavations In-depth studies	In-depth environmental studies	
Financial risk Overcost, no profitability	Temporary sports venues Sustainable permanent venues Addition of attractive facilities generating commercial revenue	Consultation to avoid delay or overcost of Games venues Addition of attractive facilities generating commercial revenue	Consultation to avoid delay or overcost of Olympic venues	

Source: Interviews, field work in Athens and London

housing, offices, retail, etc.) intended to ensure the financial viability of the associated urban project (Doustaly, 2008).

The heritagization approach may allow the reduction of risks that Olympic and associated urban projects can face, as the following matrix shows. It presents examples of heritagization forms associated to risks types from Athens and London Olympic Games projects. Devised to crossreference our expertise and extensive review of literature on risk and heritagization, the HERITRISK matrix was used as a methodology for analysis and filled with data drawn from fieldwork, interviews and the media. First, risks and opportunities were identified faced by the actors (associations, elected representatives, citizens, owners, etc.) between the date of the announcement of the winner for host city and 2018. Then, analysis of heritagization forms was carried out drawing on examples included in the matrix. These result from the analytical study of Athens 2004 and

London 2012 candidacy files and subsequent overview of achieved, in progress, or never achieved heritagization projects.

Olympic urban projects for Athens 2004 and London 2012: risks and opportunities

The organizational, media and financial stakes are extremely high for Olympic Games which are worldwide events, affect entire neighbourhoods, imply substantial investment in human, financial and natural resources and have long-term impacts on the host city.

Archaeological and historical risks and opportunities

Given the scale of construction works typically associated with Olympic Games, the risks and opportunities of this kind are numerous.

The archaeological risk can take two forms. The building of a sports venue can be delayed by the discovery of a site deserving exploratory excavations usually enforced by preventive archaeology regulations. The opposite risk can also be for archaeological or historical remains to be threatened by building works.

In Athens, numerous major sites, mainly dating from ancient Greece, but also Byzantian times, were discovered during the building of the sport and transport infrastructures. The site of Schinias in Athens faced both risks. Archaeologists feared that works would spoil a totally preserved ancient village and obtained the transfer of the Olympic canoe kayak course project to the old seafront Hellinikon Airport. This transfer allowed a compromise between the preservation of ancient heritage and the need to build the sports venue in time for the Olympics. The construction of the riding centre revealed the site of Merenda; the works for a new airport in Eastern Athens uncovered other ancient remains. During the construction of two metro lines in Syntagma Square in the centre of Athens, 70,000m^2 were excavated, causing delays, but allowing the collection of 10,000 antique objects, some exhibited in Syntagma station and others in the Athens' National Archaeology Museum (Henry, 2005; fieldwork).

In London, the archaeological risk was present, but to a lesser extent than in Athens. The works uncovered remains in the subsoil, mainly dating from the Neolithic period, the Bronze Age, the Iron Age (a settlement with farmhouses and ancient burial site with four skeletons), the 18th and 19th centuries (a wooden boat, a paved Victorian street). None are visible today onsite, but the most precious finds have been saved to be included in museum collections, notably the Museum of London, and were also shown in local temporary exhibitions (Powell, 2012).

If the archaeological risk can be avoided, the discovery of a site with historical value can turn into a patrimonial, touristic and economic opportunity.

Environmental risks and opportunities

Environmental risks can be identified before building Olympic venues or may happen as a consequence of building works.

The Athenian public authority decided to use numerous urban wastelands for Athens 2004, even if they were already exposed to environmental risks. Phalerum Bay provides a revealing example. The 500 hectares of ground were then a no man's lands between the sea and residential areas of the 1970s. The zone was encircled by a traffic barrier (Poseidon Avenue) which generated considerable noise and air pollution. The avenue stopped the flow of rain-water towards the sea, generating floods. The estuaries of the two rivers flowing into the sea were also polluted and the residents' landscape was spoiled. Today, only 17 hectares of the site have been cleaned-up and rejuvenated with the building of the Opera, the National Library and a park financed by the Niarchos Foundation (see p. 117).

In Athens, ecologists underlined the threat of building the canoe kayak river in Schinias ornithological reserve whose biodiversity is unique in the Mediterranean. Hellinikon is another example of Athens' local elected representatives and inhabitants' general pressure regarding planned Olympic sites to increase the surface of urban parks and green areas and limit new buildings harmful to the environment (Garcia, 2018).

In London, the ODA site where the Olympic park was created included a brownfield area which was rejuvenated together with 5 km of disused canals. The 1980s had seen the renovation of the footpath on the sewer embankment to create a Greenway, which was extended to include cycle routes for the Olympics. Collaborating with the Environment Agency, the ODA had to clear a vast quantity of litter accumulated over the 20th century, notably the "Fridge Mountain" and abandoned vehicles, before carrying out the cleaning of 2 million tonnes of soil which was heavily contaminated with oil, arsenic and lead residues and other chemical waste, as a consequence of past heavy industrial activity. If the extent and methods to decontaminate were challenging and contested, they eventually generated opportunities for an ambitious environmental strategy. The building works respected environmental standards (LLDC, 2012b; ODA, 2015).

In both cases some land facing a diversity of pollution issues was cleaned, but to a much lesser extent in Athens than was initially planned.

Social risks and opportunities

The social risks in Olympic projects are mainly two-fold: before and after the Games. Before, the environmental risks generated by Olympic Projects can raise social risks such as criticism of the project and controversy. Afterwards, risks of socio-spatial segregation often appear in relation to job creations and the inflationary effect on real estate valuations of the Games and related urban project.

In Athens, the ecologists protest was successful in protecting the ornithological reserve and ancient remains of Schinias and transfering the canoe kayak course to Hellinikon. Generally, Athenians and local elected representatives have criticized environmental and archaeological damage (Morvan, 2018; Papanikolaou, 2013; Garcia, 2018). As no housing projects were included in Athens' Olympic sites, no gentrification has been observed yet. The controversial "world class" private mixed-use development of Hellinikon, which targets its housing and amenities at high-income households, was initiated in 2000 and only signed in 2017 by the Greek State, following lengthy bidding procedures and widespread general public disapproval towards the privatization of the Greek State assets (Garcia, 2018).

The London case is strikingly different. The social risk appeared in three stages. Before the Games, conflicts focused on the quality of depollution and the Olympic Park area which was not as empty as presented (1,000 often deprived inhabitants and professionals). During the building of Olympic infrastructures and the event, tensions crystallized around keeping bid promises for local inhabitants regarding job creations, retail activity and affordable housing – a national bone of contention as cheaper social housing was being cut by Conservative policies. In this regards, the Olympic village fairs better than the five neighbourhoods developed in a second phase. Last, the speculative luxury towers built in the Eastern margin of the park create a striking visual, cultural et socioeconomic divide with surrounding heritage buildings and social housing (Carpenter's Estate), and feed gentrification (LLDC, 2012a: 42, 68; Poynter et al., 2015; Wagg, 2015).

Financial risks and opportunities

In comparison with other mega urban projects, Olympic projects face the constraint of an imperative deadline imposed by the IOC. If not met, the correct running of the Games can be called into question. The contract signed between the IOC and the host city commits the latter with written warranties. Risk matrices allow the identification, analysis and treatment of all types of risks which could prevent the delivery of Olympic events on time. The host city must meet objectives regarding the availability of lands, the delivery of public transport services to OG venues, the building and operating of several dozens of specialized sports venues and must present a clear planning structure and financial guarantees. Characteristics to be respected for each sports venue are also very specific (dimensions of the tracks, coatings, etc.). Careful quality control of these requirements is also carried out during the construction of venues by the OCOG. The latter (which includes national and local public authorities, as well as the NOC) is legally responsible for the preparation and organization of the Olympic and Paralympic games. The question of compliance with criteria and deadlines is therefore crucial for the OCOG and associated public authorities. Whatever the quality of planning, various risks can postpone the project and generate overcosts. Moreover, Olympic projects are often built in an emergency, which can easily lead to additional expenses.

In Athens, for instance, construction began 18 months late in Hellinikon because Second-World-War bombs were discovered, and the Air Force and airline companies were reluctant to leave the airport (Henry, 2005: 93). The wage overcost due to round-the-clock construction work served to double the total cost of the project. Public authorities preferred to scatter venues around the centre of the metropolitan area and near the seafront to avoid impacting the environment and help regenerate several suburbs, with the results presented above. Very little had been foreseen to finance and organize the maintenance of the venues after the Games (the cost was assessed at about 100 million euros per year in 2005) (Henry, 2005).

In London, planning took into account the failures of previous Games and closely followed recommendations of the IOC studies commission to gather the Olympic venues in a limited number of places to reduce building costs and maximize their reuse after the Games. In 2008, a detailed costing exercise led to the vote of an emergency fund including a high-risk margin (£2.7 billion) intended to cover higher security costs than calculated prior to the 2005 terrorist attacks, the effects of the 2008 financial crisis, unanticipatedly high inflation, decreased price of goods and services changing the profitability of subcontractors and developers, VAT imposed on the development body (ODA) because of its private status and finally a wider urban renewal plan. Delays were constrained and had a limited impact on the final budget (four months in the case of the stadium and the aquatic centre). The additional costs allowed in 2008 (of about 50% over the initial budget) were not fully used thanks to lower security fees and higher private funds in the final LOCOG budget (Jennings, 2012b; LOCOG 2013). However, this resulted from decreased social objectives in the sustainability programme (legacy), in favour of commercial resources, the former being used as an adjustment variable in the context of public budget restrictions (Cohen & Watt 2017).

In order to limit the financial risk, the usual overcosts or cost of the legacy of the Games can be financed by public authorities and/or by an enhancement and reuse strategy of venues and urban facilities.

Athens did not set up a specific governance to manage and operate sports venues and ensure the implementation of the Athens 2004 project after the Games (Garcia, 2018). The initial intention to entrust the operation of sports venues to the private sector lacked political will and met with little interest from the private sector. The financial crisis of 2008, which hugely impacted Greece, postponed the achievement of the urban project (which is a potential generator of commercial revenues), and the operation of sports venues (Garcia, 2018). Only an adapted reconversion of a small part of the Olympic wasteland of Phalerum has begun while the initial project for the reconversion of Hellinikon was modified along with EU advice to make room for more luxury property developments generating increased revenue, also allowing the funding of roads and public networks improvements which the Greek public authority could no longer afford, following the drastic austerity plan and associated billions of reimbursement linked to the 2008 crisis.

The London 2012 project was to be financed both by the public sector, the National Lottery and private funds (52% of funds were provided by suppliers, licences and ticketing). It included a British government guarantee in case of a deficit of the Games (IOC, 2005). The payback of Olympic venues is under way, but the difficulty to find stadium tenants affected forecasts and caused great public controversy. The financial equilibrium of the site will be facilitated by the commitment of the private sector in the project, the LLDC planning more housing, offices and retail building to be built until 2030. The sustainability of the financial project of the Olympics therefore relied on the creation of a planning authority (LLDC) independent from boroughs, still operational today, and responsible for a larger perimeter than initially, to complement the LOCOG and local authorities. If construction has been dynamic in Stratford, the budding atypical neighbourhood has faced attractivity challenges which a continued heritagization strategy may help to gather identity (LLDC, 2014, 2015; ODA, 2015).

Financial risks are thus numerous, varied and bear heavily on all the stages of the project, which makes the case for taking the time and resources to produce finely tuned, bottom-up, contextualized and publicly supported project planning.

Figure 6.1 Buildings under construction (Stratford, London)
Photo: G. Zembri-Mary

Heritagization as a means to support mega project legacies, under certain conditions

If the notions of heritage, preservation and transmission are central to complete these Olympic urban projects, characterized by uncertainties, risks, and fixed deadlines, how can a heritagization approach answer these? Compared with risk analysis, environmental and socio-economic feasibility or other types of pre-project studies, the latter lasts during the entire life time of the urban project associated with the Olympics, from design, through planning and legacy and even references the past situation. This can endow the project with territorial and national identity anchorage.

What heritage planning and governance could be recommended for host cities? The examples of Athens and London point to four heritagization practices: architectural and urban, archaeological, environmental, and intangible heritagization.

Heritagization practices for sustainable Olympic urban projects

From the beginning of the 2000s, the notion of sustainable development included in IOC recommendations for candidate cities has not only tackled the environment but also Olympic heritage, in relation to sites, infrastructure, knowledge and experiences. Rule 2–13 of the Olympic charter specified in 2003 that the IOC was to take "measures to promote a positive legacy of the host city and country, notably a reasonable control of the size and the costs of the Olympic Games, and encourages the OCOG and the local authorities of the host country and stakeholders in the Olympic movement to act accordingly." To ensure an Olympic legacy, the IOC recommended minimizing costs, maximising competition and training and other venues use, efficient time, usage and services management. Quality planning was put forward to deliver the Games for the date, but no reference was then made to post Olympic planning legacy of the physical project (IOC, 2003: 5).

Architectural and urban heritagization

This heritagization concerns mainly two aspects of the future urban fabric: the renovation of historic buildings and the transformation of some Olympic venues into permanent ones.

The embellishment programme of the centre of Athens as laid out in Athens 2004 included the renovation of facades, the upkeep of sculptures and monuments, the restauration of major buildings from the Athenian heritage following the deterioration of the city centre from the 1970s onwards (ATHOC, 1996; Law 2730/1999). For example, the historical Panathenian stadium of the 1896 Games was renovated. Another stadium constructed in 1982 was used for the 2004 Olympics, after a redesign and refurbishment by the famous architect Santiago Calatrava (Henry, 2005). The purpose was to turn it into an iconic building of unique architecture, a new visual reference for a Modern Olympic Athens, while hosting cultural and sport events. It hosted the 2007 football league finals, and the very vast area is sometimes used for popular events (festivals, sports). However, the building, with its unusable main swimming pool, has badly lacked upkeep, as well as its surroundings: the Agora, its central square, shops and green spaces.

In Stratford, the LLDC zone includes several conservation areas, valued reminders of London's industrial heyday (Hackney Wick, Fish Island and White Post Lane, Sugar House Lane, Three Mills – whose Grade I-listed oldest Mill dates back to 1776) which are connected by renovated canals. The LLDC produced numerous studies before publishing its 2015 Local Plan underlining the necessity of preserving this local heritage, obtaining further extend protected areas, supporting conservation programmes, and adding new buildings of high standards (quality mark "building for life 2012"). This strong industrial identity influenced the style and kind of new mixed developments. The 8,000 housing units to be built before 2030 are attractive in a context of intense housing market pressure.

Contrary to Athens where new sports venues were abandoned, in Stratford, heritagization also took the form of five permanent buildings for the Olympics, giving the park a resolutely contemporary identity. These won 12 design awards, and the London Aquatics centre (by world-renowned architect Zaha Hadid) was shortlisted for the RIBA Stirling prize. With the stadium, it became immediately iconic and still holds strong symbolic value. All buildings are in operation and managed by social enterprises. The athletes' village was transformed into housing (East Village), the media centre turned – with delays – into an innovation centre (Here East). Last, the emblem of London 2012 was the privately funded ArcelorMittal Orbit (the tallest sculpture in the UK, which has become a visitor attraction through the addition of a giant slide against the will of its creator, the famous artist Anish Kapoor).

Thanks to these sustainable developments in an area larger than the Park itself, the financial balance of the LLDC is planned to be reached by 2025, although rents and charges imply commercial negotiations, adaptations and strategies (LLDC, 2015: 14–16, 26; ODA, 2015). Contrary to Athens, by associating a diversity of stakeholders, from heritage organizations to real estate investors, the London example illustrates how rehabilitation of architectural and urban assets can guarantee their conservation and enhancement and can be articulated with the maintenance and use of Olympic iconic buildings within a larger regeneration area.

Archaeological and historical heritagization

Archaeological and historical heritagization can include excavation of objects and ancient sites, their preservation and enhancement, notably related to urban development.

Figure 6.2 The ArcelorMittal Orbit (Queen Elizabeth Park, London)
Photo: G. Zembri-Mary

Athens 2004 aimed at finalizing the unification of the historic city centre's archaeological sites to create "the largest open-air archaeological park in Europe" (ATHOC, 1996). The sites and the various cultural venues (leisure, cultural and educational centres) were linked to a network of pedestrian alleys and green spaces, through a 2.7 km trail out of the 4 km initially planned to conduct parts of the expropriations and excavations (Palyvou, 2007). The park covers wide historical periods: antique (fifth century), Byzantine (until fifteenth century) and modern (nineteenth century), from the Panathenaic Stadium, through the Acropolis hill, the historic quarter of Plaka, the new Acropolis museum to the old Ceramics cemetery. Urban planning choices played a role in this heritagization process: the Olympic village was integrated in its surrounding archaeological heritage as its design followed the structural axis allowing views on the Acropolis.

Figure 6.3 An old house and a renovated house in Plaka (centre of Athens)
Photo: G. Zembri-Mary

In London, 1% of the site was excavated, as compulsory in the planning permit. Digs notably unearthed remains from prehistoric hunters and farmers, a skeleton from the Bronze Age, and mostly industrial assets (related to the major railway depot and chemistry hub). These finds were mediated to the public as one of the ten learning legacy programme's themes and the LLDC followed English Heritage's advice to register the largest part of its zone as an archaeological protection area, indicating that it may contain archaeological remains deserving protection, requiring for any development project to be preceded by preventive digs (LLDC, 2015; http://learninglegacy.independent. gov.uk/themes/archaeology/index.php).

Considering the rich industrial past of the area, and the strong tradition of industrial archaeology in the UK, there were already listed areas and build-ings, mainly in Hackney Wick and Fish Island. The historic canals of the Lea River were renovated. During concertation over the 2015 LLDC Plan, Eng-lish Heritage managed to obtain the respect of its recommendation on the protection of historic views and the limitation of height for new builds (in Stratford centre, along the listed conservation area of St John). With the Royal Institute of Chartered Surveyors, it lobbied for the conservation through renovation of industrial buildings so that the neighbourhood would not only look towards the future, but kept its past anchors to identify with.

However, English Heritage concerns in favour of vernacular cultural assets were not heeded, regardless of the LLDC prior engagement to "maintaining the character and strength of existing communities and creating new neighbourhoods with distinct identities" (LLDC, 2014: 34; 2012b).

Environmental heritagization

Environmental heritagization implies considering the natural environment in its wide sense (natural space, fauna, flora, air, water etc.) as a common good which should be preserved and enhanced.

Initiatives included in Athens 2004, notably to depollute wasteland and enhance green space, were only partially implemented. In Schinias, following environmentalists' opposition to some Olympic projects (see p. 000), natural space was heritagized with the creation of a 1,500 ha Natura 2000 protected area forbidding construction to protect the ornithological reserve (Henry, 2005). However, the project for the old Hellinikon airport to become a large urban park of about 520 ha completed with 100 ha of housing, offices and cultural and leisure venues has been on hold (Henry, 2005). Since 2004, 270 ha have been set aside for a highly contested vast urban private development and only 290 ha left for the strongly publically supported urban park (Astier, 2015). Following public demand, the wasteland around the Phalerum Bay was also to be converted into a park, but to this day, for lack of public investment, only 17 ha (out of about 500 ha) have been reclaimed for the construction of new Opera, the National library and an urban park.

A variety of environmental protection initiatives introduced to limit the energy consumption of the Olympic village (bioclimatic construction involving building orientation and green space) allowed a three degree cooler average temperature. They also involved limiting fossil energy consumption through street pedestrianization and greening, as well as the Syntgama and Omonia squares, the heart of the capital, limiting the use of cars in the centre and associated oil consumption, pollution and blackened façades.

In London, the sustainable strategy for 2012 was to create a model of green urban regeneration, replacing industrial waste from past activities while reclaiming natural assets for modern use. The nine-metre-deep depollution of the site meant it was impossible to plant deep-rooted high trees, but 2,000 native trees and 300,000 wetland plants were introduced. A natural wild reserve with wetlands, woodlands, wildlife habitats was created as well as 110 hectares of public parkland with lawns and meadows, 45 of which respect an action plan for biodiversity also allowing limitation of flood risks. Five miles of river Lea were restored with 22 miles of paths and cycle ways. To reduce carbon print, a renewable Energy Centre (capable of producing low carbon energy for about 10,000 homes), water plants and energy efficient buildings were built. Transport related pollution has been limited as the Park is only open to buggies for disabled people and public transport has been improved (three expanded stations by 2019) (LLDC, 2012b: 9, 59; ODA, 2015).

Figure 6.4a Schinias (Athens): the rowing pool which could be built near the Natura
2000 protected area. The canoe kayak course foreseen in Schinias with the
rowing pool was transferred to Hellenikon.
Photo: D. Sengouni

Figure 6.4b Schinias (Athens): the rowing pool which could be built near the Natura
2000 protected area. The canoe kayak course foreseen in Schinias with the
rowing pool was transferred to Hellenikon.
Photo: D. Sengouni

Figure 6.5 The Queen Elizabeth Park (Stratford, London)
Photo: G. Zembri-Mary

In both Olympic cases under study, the density of construction in the Olympic areas was regulated and land use controlled, to allow homogeneous and quality constructions and to restrain the urban sprawl detrimental to natural space. Less polluting public transport was supported to limit or ban cars. This reflects policies co-constructed between planners, inhabitants and elected representatives calling for better environmental preservation in urban projects.

Intangible heritagization

The Athenian Olympic project was associated with programmes preserving and enhancing such practices as dance, music and theatre. Intangible heritagization is sometimes difficult to isolate from its material dimension. Athens 2004 planned for many cultural centres to be built close to Olympic venues, but the Ano Liossia was the only one to become reality and very recently the Opera and National Library in Phalerum. The media centre was to be rehabilitated into an Olympic Games museum, but was turned into a shopping centre (Garcia, 2018); the Athletics Museum project was dropped for lack of adequate planning structure, tools and financing.

In London, a cultural and educational quarter (the East Bank, to balance the South Bank) with high culture and academic venues with an international

Figure 6.6 The Opera and the National Library in Phalerum, Athens
Photo: G. Zembri-Mary

reputation (Sadler's Wells, a ballet company; the Victoria and Albert Museum; BBC Music; two universities) are to open in the coming years. This, together with ongoing gentrification introduces a break with the traditional East-end popular and multi-ethnic cultural ecosystem based on different cultural practices which are endangered, in particular in the south and the east of the site. Little has been done by the LLDC (apart from the organization of markets and community activities in the park) to include this local cultural identity, minority issues being focused on job creation. In their strategies, the ODA and the LLDC interpreted the notion of heritage in a tangible manner, and initial promises to "stitch the fringes" have been subsumed by the need to build more private housing, notably luxury towers in the south-eastern margin of the park, which illustrate urban change through fracture rather than transition (Doustaly, 2019a).

Conclusion

The epistemological and theoretical HERITRISK matrix crossing risk and heritagization has been proven effective to compare mega urban projects and shed light on their sustainability and legacy. When applied to analyse Athens' and London's Olympic Games projects, the following conclusions can be drawn on the urban change brought about.

First, Olympic urban projects which include a heritagization approach to the functional development of the city (improvement of transport, urban regeneration, building renewal and green space enhancement) have been used as catalysts (Cartalis, 2015) and accelerator for urban projects unrelated to sport, some of which have been delayed for urban planning, political and financial reasons for decades. Second, the heritagization approach allows sustainable projects to be devised and implemented and limits the numerous risks they incur by taking into account local inhabitants' insights and wishes, but sometimes after negotiations with the plannners.

Nevertheless, the future of these sites is uncertain and raises a variety of questions. Heritagization approaches can rely on or encourage a privatization of the sites, which allows the funding of urban development with less public spending, but reinforces gentrification and may only marginally tackle local lack of affordable housing, as in London. The risks in London have been associated with a project going at full speed around the construction of international venues (Westfield, the biggest commercial centre in Europe, hotels, fourth international business centre in London, prestigious sports, new cultural and academic institutions), with less democratic counterbalance, social value and power for the boroughs than initially planned. Some Athenians fear a similar future for Phalerum and Hellinikon luxurious urban projects. In Athens, we can note a desynchronization between the population's expectations to enhance the Olympic sites by preserving nature in the city and the political will supported by the Troïka but contested by the opposition, to sell the Olympic urban wasteland to the private sector. We do not know yet if and how fast these projects will be delivered.

Olympic projects use exceptional governance, time-limited and often relying on derogation to usual planning regulations, which accounts for some unachieved projects. This was the case in Athens where the ORSA, a metropolitan-level State body, was in charge of the Olympic venues and urban project development, but the public sector was not able to regain the management of sports venues and pursue the ambitious development programmes of Phalerum Bay or Hellinikon. In London, the creation of private exceptional planning bodies (ODA then LLDC after the Games) which devised and extended the ad-hoc local plan for the area has gone a long way to facilitate long-term planning to 2030, though restraining its social and heritage value. While the ODA was under ministerial authority, the LLDC is a municipal corporation responsible to the Mayor of London. As well as being stirred by a different level of government, the Greek economic crisis and insufficient local planning practices explain the difference in legacy.

Last, processes of heritagization seem particularly useful to study for developers, urban planners, heritage and urban studies scholars. While environmental, archaeological and architectural heritagization policies can be sustained through the use of labels and regulations, urban heritagization is more complex as it is potentially exposed to a wider number of risks. Planners lack methods to ensure that their post-Olympic site-use plans will meet with user's expectations. This is where further research on the heritagization model is most needed, as well as on other Olympic cities, including Tokyo 2020 and Paris 2024, especially since the latter's candidacy has attempted to strike a challenging balance between internationalization, local heritage preservation and urban tourism reflecting the development of more varied tourism and heritagization practices (Delaplace & Gravari-Barbas, 2015), but also where risks have already arisen (archaeological, budgetary, transport wise) (Cour des Comptes, 2017).

Notes

1 In 2008 labour costs in Greece were 16.7 euros per hour compared to 20.9 euros in the United Kingdom. http://www.clesdusocial.com/IMG/pdf/cout-du-travail-e n-europe-en-2013.pdf
2 The Troïka including EU, European Central Bank and International Monetary Fund experts was created after the 2008 crisis.

References

Arndt, R. (1998). Risk allocation in the Melbourne city link project. *Journal of Project Finance* 4(3), 11–24.

Astier, M. (2015). Un Notre-Dame-des-Landes résiste aux portes d'Athènes. *Reporterre*, 22/11/2015, https://reporterre.net/Un-Notre-Dame-des-Landes-resiste

ATHOC (1996). *Dossier de candidature d'Athènes aux Jeux Olympiques d'été de 2004*, Athens. 3 volumes.

Bellanger, A. and Pouchard, E. (2018). Les Jeux Olympiques, un budget difficile à maitriser. *Le Monde* 15/05/2018.

Beriatos, E. and Gospodini, A. (2004). "Glocalising" urban landscapes: Athens and the 2004 Olympics. *Cities* 21(3), 187–202.

Boukas, N., Ziakas, V. and Boustras, G. (2013). Olympic legacy and cultural tourism: Exploring the facets of Athens' Olympic heritage. *International Journal of Heritage Studies* 19(2), 203–228.

Campbell, D. and Harris, D. (1993). Flexibility in long term contractual relationships: The role of co-operation. *Journal of Law and Society* 20(2), 166–191.

Cartalis, C. (2015). Sport mega-events as catalysts for sustainable urban development: The case of Athens 2004. In Viehoff, V. and Poynter, G. (eds). *Mega-event Cities: Urban Legacies of Global Sports Events*. London and New York: Routledge. 185–198.

Chaboche, J. and Schoeny, A. (2018). Les enjeux territoriaux et urbains des Jeux Olympiques: un état de la recherche géographique, aménagiste et managérial. Conference Paper, Olympic Games: State of the Art. ORME, Université Marne la Vallée, 18 June 2018.

Coaffee, J. (2011). Urban regeneration and renewal. In Gold, J. R. and Gold, M. (eds) *Olympic Cities. City Agendas, Planning, and the World's Games. 1896–2016*. London and New York: Routledge. 180–193.

Coanus, T., Duchêne, F. and Martinais, E. (1999). Les relations des gestionnaires du risque urbain avec les populations riveraines. Critique d'une certaine idée de la "communication". *Annales des Mines* Janvier n°13.

Cohen, P. and Watt, P. (eds) (2017). *London 2012 and the Post Olympic City: A Hollow Legacy?*London: Palgrave.

Council of Europe (2005). *Convention on the Value of Heritage for Society* (Faro Framework Convention) 27/10/2005, Treaty n°199. Brussels.

Cour des Comptes (2017). *Rapport: La société du Grand Paris*. Décembre, Paris.

Crivello, M., Garcia, P., OffenstadtN. and Vadelorge, L. (eds) (2006). *La concurrence des passés. Usages politiques du passé dans la France contemporaine*. Aix-en-Provence: Publications de l'Université de Provence.

Delaplace, M. and Gravari-Barbas, M. (2015). Le tourisme urbain "hors des sentiers battus". *Téoros* 34(1–2). http://journals.openedition.org/teoros/2790

Di Méo, G. (2008). Processus de patrimonialisation et construction des territoires. *Colloque « Patrimoine et industrie en Poitou-Charentes: connaître pour valoriser »*. Poitiers-Châtellerault: Geste éditions. 87–109.

Doustaly, C. (2008). Le rôle de la culture dans la renaissance urbaine depuis 1997 en Angleterre: de l'économique au socioculturel ? In Nail, S. and Fee, D. (eds), *Vers une renaissance urbaine britannique ? Dix ans de politique travailliste de la ville*. Paris: Presses de la Sorbonne Nouvelle. 75–95.

Doustaly, C. (2013). Arts Council England in the 2000s: Towards Digital Era Governance?. In Zumello, C. and Avril, E. (eds). *New Technology, Organizational Change and Governance*. London: Palgrave. 23–38.

Doustaly, C. (2019a). Heritage, cities and sustainable development. Challenges and opportunities between theory and practice. In Doustaly, C. (ed.). *Heritage, Cities and Sustainable Development*. Brussels: Peter Lang.

Doustaly, C. (2019b). Participative budgeting and progressive cities: Are London and Paris listening to their own voices? In Douglas, M., Ho, K. and Garbaye, R. (eds), *The Rise of Progressive Cities East and West*. Singapore, London, New York: Springer. 117–136.

Doustaly, C. and Peng, L. (2019). Implementing the historic urban landscape approach: Exploring participatory planning in China. In Doustaly, C. (ed.). *Heritage, Cities and Sustainable Development*. Brussels: Peter Lang.

Faugères, L. and Vasarhelyi, P. (1988). Aménagement et risques. *Aménagement et nature*91, 17–21.

Faruqi, S.N.J. (1997). Karachi Light Rail Transit: A private finance proposal. *Engineering, Construction and Architectural Management* 4(3), 233–246.

Flyvbjerg, B., Bruzelius, N. and Rothengatter, W. (2003). *Megaprojects and Risks: an Anatomy of an Ambition*. Cambridge: Cambridge University Press.

Forshaw, A. (1999). The UK revolution in public procurement and the value of project finance. *Journal of Project Finance* 5(1), 49–54.

Garcia, B. (2008). One hundred years of cultural programming within the Olympic Games (1912–2012): Origins, evolution and projections. *International Journal of Cultural Policy* 14(4), 361–376.

Garcia, B. (2015). Placing culture at the heart of the Games: Achievement and challenges within the London 2012 cultural Olympiads. In Poynter, G., Viehoff, V. and Li, Y. (eds), (2015). *The London Olympics and Urban Development: The Mega Event City*. London and New York: Routledge. 255–269.

Garcia, D. (2018). Pertes publiques et gains privés à Athènes. *Le Monde diplomatique.* February 2018, 22–23.

Gold, J. R. and Gold, M. M. (eds) (2017). *Olympic Cities: City Agendas, Planning, and the World's Games, 1896–2016.* London and New York: Routledge.

Gralepois, M. (2012). *Face aux risques d'inondation.* Paris: Éditions d'Ulm.

Grimsey, D. and Lewis, M.-K. (2002). Evaluating the risks of public–private partnerships for infrastructure projects. *International Journal of Project Management* 20(2), 107–118.

Harrison, R. (2013). *Critical Approaches to Heritage.* London and New York: Routledge.

Harvey, D. (2015). Landscape and heritage: Trajectories and consequences. *Landscape Research* 40(8), 911–924.

Heinich, N. (2009). *La Fabrique du patrimoine.* Paris: Maison des sciences de l'homme.

HenryA. (2005). Projet urbain et Jeux Olympiques: le cas d'Athènes 2004. Doctoral dissertation, Université de Franche-Comté.

Hewison, R. (1987). *The Heritage Industry: Britain in a Climate of Decline.* London: Methuen.

Horne, J. and Whannel, G. (2016). *Understanding the Olympics,* 2nd edition. London and New York: Routledge.

International Olympic Committee (IOC) (2003). *Olympic Games Study Commission, Report to the 115th IOC session.* Lausanne.

International Olympic Committee (IOC) (2005). *Report of the IOC Evaluation Commission for the XXX Olympiad 2012.* Lausanne.

Jennings, W. (2010). Governing the Games in an age of uncertainty: The Olympics and organizational responses to risk. In Richards, A., Fussey, P. and Silke, A. (eds), *Terrorism and the Olympics: Major Event Security and Lessons for the Future.* London and New York: Routledge. 135–162.

Jennings, W. (2012a). *Olympic Risks.* Basingstoke: Palgrave Macmillan.

Jennings, W. (2012b). Why costs over-run: Risk, optimism and uncertainty in budgeting for the London 2012 Olympics. *Journal of Construction Management and Economics* 30(6): 455–462.

Jennings, W. and Lodge, M. (2010). Critical infrastructures, resilience and organization of mega-projects: The Olympic Games. In Hutter, B. (ed.), *Anticipating Risks and Organising Risk Regulation.* Cambridge: Cambridge University Press. 161–184.

Jennings, W. and Lodge, M. (2011). Governing mega-events: Tools of security risk management for the London 2012 Olympic Games and FIFA 2006 World Cup in Germany. *Government and Opposition* 46(2), 192–222.

Jennings, W. and Lodge, M. (2012). The Olympic Games: Coping with risks and crises at a mega-event. In Helsloot, I., Boin, A. and Jacobs, B. (eds), *Mega-Crises: Understanding the Prospects, Nature, Characteristics and Effects of Cataclysmic Events.* Springfield, IL: Charles C. Thomas.

London Legacy Development Corporation (LLDC) (2005). *2012 London Olympic Bid Candidate File.* London: LLDC.

London Legacy Development Corporation (LLDC) (2014). *Our Area: Spacial Portrait Background Paper.* London: LLDC.

London Legacy Development Corporation (LLDC) (2012a). *Olympic Legacy Supplementary Planning Guidance (OLSPG).* London: LLDC.

London Legacy Development Corporation (LLDC) (2012b). *Your Sustainability Guide to the Queen Elizabeth Park 2030.* London: LLDC.

London Legacy Development Corporation (LLDC) (2015). *Local Plan.* London: LLDC.

London Organising Committee of the Olympic Games (LOCOG) (2013). *Final Reports and Accounts.* London: LOCOG.

Macharis, C., Nijkamp, P. (2013). Multi-actor and multi-criteria analysis in evaluating mega-projects. In Priemus, H. and Van Wee, B. (eds), *International Handbook on Mega-projects.* London: Edward Edgar. 242–246.

Miller, R. and Lessard, D. (2008). Evolving strategy: Risk management and the shaping of mega projects. In Flyvbjerg, B., Priemus, H. and Van Wee, B. (eds). *Decision Making on Mega Projects, Cost Benefit Analysis, Planning and Innovation.* Cheltenham: Edward Elgar. 145–172.

Morvan, O. (2018). *Le dilemme grec, Helliniko: une reconversion controversée.* Masters thesis in Architecture, École d'Architecture de Nantes.

Olympic Delivery Authority (ODA) (2007). *Olympic, Paralympic & Legacy Transformation Planning Applications.* London: ODA.

Olympic Delivery Authority (ODA) (2015). *Final Report (2006–2014).* London: HMSO.

Osadtchy, C. (2014). Mobilizations et conflits liés à la maitrise de l'urbanisation autour des industries à risque. *Territoire en mouvement*23–24/2014, 129–142.

Palyvou, C. (2007). La mise en image d'un paysage historique, l'unification des sites archéologiques d'Athènes reconsidérée. *Études balkaniques* 14(2007): 215–229.

Papanikolaou, P. (2013). Cultural Olympiad: The legacy of the Olympic Games Athens 1896, 2004. *American International Journal of Contemporary Research* 3(7), 18–22.

Potsiou, C. and Apostolatos, G. (2006). Legal reforms in land management. Aspects to support the construction and the continuing use of the Olympic Infrastructure. An example of good practice in Greece. Promoting Land Administration and Good Governance, XXIII FIG Congress, 1–21.

Powell, A. (2012). *The Making of the Lower Lea Valley Archaeological and Cultural Heritage Investigations on the Site of the London 2012 Olympic and Paralympic Games.* Wessex Archaeology.

Poynter, G., Viehoff, V. and Li, Y. (eds) (2015). *The London Olympics and Urban Development: The Mega Event City.* London and New York: Routledge.

Roult, R. and Lefebvre, S. (2010). Reconversion de l'espace Olympique et rénovation de l'espace urbain: le cas des stades olympiques. *Géographie, économie, Société*12, 367–369.

Siemiatycki, M. (2013). Public-private partnerships in mega-projects: Successes and tensions. In Priemus, H. and Van Wee, B. *International Handbook on Mega-projects.* London: Edward Edgar. 133–157.

Smith, L. (2006). *Uses of Heritage.* London: Routledge.

Stevenson, N. (2012). Culture and the 2012 Games: Creating a tourism legacy? *Journal of Tourism and Cultural Change* 10(2), 137–149.

Stögerer, M. (2015). *Mega Events in the Complex City: A Case Study of the 2004 Olympic Games in Athens, Greece.* Munich: GRIN Verlag.

Suraud, M.-G., Blin, M.-P. and de Terssac, G. (2009.) *Risques industriels, quelle ouverture publique ?*Toulouse: Octarès Editions.

UN (2016). New Urban Agenda. The United Nations Conference on Housing and Sustainable Urban Development (Habitat III), 68th Plenary Meeting, 71st Session. General Assembly, December 2016.

UNESCO (2011). *Recommendation on the Historic Urban Landscape*, 10/11/2011, 36C Resolution. Paris.

UNESCO (2003). Intangible Cultural Heritage convention. MISC/2003/CLT/CH/14; Paris.

Wagg, S. (2015). *The London Olympics of 2012. Policies, Promises and Legacy.* London, New York, Shanghai: Palgrave Macmillan.

Ward, S.-C., Chapman, C.-B. and Curtis, B.(1991). On the allocation of risks in construction projects. *International Journal of Project Management* 9(3), 140–147.

Waterton, E. and Winter, T. (2013). Critical Heritage Studies. *International Journal of Heritage Studies* 19(6), 529–531.

World Bank, *GDP Statistics.* https://data.worldbank.org/indicator/ny.gdp.mktp.cd? most_recent_year_desc=true

Zembri-Mary, G. (2019a). *Appréhender le risque projet. Jeux d'acteurs autour de l'incertitude et du risque en Aménagement et Urbanisme.* Paris: ISTE éditions (forthcoming).

Zembri-Mary, G. (ed.) (2019b). *Produire des projets d'aménagement dans l'incertitude.* Paris: Editions du Manuscrit. (forthcoming).

Zembri-Mary, G. (2016). Planifier les projets d'aménagement dans un contexte incertain: le cas de la LGV Bretagne Pays de Loire et de la ZAC Eurorennes. *Revue internationale d'Urbanisme* 2.

Zembri-Mary, G. (2014). Risques, incertitudes et flexibilité du processus de décision et de planification des projets d'infrastructures de transport. Habilitation thesis (Urban planning), Université de Lille 1.

Zifou, M., Ioannou, B., Serraos, K., Tsikli, A. and Polychronopoulos, D. (2004). The 2004 Olympic Games: A Non-Planning Paradigm?AESOP Conference. July 2004.

7 The relationship between Olympic Games and tourism: Why such heterogeneity?

Towards a place-based approach

Marie Delaplace

Introduction

The Olympic and Paralympic Games (OPGs) raise many expectations for tourism in host cities: they are likely to attract many visitors and increase revenues and employment from tourism (Nunkoo and Gursoy, 2012). But, as underlined by Faulkner et al. in 2000 with regard to Sydney the impacts of OPGs on tourism in a host city are very uncertain. The analyses carried out on previous editions of the OPGs show that the expansion of tourism is not always proven. OPGs are associated with the crowding-out of tourists: the announcement of the scale of the event and the anticipated congestion discourage leisure visitors and professionals from coming to the city during this period (Matheson, 2006; Preuss, 2011). There is also frequently a substitution effect in terms of spending: expenses associated with OPGs replace other expenses (Matheson, 2006). In tourist cities, these eviction and substitution effects have a spatial and temporal dimension, with tourists coming to OPG sites but visiting other sites less and many tourists arriving before or after the event. Using a review of the literature and case studies on this issue and in different countries since 1964, the objective of this chapter is to highlight that there is a strong heterogeneity in the link between OPGs and tourism, that is to say, a variety of spatial and temporal expressions of the interactions between OPGs and tourism. Specifically, the expectations raised by OPGs in terms of tourism development are not always realized either during the OPGs or after they take place.

Olympic and Paralympic Games and tourism

The literature on tourism in OPG-hosted destinations highlights significant *ex ante* expectations but controversial *ex post* results.

OPGs with significant expectations

At the time of bidding, OPGs are often presented and designed by cities and host countries as a tool to boost tourism (Boukas et al., 2013; Sant et al., 2013; Williams and Elkhashab, 2012; Li and Blake, 2009, etc.).[1] Furthermore, candidate countries that are not selected to organize the Games can also benefit from the event itself (Fourie, Santana-Gallego, 2011).

For example, the first goal of the organizers of the Sydney Games was to stimulate tourism, promoting Sydney and Australia as tourist destinations (Vettas, 2015). In 2001, the main goal of the 2008 Beijing bid was to promote China as a tourist destination (Minnaert, 2012). London 2012 was seen as an asset that would help the UK to achieve annual visitor numbers of 40 million by 2020 (Visit Britain, 2012). Tokyo 2020 is also seen as a tool to boost tourism. The goal here is for the number of inbound tourists to Japan to reach 40 million by 2020 and 60 million by 2030 compared with 19 million in 2015.[2] Expectations in terms of tourism development also seem to exist in Paris as evidenced by the recent interview with Tony Estanguet[3] or the comments of Frédéric Valletoux, chair of the Paris Île-de-France Regional Tourism Committee: "This is excellent news. It will inevitably be positive for tourism."

However, analysis of past OPGs shows a significant variability of results, linked to the inaccuracy of the data themselves (tourists), but also to spatial and temporal inaccuracies raised by the media. These data sometimes relate to the overall number of tourists at the destination where OPGs are held, sometimes to the number of hotel arrivals, sometimes to the number of tourists specifically coming for these OPGs, sometimes to the number of spectators who bought a ticket, sometimes to the number of tourists from the host region or country, and, lastly, sometimes the data only concern international visitors. In addition, the time frame used often also differs. Sometimes it is exclusively the period of the OPGs, in other cases, it is August the month in which the main events are concentrated, while for others it is the third quarter of the year and for others still the whole calendar year. But whatever data are used, expectations are far from being realized (Table 7.1).

This perfectly illustrates all the vagueness concerning both expectations and the actual results.

Unsystematic growth in the number of tourists during the Games

The literature on the effect of mega-events including the OPGs, on tourism is highly contradictory. By examining the bilateral flows of tourism between 200 countries from 1995 to 2006 and during 18 mega-events including three Summer Olympic Games (1996, 2000 and 2004), Fourie and Santana-Gallego (2011) show that events do not always have the same impact on tourism. Benefits vary according to the type of mega-events (however, they are always positive for Summer OPGs), the participating countries, and whether the mega-event takes place in low or peak season. During peak season, events are, on average, associated with a smaller number of tourists than expected while in low season[8] these events attract significantly more people than expected. They show that international tourist arrivals in the host country tend to grow on average by about 8% in the year of the Games. With this in mind, it should be pointed out that these data concern countries.

Table 7.1 Expectations and achievements in terms of tourism during previous Games

Year	City	Tourists expected	Tourists received
1964	Tokyo	130,000[a]	70,000[a]
1968	Mexico City	200,000[a]	Not known[a]
1972	Munich	1,800,000 [a]	Not known[a]
1976	Montreal	1,500,000 [a]	1,600,000[p]
1980	Moscow	30,000–300,000[a]; 120,000 foreigners and 120,000 Russian tourists[s]; 600,000 visitors (including 200,000 from abroad)[t]; 240,000 visitors expected in1978, 160,000 expected in 1980[t]	30,000[a]; 1,323,790 tickets sold to foreigners[r]; Millions of soviet tourists and hundreds of thousands of foreign visitors in Moscow and other Olympic cities[r]
1984	Los Angeles	625,000[a]; 600,000[q]	400,000[a]–770,000[c]
1988	Seoul	270,000 (1984), then 240,000 (1987)[b]	211,000[2] 240,000[c]
1992	Barcelona	400,000[q]	450,000[c] ; 10 million[f]
1996	Atlanta	400,000-1.1 million[q]	968,000[c]–2,000,000[c]
2000	Sydney	132,000[h]	475,000[c]; +8.7% more visitors in 2000 than in the previous year[f]; 97,000 during the Games[h]; 111,000 visitors attending the Games[j] (estimate, Tourism Forecasting Council)
2004	Athens	30% more tourists than usual 4.9 million–5.7 million[q]	660,000[c] (20–30% less than expected)
2008	Beijing	4,500,000 including 550,000 international visitors[f]; 400,000 international visitors[h]	3,900,000 including 390,000 international visitors[f]–660,000[c]; 235,000 international visitors[h]
2012	London	2 million in London during the Games[j]; 3 million during the Games[k]	698,000 international visitors attending the Games[d] +English tourists (1.4 million spectators travelled on foot or by bike, bus or coach, and used park-and-ride facilities); 680,000 from July to September[i]
2016	Rio	380,000–500,000[g] international tourists	541,000 international tourists in Brazil[e] A total of 1.17 million
2020	Tokyo	More than 2 million visitors (more than London)[l] More than 20 million tourists in Japan[m]	

Year	City	Tourists expected	Tourists received
2024	Paris	15–20 million visitors[n] 4 million spectators[o]	

Source: Compiled by the author based on: [a]Pyo et al., 1988a and b, [b] Seoul OG Report, Official Data; [c] Preuss, 2004 (external tourists from the city attending the games including families), [d] ONS–London-International Passenger Survey (IPS) (471,000 whose main reason for travel was the OPGs and 227,000 who took part in an Olympic event with a ticket but whose main reason for travel was not the OPGs, to which it was necessary to add domestic tourists); [e] from July to August 15, Tourmag, September 2016[4]; [f]Vettas, 2015; [g]Castro, 2016; [h] ETOA; [i] Visit Britain, 2012; [j] De Groote, 2005; [k]*Le Point* [5] and *La Croix* [6]; [l] IAU, 2018; [m] Mizuho, 2014; [n] Le Parisien[7]; [o] Bilan carbone Paris 2024, 2017; [p] international tourists, Khomsi, 2015; [q] Data from Kasimati, 2003; [r]Moscow Official Report V2, 1981; [s]*New York Times*, https://www.nytimes.com/1976/05/19/archives/moscow-preparing-for-1980-olympics.html; [t] CIA, 1980, https://www.cia.gov/library/readingroom/docs/DOC_0003387227.pdf; [u]Morrison, 1982.

For cities, however, the results can sometimes be quite different (see Table 7.2): the crowding-out effects that are widely discussed in the literature are present to a greater or lesser extent.

Accordingly, tourist attendance has declined during different OPGs, albeit sometimes in specific contexts (Beijing 2008 at the height of the subprime crisis, Moscow 1980 with the boycott of the Games). In Los Angeles in 1984, the results were worse than in 1982, when a record number of tourists was attained. Athens received fewer visitors during the Games and lost international arrivals in 2004 in times of recession.

If we look at London for example, the number of tourists decreased by 4% in July 2012 (see Figure 7.1) compared with the same period in 2011, even if this figure grew overall in 2012 by 1.1%. During the first week of the OPGs, many media, such as *The Telegraph* [10] or *The Financial Times* [11] portrayed London as a ghost city characterized by the lack of tourist customers in the usual touristic locations.

Conversely, Brazil was characterized by a +40.8% increase in international tourists from July 1 to August 15, 2016 compared with the same period the previous year and Rio by 7.8% more tourists in 2016 compared with 2015 (Embratur).

In analysing London 2012, Weed (2014) considers that tourism impacts should have had a key place in strategies to optimize the legacy of the Games, which was not the case.

Based on airport arrival data during the Summer Olympics in Atlanta, London and Sydney, and the Winter Olympic Games in Salt Lake City, Turin and Vancouver, Moss et al. (2019) show that only Sydney seems to have experienced positive short-term effects in terms of international arrivals.

Lastly, while there is sometimes real growth in the number of tourists during the Games as in Barcelona, the wider region does not necessarily benefit. For example, resorts in the Costa Brava recorded a drop in demand during the Games (ETOA, 2006).

Besides the leisure tourism, business tourism declines in the year of the Games, once again materializing the crowding-out effects (see p. 000). During

Table 7.2 Change in the number of tourists during OPGs and/or during the year of the Games

An increased number of tourists	A decreased number of tourists
Mexico City (1968) 16,158 participants (of which 1,353 were Mexican); 188,388 including 50,522 Olympic visitors between September 15 and October 31 compared with 138,471 over the same period the previous year, i.e. an increase of 49,917 (37%) (Mexico, 1969)	**Japan (1964)** Decrease in the number of tourists in 1964 compared with 1963 (Pyo et al., 1988a)

Munich (1972): no comparative data available

Montreal (1976) +19% compared with 1975 (Khomsi, 2015)	**Los Angeles (1984)** Poorer results than in 1982 (Pyo et al., 1988a)

Moscow (1980) no comparative data available

An increased number of tourists	A decreased number of tourists
Seoul (1988) (2.3 million) A 23% increase compared with the previous year	
Barcelona (1992) 9.5% more tourists in 1992, but a decrease in 1991 (−1.8%) +16% increase in international visitors (ETOA, 2006)	
Atlanta (1996) +25% increase in international visitors (ETOA, 2006)	
Sydney (2000) +8.7% increase in international tourists compared with 1999 (official data); increases of +11.5% (ETOA, 2006) and +10.9% to for a total of 5 million (De Groote, 2005; official data)	**Athens (2004)** -20% fewer visitors during the Games; Fewer international arrivals in Greece (−6.2%) compared with 2002 (UNTWO data) in particular coming from Europa (Vettas, 2015). Hotel arrivals down by −4.9% for residents and −5.6% for non-residents in 2004 compared with 2003 (official data El-Stat)
Brazil (2016) +40,8% increase in international tourists from July 1 to August 15, 2016 compared with the same period the previous year; 4.8% more tourists in Brazil in 2016 compared with 2015 **Rio (2016)** 7.8% more tourists in 2016 compared with 2015 (Embratur, Brasilia Tourism Institut)	**Beijing (2008)** −7% fewer international visitors in August 2008, for the remainder of summer 2008, visitors numbers were down −30% on the previous year (JLL, 2014) and a −9.2 % decrease from January to July 2008 (Chinese official data); Overall there was a −13% drop from 2007 to 2008

London (2012) −4% fewer international visitors from July to September 2012 compared with the same period in 2011 (Office for National Statistics data[9]); there was an overall increase of +1.1% in 2012 compared with 2011.

Source: Compiled by the author.

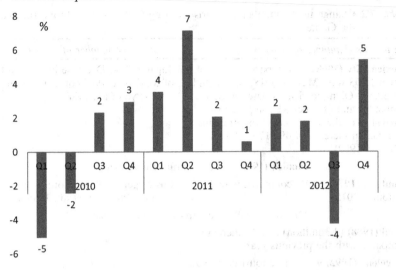

Figure 7.1 Change in the number of international visitors to London (%) compared
with the previous quarter
Source: the author based on ONS data (Office for National Statistics, see note 9)

the Olympic year, the number of delegates decreases in Atlanta, Barcelona
and Sydney (McKay and Plumb, 2001). But one year later, it grows again
(Figure 7.2).

There is therefore a first form of heterogeneity related to the number of
visitors present at the time of the Games. Tourist arrivals are likely to influence the wider effects on the tourism economy in the destination in question.

Heterogeneous wider effects on the tourism economy

The decrease in tourist number, if and when it occurs, leads to lower-than-
expected tourism revenues. But these revenues are also likely to vary in
terms of beneficiaries given the differentiated behaviour of sports tourists.
Similarly, income from tourist accommodation is likely to be differentiated. Finally, residents are also likely to change their behaviour during
the Games.

Variable tourism expenses

Tourists who come to the city for OPGs have interests that differ from those
of typical visitors who come to discover the city and so forth. These interests
induce specific expenses. For example, the "tourism budget" is transferred and
concentrated on Olympic sites and their activities at the expense of the usual
tourism sites. There is thus a substitution effect, defined as the replacement of
expenditures at the main tourist sites by expenditures associated with the
OPGs and the sites they occupy (Matheson, 2006).

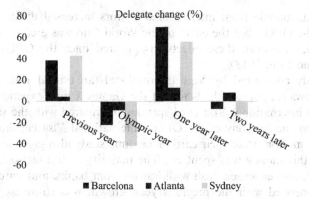

Figure 7.2 Change in the number of delegates[12] before, during and after the Olympic year
Source: the author based on data from McKay and Plumb (2001)

In Japan, following the decrease in the tourist number in 1964 compared with 1963, revenues were lower than expected. Only stores selling cameras, transistor radios and portable televisions – for which Japanese companies had a competitive advantage at this time – experienced sales growth (Pyo et al., 1988a). Tourist spending varies by sector.

In Atlanta, as in Sydney, tourism revenues were lower than those announced *ex ante*.

In Los Angeles in 1982, restaurant sales were 20% to 40% below their annual average during the first week of the Games and just at the average level thereafter. Some 80% of restaurants reported a decline in business (Pyo et al., 1988a). Most attractions in and around Los Angeles saw their sales shrink by 20% to 35% compared with a normal July and August. Visitors to Los Angeles during the Games were OPG sports fans who generated little revenue from restaurants and tours. Small businesses in Los Angeles saw their sales decrease from 15% to 25%. This was due to 1) to pre-game media coverage anticipating heavy congestion and higher hotel prices and 2) the non-arrival of Californian tourists in Los Angeles because of the Olympics (Economic Research Associates, quoted by Pyo et al., 1988a). In Athens, tourism revenues were also lower due to a decrease in the visitor number. That being said, tourism revenues do not always decrease.

The official data for London 2012 show that average spending per day grew by 6% in 2012 compared with the previous year. In London, there was a 3.6% increase in spending compared with the previous year, but a −0.3% decrease in real terms (official data). Tourists who came specifically for the OPGs spent, on average, over three times more per day (including tickets to OPG events) than those who did not come specifically for the OPGs but attended an event during the Games (London Travel Trend).

In Brazil, income from international visitors increased during the World Cup and the OPGs, but the effect of the World Cup was greater than that of OPGs and, moreover, these effects disappeared once the OPGs were over (Meurer and Lins, 2018).

The study conducted by Visa International (an official IOC partner) in Beijing shows that across the whole of the Games, China experienced a 15% increase in international Visa card spending compared with the same period in 2007. On the first day of the OPGs, international Visa cardholders spent nearly $10 million using their card. This same study also gives some insights into what this money was spent on. The majority of transactions concerned accommodation expenses, cash withdrawals from banks, and purchases from shops. Compared with the previous year, growth was strongest in gift and novelty stores, department stores, and clothing, that is sectors in which Chinese companies have a competitive advantage. By contrast, spending decreased in craft stores.

But looking beyond the overall amount spent, the Games' impact on tourism must also be considered in terms of the type of tourists and behaviour observed; in particular, sports tourists appear to form a specific population group, although the literature on this subject is scarce.

Few scientific studies regarding types of visitors and their behaviours

It is clear that few scientific studies exist on the subject of visitor behaviour during the OPGs, particularly in terms of their consumption practices, compared with those of "usual" tourists (Kwiatkowski and Könecke, 2017). Such specific studies of tourist consumption during OPGs and the possible distortions of residents' consumption as a result are nevertheless essential if we wish to accurately measure the economic impact of the Olympic Games (Preuss et al., 2007).

In Los Angeles, an exploratory study conducted between August 4 and 13, 1984 on a sample of 211 English-speaking visitors specifically there for the Los Angeles Games and interviewed at the airport, sought to identify the characteristics of tourists likely to go to the 1988 OPGs in Seoul (Pyo et al., 1988b). The results showed that 43% (50.5% of whom were North Americans) did not yet know if they would go to Seoul, while 33% stated that they would probably go. More than half (57%) of those saying they would go were Asian. The authors identified the main target market for Seoul as men aged 21 to 50 living first in Asia followed by those who lived in Europe and finally those residents in North America.

In London according to the International Passengers Survey (IPS, see note 9), 63% of international visitors who came specifically for the OPGs were also male. In terms of age profile, 29% were 25 to 34 years old, 23% were 35 to 44 years old and 21% were 45 to 54 years old; the over-55s accounted for 13%. Three quarters of these visits took place in August with the rest spread between July and September.

In research based on a survey of 1,196 spectators of the Commonwealth Games in Manchester in 2002, Preuss et al. (2007) show that different sports attract different visitors in terms of age and gender. The median age was 28 and the mean age was 40.6 overall, but the mean value from individual sports ranged from 26 for netball to 52 for pétanque. In addition, only 3% of visitors came alone; most visitors tended to come with friends or family.

In another context (namely the Rugby World Cup in France in 2007, a unique and more decentralized sporting context spread across different regions) a survey of 5,500 of match spectators aged at 15 and over that aimed to measure the economic impacts of this mega-event, Barget and Gouguet (2012) highlighted that, overall, 78.6% of the spectators were men; 67.7% were married or lived with their partner; and 47.7% had pursued higher education. These spectators had an average monthly income of 2,455 euros (29,460 euros per annum) and their average age was 39.

These studies show that sports tourists are more often men, with a mid-ranging income and an average age around 40.

In addition to their socio-demographic characteristics, the question of their practices and their expenditure is also central for analysing the impact of the OPGs in terms of tourism.

Pyo et al. (1988b), for example, sought to identify the key area of interest of tourists likely to come to Seoul in 1988. Apart from the Games, the main activities considered were shopping (60.9%), visiting the city of Seoul (59.5%), discovering Korean gastronomy (51.8%), and meeting Koreans (47.7%). Some 27% of them said they would spend more than $100 on authentic and typical souvenirs.

Regarding the Commonwealth Games, Preuss et al. (2007) highlighted several interesting results. Some are intuitive:

- Spectators with higher spending power spend more time in the destination and purchase more tickets and more goods and services;
- The amount of time and money spent in the destination is proportionate to the distance travelled by visitors from their country of origin.

Other more interesting results relate to types of visitors and expenses:

- Visitors during the Commonwealth Games consume in different way from their usual vacations. Tourists ate more at fast-food restaurants and used public transport more (public transport was free in Manchester during the Games), compared with their other holidays. In addition, day visitors tended to bring their own food.
- Furthermore, residents consume differently. Like tourists they also ate more at fast food restaurants and use more public transport (which was free). Some, however, had to leave the city, thus reducing their spending in the city and creating an opportunity cost for the city (Preuss et al., 2007).
- Visitors who would have come even without the Commonwealth Games in Manchester were more interested in cultural events.

Based on data collected during the Rugby World Cup in France in 2007, Barget and Gouguet (2012) showed that spending also varies according to visitor type (from outside the region but resident in France versus non-residents) and according to income level. Findings were once again quite intuitive. Foreigners spend more than the French, and the richest spend more than the poorest. So, for example, the 66.1% of French residents with monthly incomes of less than 4,000 euros spent 44.90 euros on average. For the 33.9% with incomes of more than 4,000 euros, average expenditure was 83.10 euros during the World Cup. Residents' expenditure is therefore related to their income, as might be expected. The same is true for non-residents except that they spend a lot more than residents. The 46.3% of non-residents with incomes below 4,000 euros spent 194.70 euros on average while the 53.7% with incomes above 4,000 euros spent an average of 553.60 euros.

The authors also showed that the main expenditures (excluding transport) concern stadium shopping (27.3%), food (26.8%), accommodation (15.1%), tourism (12.7%), outings (10.3%), services (0.4%) and other expenses (7.5%).

Finally, the duration of sports tourists' stays differs from that of typical tourists. For example, in London during the 2012 OPGs, this duration was 9–10 days, with most stays lasting between 4 and 13 nights, followed by stays of 1 to 3 nights (IPS, see note 9).

However, it is not just tourists attending the Olympics that consume differently; residents' habits are also affected. In Los Angeles, for example, residents spent more on OPGs than on other recreational activities, either in Southern California or outside the region (Pyo et al., 1988a). In addition, it seems that, during the Olympics, they also ate more fast-food products (see p. 000).

Significant effects on the hotel industry

OPGs induce a growth in hotel capacity. The number of rooms grew by 40% in Sydney between 1994 and 2000. In Rio, it grew by 93% between 2009 and 2016; there was also similar growth in Barcelona, Seoul and Atlanta (McKay and Plumb, 2001).

They also induce an increase in the supply of temporary housing on platforms such as Airbnb and a rise in prices. In Rio, Airbnb was even designated an official host (due to a shortage of hotels in the city[13]) and 85,000 visitors were accommodated in this way according to Airbnb. TripAdvisor observed a 122% price increase during the 2016 OPGs compared with the same period in 2015. The French daily newspaper *Le Figaro* even published this headline on August 5, 2016: "The Olympics make Rio the most expensive city in the world on Airbnb".[14]

In London in 2012 in the Stratford district near the Olympic Village, some rents increased fivefold. Airbnb stated that 9,700 visitors from more than 100 countries were welcomed by more than 1,800 hosts during the Olympic Games, providing them with more than $4 million in revenue.[15]

But in addition to the effects before and during the Games, there are also possible long-term effects after the Games.

Heterogeneous medium- and long-term impacts on tourism

A frequent positive change in the number of visitors in the medium term but not always in the long term

Sometimes, tourism attendance benefits from the OPGs in the medium term but not always in the long run (Song, 2010; Poncet, 2001, quoted by Augustin, 2008). In Montreal, although the number of tourists grew in 1976, it shrank by 10% in 1977. In 1981, however, the number of tourists was still higher than in 1975. In Sydney, this figure has been decreasing since 2001. In Beijing, it was lower in 2016 than in 2007. In London, it increased from 2013 to 2017 (See Figure 7.3).

In Brazil, the effects were short-lived (Meurer and Lins, 2018).[16] In Rio de Janeiro, the overall growth in the number of international visitors in 2016 is only 7.6% and -8.4% in 2017 compared with 2016 (Figure 7.4).

These changes are once again contrasted (See Table 7.3).

In Athens, during the huge economic crisis, the total number of hotel arrivals decreased every year from 2008 to 2011. In Barcelona, often presented as a successful example of OPGs in terms of tourism, the number of tourists grew in 1992 as well as in 1993. However, this figure would later begin to fall (in 1996 (−0.9%) and 1997 (−8.5%)). Growth would not accelerate again until the beginning of the 2000s. But it is clear that, ten years on, this trend is no longer directly linked to the Olympic Games. It is due more to the general development of urban tourism linked to the expansion of low-cost airlines (Figure 7.5).

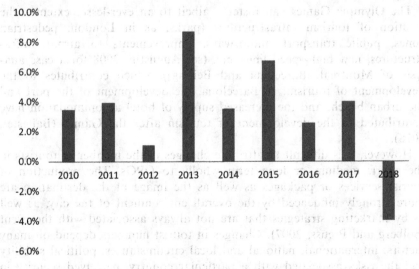

Figure 7.3 Change in the number of international visitors (%) compared with the previous year in Greater London

Source: the author based on data from ONS (Office for National Statistics)

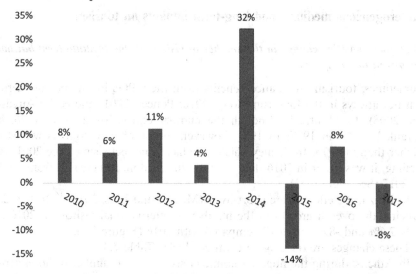

Figure 7.4 Change in the number of international visitors (%) compared with the previous year in Rio de Janeiro
Source: the author based on *Anuário Estatístico de Turismo* [17]

In addition, the origin of visitors has changed as the case of London shows (see Figure 7.6). Tourism from countries participating in the event has grown more than that of countries not participating (Fourie and Santana-Gallego, 2011).

The Olympic Games can foster – albeit to an ever-lesser extent – the creation of tourism infrastructures (parks, as in London, pedestrian zones, public transport, motorways, improvements to airport infra-structures, new high-speed lines, etc. (see Augustin, 2008 for a case ana-lysis of Montreal, Barcelona and Beijing)), which contributes to the development of tourism. In Barcelona, the development of the port and the urban beach, and the increased supply of hotel accommodation have contributed to the development of tourism after the Games (Ballester, 2018).

However, it is difficult to attribute changes in the number of tourists in the short, medium or long term wholly to OPGs. The production of tourist services or packages as well as the image of the destination are more strongly influenced by the overall environment of the city, as well as by marketing strategies that are not always associated with the event (Solberg and Preuss, 2007). Changes in tourist numbers depend on many factors: international, national and local circumstances, political stability and the risks associated with a particular country, perceived security in different cities, weather and climate, exchange rates, local policies that help to transform the city, etc. Moreover, these many variables sometimes combine forces to pull in the same direction, and sometimes work in the

Table 7.3 Medium- and long-term change in the number of tourists in host cities

Medium-term change in tourist numbers	Long-term change in tourist numbers
Montreal (1976) −10% from 1976 to 1977, +5% from 1977 to 1978 (Khomsi, 2015)	In 1981, a lower number of tourists than in 1976 (Khomsi, 2015)
Moscow (1980) N/K	N/K
Los Angeles (1984) N/K	N/K
Seoul (1988) + 78% more international visitors between 1986 and 1990 (JLL, 2014); +17% in 1988 and +8% in 1989 compared with 1986 (ETOA, 2006)	In 2002 (+222% compared with 1986) (JLL, 2014)
Barcelona (1992)* +9.3% more tourists in the city hotels in 1992, +23.6% in 1993, 7.8% in 1994, +13.8% in 1995; −10% in 1993, +4% in 1994 (ETOA, 2006)	*In 1996 (−0.9%) and 1997 (−8.5%) From 1992 to 2017, there was 384% growth, with particularly significant growth during the 2000s.
Atlanta (1996) +4% between 1994 and 1998 (JLL, 2014): +5% in 1997; −4% in 1998 (compared with 1994)	A decrease in visitors from 2001 to 2003 (JLL, 2014)
Sydney (2000) +16% more visitors to Australia between 1998 and 2002 (+48% between 1994 and 2000) (JLL, 2014)[18]	A decrease in visitors (−0.1% in 2001, 0.9% in 2002 (Overmyer, 2017; ETOA, 2006)) but a long-term increase. Olympics-induced visitors 1997–2004: 1.7 million (Tourism Forecasting Council (TFC)[19]
Athens (2004)* +6.7% increase in Greek hotel arrivals and +21.7% increase in foreign hotel arrivals in 2005 compared with 2004, and +3.3% Greek tourists and +11.7% more foreign tourists in 2006 compared with 2005	* + 11.7% more Greek hotel arrivals and 10.3% foreign hotel arrivals in 2007 falling to respectively −0.7% and −7.1% in 2008; −1% and −4.9% in 2009 and −7.5% and −0.4% in 2010
Beijing (2008) +7.9% in 2009, +17% in 2010; +6% in 2011 (UNWTO-WTCF, 2018)	A lower total in 2016 than in 2007 (UNWTO-WTCF, 2018)
London (2012)* Growth of 8.7% in 2013	* There was an overall increase in the number of tourists of 23.2% from 2012 to 2018
Rio (2016)* −8.4% in 2017 compared with 2016	

Source: the author based on official data from different countries (*) and on the literature

opposite direction. For example, in Los Angeles, the decline in tourism during the 1984 OPGs (see p. 000) was also related to the overall decline in tourism in USA during this period due to the dollar's high exchange rate.

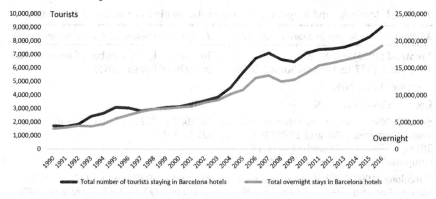

Figure 7.5 Number of overnights and tourists in Barcelona city
Source: the author, based on official data from the city of Barcelona[20]

A hotel sector sometimes characterized by long-term difficulties

The observed growth in hotel capacity (see p. 000) is not always profitable. The number of hotel rooms grew by 40% in Sydney between 1994 and 2000. In Rio, it grew by 93% between 2009 and 2016. There was also growth in Barcelona, Seoul, and Atlanta (McKay and Plumb, 2001).

But the construction of hotels can sometimes lead to a decrease in occupancy rates at the time of the event. For instance, in Montreal during August 1976, the hotel occupancy rate dropped to 69% (compared with 97% in August 1974 and 91% in August 1975). One year after the Olympic Games, occupancy rates were low in Rio, Barcelona, Seoul, and Atlanta (McKay and Plumb, 2001).

In Rio, around the Olympic Park, these rates did not exceed 12%, and in tourist areas they are lower than expected. For example, according to managing director, Douglas Viegas, Arena Ipanema, a 136-room and four-star hotel built for the OPGs, is experiencing a very serious occupancy crisis. "It is absolutely not what we expected": instead of an occupancy rate of 75%, we are now running at around 40%" (Interview for French weekly news magazine *Le Point* [21]). This led him to lower his prices by about 30% to attract customers. In London, while occupancy rates increased during the last four days of July and the first 11 days of August, they decreased before and after the Games (ETOA, 2006). Throughout June and July, occupancy was lower than in 2011 and 2013 while it was stable in August compared with 2011 (see Figure 7.7).

Owing to this additional supply of rooms, income per room often decreases after OPGs (Solberg and Preuss, 2007). In Barcelona, for example, revenue per room fell by nearly 60% in the two years following the Games (McKay and Plumb, 2001). The years following the OPGs were a period of reduced profitability in Barcelona and generated numerous bankruptcies in the tourism industry.

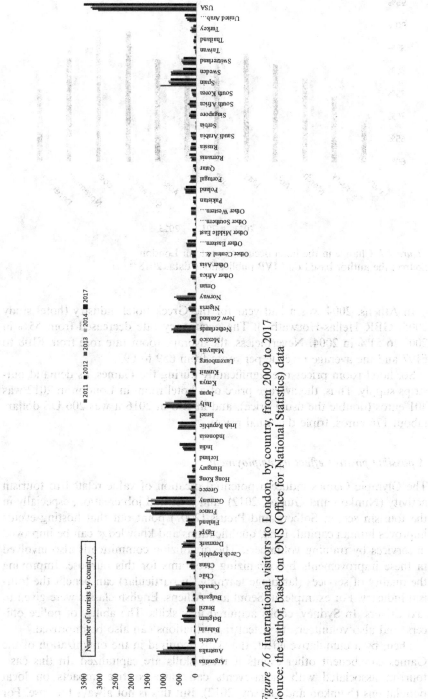

Figure 7.6 International visitors to London, by country, from 2009 to 2017
Source: the author, based on ONS (Office for National Statistics) data

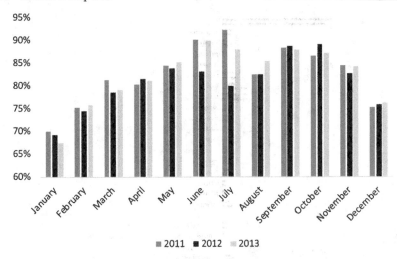

Figure 7.7 Change in the hotel occupancy rate in London
Source: the author based on MVP publications data, 2018[22]

In Athens, 2004 was a bad year for the Greek hotel industry (hotel study 2005, GBR Hellas-Horwath[23]). The occupancy rate decreased from 55% in 2003 to 51% in 2004. Nevertheless, the average room rate rose from €108 to €197 and the average revenue per room from €59 to €93.

So, hotel room prices rise significantly during the Games, as demand outstrips supply. Thus, the average price of a hotel room in London in 2012 was 401 euros (double the usual price), and in Rio in 2016 it was 206 US dollars (about 176 euros, triple the usual price).

A possible positive effect on employment

The Olympic Games induce a potential creation of value related to tourism activity (Nunkoo and Gursoy, 2012), and potential job creation, especially in the tourism sector. Solberg and Preuss (2007) point out that hosting events improves human capital. First, qualifications and knowledge can be improved in services by training volunteers. The organizing committee is also involved in these improvements by organizing programs for this purpose. Improving the quality of services (language learning, in particular) can benefit the tourism industry. For example, in Seoul and Athens, English classes were given to taxi drivers. In Sydney, cooks acquired new skills. The ability of police officers, and also volunteers, to detect risk situations can also be improved.

Then, by a cumulative effect, the skills acquired in the organization of the Games can benefit other events if these skills are capitalized. In this case, tourism associated with mega-events can have positive impacts on local populations (Nunkoo and Gursoy, 2012). But this is not always the case. For example, employment in hotels and restaurants in the Sydney area has declined every year since the 2000 OPGs (Solberg and Preuss, 2007).

It must be noted that when tourism growth occurs, it can also have negative effects on the economy (Massiani, 2018), particularly in relation to what is called the "Dutch disease": the appreciation of the value of money diminishes the competitiveness of other sectors. Moreover the growth in employment and/or salaries in the tourist sector can affect the other sectors' ability to find employees.

Conclusion: effects on tourism based on contextualized conditions in time and space

This analysis shows that the interrelation between OPGs and tourism varies over time and in space. Following on from the work of Barca et al. (2012), we have qualified these as "place-based" interrelations (Figure 7.8) because they depend on local considerations and policies.

These interrelations depend on the contract binding the IOC, the host city and the relevant National Olympic Committee. They also depend on the strategies of local actors and the State regarding the Olympic Games and tourism. Long-term success in terms of tourism requires the destination to introduce new products and services, and to continue to promote itself (Solberg and Preuss, 2007). For example, in Sydney, post-Games resource mobilization programs were put in place to boost tourism. These programs have led to cooperation between the organizers of the Olympic Games and the Australian Tourist Commission, with

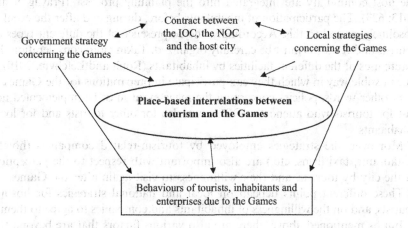

Figure 7.8 Place-based interrelations between tourism and the Games
Source: the author

a view to promoting the destination and enhancing the positive advertising generated by the Games. As is always the case in tourism, local cooperation strategies between tourism stakeholders and with OPG players undoubtedly play an important role in the sustainability of the effects on tourism. In London, on the other hand, tourism has been seen as a less important part of the Olympic and Paralympic legacy strategy (Weed, 2014).

These interrelations are ultimately part of a socio-economic and touristic context that can be seen at different scales (international, national and local). For instance, it seems at first glance that the benefits in terms of tourism are greater in countries where tourism was previously less developed. Without usual tourists, there is no crowding out effect. This is also partly the case because these countries lifted visa restrictions at the time of the Games in order to facilitate the arrival of tourists. If this visa policy continues after the Games, there may be an increase in tourism.

These interrelations also depend on the behaviour of tourists, inhabitants and companies *vis-à-vis* the Games. Indeed, a mega-event such as the Olympics can generate conflicts between tourists and locals before, during and after the event (Chen and Tian, 2015; Nunkoo and Gursoy, 2012) owing to cultural, social and economic differences, environmental pollution, noise and even the destruction of cultural and historical resources. These conflicts affect a country's ability to continue to attract tourists. Many authors stress the need to take account of participation in the planning process in order to guarantee the success of the event in terms of tourism (Pappas, 2014; Rocha and Barbanti, 2015). "The sustainability of mega sporting events depends on the extent to which the views of the host community are integrated into the planning process" (Prayag et al., 2013: 629). The participation of inhabitants before, during and after the event is absolutely central to this. Accordingly, the co-presence of the different types of tourists and residents must be carefully organized. Taking into consideration the future uses of the different facilities by inhabitants (Roult and Lefebvre, 2010) is one possible way in which they can participate in preparations for the Games.

In other words, policies concerning the mega-event must be implemented not just for tourists who attend the OPGs but also for other tourists and for local inhabitants.

Moreover, the strategies employed by tourism-related companies (hotels, restaurants, taxi firms, etc.) are also important with respect to the perception of the city by tourists, and their willingness to visit again after the Games.

These different points depend on local and national strategies for hosting tourists, and on the willingness of inhabitants and companies to agree to them.

But as mentioned above, there are also various factors that are beyond the control of the organizers of mega-events and which influence tourism in the long run. These factors include the political climate and the exchange rate in the host country, and more generally the prevailing international context at a given period in time. In addition, the production of tourist services and the image of the host destination are both strongly influenced by the overall environment of the host city as well as by marketing strategies that are not always associated with the event (Solberg and Preuss, 2007).

This literature review of the links between OPGs and tourism highlights the diverse range of situations that exist, at the heart of which lie not just the host locations and their socio-economic characteristics but also the expectations, projects and strategies of the various stakeholders involved and the different behaviours of tourists and inhabitants alike.

Notes

1 Tourism is not always, however, the primary motivation for hosting Games in developed countries (Rocha and Fink, 2017); urban regeneration and the development of sports are sometimes other motives.
2 https://www.japantimes.co.jp/news/2016/03/30/national/japan-doubles-overseas-tour ist-target-2020/
3 https://twitter.com/Challenges/status/1071112836468957184
4 https://www.tourmag.com/Bresil-les-Jeux-Olympiques-ont-booste-la-frequentation-touristique_a82444.html
5 According to the British Minister of Culture at the time, Jeremy Hunt, three million additional visitors to the city were expected. https://www.lepoint.fr/sport/jeux-olympiques/londres-ville-fantome-pendant-les-jo-08-08-2012-1494206_761.php
6 According to the British Minister for Sport and the Olympics at the time, Hugh Robertson, two million visitors were expected https://www.la-croix.com/Actualite/Sport/Les-Jeux-olympiques-de-Londres-en-10-chiffres-cles-_NG_-2012-07-27-836087
7 According to Roland Héguy, President of the Union des Métiers et des Industries de l'Hôtellerie (Union of the Hotel Industries and Professions) http://www.lepa risien.fr/sports/JO/paris-2024/paris-2024-a-la-cle-entre-120-000-et-250-000-crea tions-d-emplois-14-09-2017-7258923.php
8 No definition of low season and peak season is given. However this definition depends on the type of tourism and places concerned. While July and August is the peak season for Nice and Marseille in terms of tourism, this is not the case for Paris as business tourism is lower in the summer months.
9 https://www.ons.gov.uk/businessindustryandtrade/tourismindustry
10 https://www.telegraph.co.uk/sport/olympics/picturegalleries/9443898/Londo n-2012-Olympics-has-the-West-End-become-a-ghost-town.html
11 https://www.ft.com/content/0767327a-da6d-11e1-902d-00144feab49a
12 While Atlanta refers to international and domestic delegates, for Barcelona and Sydney, only the international delegates are considered.
13 A study conducted by the World Economic Forum in partnership with MIT showed that 257 hotels should have been built to accommodate tourists coming for the Games (World Economic Forum, 2016).
14 http://www.lefigaro.fr/conjoncture/2016/08/05/20002-20160805ARTFIG00007-le s-jo-font-de-rio-la-ville-la-plus-chere-au-monde-sur-airbnb.php
15 https://www.airbnbcitizen.com/airbnb-and-big-events/
16 By using a gravity model of international trade, Song shows that the long-term effects on tourism are negative while they are positive on exports as has already been shown by Rose and Spiegel, 2011 (Song, 2010, p. 106).
17 Annuário Estatístico de Turismo (2010–2017)
18 Different data exhibiting a lower growth rate are, however, presented by other authors (Overmyer, 2017)..
19 https://www.abs.gov.au/AUSSTATS/abs@.nsf/Previousproducts/1350.0Main% 20Features100Jan%202006?opendocument&tabname=Summary&prodno=1350. 0&issue=Jan%202006&num=&view=

20 The author thanks Salvador Anton Clave of Rovira y Virgili University of Catalonia and his team for the data concerning Barcelona.
21 https://www.lepoint.fr/monde/rio-un-an-apres-les-jo-la-frequentation-de s-hotels-en-chute-libre-03-08-2017-2147763_24.php
22 https://www.ukinbound.org/wp-content/uploads/2018/07/LondonHotelOccupa ncy-incl-June2018.pdf
23 https://www.gbrconsulting.gr/sectors/tourism/hotelstudy_results2005.html

References

Augustin, J-P. (2008). Installations olympiques, régénération urbaine et tourisme, *Téoros*, 27(2). Online since 1 June 2009, accessed 11 January 2018. http://journals.op enedition.org/teoros/133

BallesterP. (2018). Barcelone face au tourisme de masse: « tourismophobie » et vivre ensemble, *Téoros* 37(2). Online since 28 May 2018, accessed 20 June 2018. http:// journals.openedition.org/teoros/3367

Barca, F., McCannP., and Rodríguez-PoseA. (2012). The case for regional development intervention: place-based versus place-neutral approaches, *Journal of Regional Science*, 52(1), 134–152

Barget, E., Gouguet, J.-J. (2012). The importance of foreign spectators' expenditure in the tourism impact of mega-sporting events. *Papeles de Europa*, 25, 27–50 doi:10.5209/rev_PADE.2012.n25.41094

Boukas, N., Ziakas, V., Boustras, G. (2013). Olympic legacy and cultural tourism: exploring the facets of Athens' Olympic heritage. *International Journal of Heritage Studies* 19, 203–228. doi:10.1080/13527258.2011.651735

Castro, C. (2016). Les Jeux Olympiques 2016 et le tourisme à Rio de Janeiro, *IdeAs*, 7 (Spring/Summer), Online since 9 June 2016, accessed 4 December 2018. http:// journals.openedition.org/ideas/1408 doi:10.4000/ideas.1408

Chen, F., Tian, L. (2015). Comparative study on residents' perceptions of follow-up impacts of the 2008 Olympics, *Tourism Management*, 51, 263–281

Embratur (2018). Brazilian Tourism Institute, accessed 4 December 2018. http://www. embratur.gov.br/

European Tour Operators Association (ETOA) (2006). *Olympic Report*

Faulkner, B., ChalipL., Brown, G., Jago, L., MarchR., Woodside, A. (2000). Monitoring the Tourism Impacts of the Sydney 2000 Olympics, *Event Management*, 6, 231–246. doi:10.3727/152599500108751390

Fourie, J., Santana-Gallego, M. (2011). The impact of mega-sport events on tourist arrivals, *Tourism Management*, 32, 1364–1370. doi:10.1016/j.tourman.2011.01.011

De Groote, P. (2005), Economic and tourism aspects of the Olympic Games, *Tourism Review*, 60(1), 12–19

IAU ÎdF (Institut d'Aménagement et d'Urbanisme d'Île de France) (2008). *Benchmark Mass Transit 11 villes*

JLL (John Lang Lassalle) (2014). *Tokyo 2020: Expectations for the Hotel Industry, November*, accessed 8 December 2018. https://nanopdf.com/download/tokyo-2020-o lympics-expectations-for-the-hotel-industry_pdf

Kasimati, E. (2003). Economic aspects and the Summer Olympics: a review of related research, *International Journal of Tourism Research*, 5, 433–444. doi:10.1002/jtr.449

Khomsi, M.R. (2015). Le rôle des grands événements dans le développement touristique d'une destination métropolitaine: cas de la ville de Montréal 1960–1992, Doctoral thesis, Université du Québec à Montréal

Kwiatkowski, G., Könecke, T. (2017). Tourism and recurring sport events: event tourists' and regular tourists' profiles and expenditures at the Windsurf World Cup on Sylt, *Sport, Business and Management: An International Journal*, 7(5), 464–482, doi:10.1108/SBM-11-2016-0070

Li, S., Blake, A. (2009). Estimating Olympic-related investment and expenditure, *International Journal of Tourism Research*, 11, 337–356. doi:10.1002/jtr.694

McKay, M., Plumb, C. (2001). *Reaching Beyond the Gold: The Impact of the Olympic Games on Real Estate Markets*, John Lang Lassalle

Massiani, J. (2018). Assessing the economic impact of mega events using Computable General Equilibrium models: promises and compromises. *Economic Modelling*, 75, 1–9 doi:10.1016/j.econmod.2018.05.021

Matheson, V.A. (2006). Mega-events: the effect of the world's biggest sporting events on local, regional, and national economies, College of the Holy Cross, Department of Economics, Faculty Research Series, Paper No. 06–10

Meurer, R., Lins, H.N. (2018). The effects of the 2014 World Cup and the 2016 Olympic Games on Brazilian international travel receipts. *Tourism Economics*, 24, 486–491. doi:10.1177/1354816617746261

Mexico (1969). *Rapport officiel des Jeux Olympiques d'été de Mexico 1968/Official report of the Summer Olympic Games Mexico 1968*. Vol. 2. Comité organisateur des Jeux de la XIXe olympiade

Minnaert, L. (2012). An Olympic legacy for all? The non-infrastructural outcomes of the Olympic Games for socially excluded groups (Atlanta 1996–Beijing 2008). *Tourism Management*, 33, 361–370. doi:10.1016/j.tourman.2011.04.005

Mizuho Economic Outlook & Analysis (2014). *The Economic Impact of the 2020 Tokyo Olympic Games*, October 17, Economic Research Department

Morrison, R. (1982). *Government Documents Relating to the 1980 Olympic Games Boycott: A Contents Analysis and Bibliography*

Moscow Official Report (1981). *Games of the XXII Olympiad, Moscow 1980*, Official Report of the Organising Committee of the Games of the XXII Olympiad, Vol. 2

Moss, S.E., Gruben, K.H., Moss, J. (2019). An empirical test of the Olympic tourism legacy. *Journal of Policy Research in Tourism, Leisure and Events*, 11(1) 16–34. doi:10.1080/19407963.2017.1418750

Novikov, I.T. (Ed.) (1979). *Games of the XXII Olympiad Moscow 1980*, Official Report of the Organising Committee of the Games of the XXII Olympiad

Nunkoo, R., Gursoy, D. (2012). Residents' support for tourism: an identity perspective, *Annals of Tourism Research*, 39(1), 243–268

Overmyer, M.P. (2017). Economic impact analysis on Olympic host-cities, *Honors Projects*, 647. http://scholarworks.gvsu.edu/honorsprojects/647

Pappas, N. (2014). Hosting mega events: Londoners' support of the 2012 Olympics, *Journal of Hospitality and Tourism Management*, 21, 10–17

Paris2024 (2017). *Bilan carbone*, 14 03 Organizing Committee

Poncet, P.P. (2001). Sydney et les JO ou le complexe de Cendrillon, *Pouvoirs locaux*, 49, 78–81

Prayag, G., Hosany, S., Nunkoo, R., Alders, T. (2013). London residents' support for the 2012 Olympic Games: the mediating effect of overall attitude, *Tourism Management*, 36, 629–640

Pyo, S., Cook, R., Howell, R.L. (1988a). Summer olympic tourist market — learning from the past, *Tourism Management*, 9, 137–144. doi:10.1016/0261-5177(88)90023-4

Pyo, S., Uysal, M., Howell, R. (1988b) 1988 Seoul Olympics — visitor preferences. *Tourism Management*, 9, 68–72. doi:10.1016/0261-5177(88)90060-X

Preuss, H. (2011). A method for calculating the crowding-out effect in sport mega-event impact studies: the 2010 FIFA World Cup, *Development Southern Africa*, 28 (3), 367–385, doi:10.1080/0376835X.2011.595995

Preuss, H. (2004). Aspects of Olympic Games tourism, Paper presented at the 3rd SETE Tourism & Development Conference, Vouliagmeni, Greece

Preuss, H., SeguinB., O'Reilly, N. (2007). Profiling major sport event visitors: the 2002 Commonwealth Games, *Journal of Sport & Tourism*, 12(1), 5–23

Rocha, C.M., Fink, J.S. (2017). Attitudes toward attending the 2016 Olympic Games and visiting Brazil after the games, *Tourism Management Perspectives* 22, 17–26. doi:10.1016/j.tmp.2017.01.001

Rocha, C., Barbanti, V. (2015). Support for the 2014 FIFA World Cup and the 2016 Olympic Games, *Journal of Physical Education and Sports Management*, 2(2), 66–68

Rose, A.K., Spiegel, M.M. (2011). The Olympic effect, *The Economic Journal*, 121 (553), 652–677

Roult, R., Lefebvre, S. (2010). Reconversion des héritages olympiques et rénovation de l'espace urbain: le cas des stades olympiques. *Géographie, économie, société*, 12, 367–391

Sant, S.-L., Mason, D.S., Hinch, T.D. (2013). Conceptualising Olympic tourism legacy: destination marketing organisations and Vancouver 2010, *Journal of Sport & Tourism*, 18, 287–312. doi:10.1080/14775085.2014.947312

Solberg, H.A., Preuss, H. (2007). Major sport events and long-term tourism impacts, *Journal of Sport Management*, 21, 213–234. doi:10.1123/jsm.21.2.213

Song, W. (2010). Impacts of Olympics on exports and tourism, *Journal of Economic Development*, 35(4), 93–110

UNWTO-WTCF (2018). *City Tourism Performance Research*, UNWTO Publications, accessed 4 December 2018. http://publications.unwto.org/publication/unwtowtcf-city-tourism-performance-research

Vettas, N. (ed) (2015). *The Impact of the 2004 Olympic Games on the Greek Economy*, Athens: Foundation for Economic & Industrial Research

Visa (2011). *Mega-sporting Events: Generating Visitor Spending*

Visit Britain (2012). The London 2012 Olympic & Paralympic Games, Interim Report, November

Weed, M. (2014). Is tourism a legitimate legacy from the Olympic and Paralympic Games? An analysis of London 2012 legacy strategy using program theory, *Journal of Sport & Tourism*, 19, 101–126. doi:10.1080/14775085.2015.1053968

Williams, P., & Elkhashab, A. (2012). Leveraging tourism social capital: the case of the 2010 Olympic Tourism Consortium, *International Journal of Event and Festival Management*, 3(3), 317–334

World Economic Forum (2016). Understanding the sharing economy, accessed 4 December 2018. http://www3.weforum.org/docs/WEF_Understanding_the_Sharing_Economy_report_2016.pdf

Part III

Risk, uncertainty and environmental issues

8 Integrating public behaviours into operational responses to crisis situations

A way to improve security of major events?

Paul-Henri Richard, Patrick Laclémence, Audrey Morel Senatore and Guillaume Delatour

Introduction

The modern Olympic Games, resurrected by Pierre de Coubertin and first staged in Athens in 1896 is, alongside the FIFA World Cup, one of the most widely followed sporting events on the planet. Billions of people tune in to watch the opening and closing ceremonies and competitions, and millions of spectators attend in person. Managing security at these events poses a major challenge for host societies, amid the growing threat of social uprisings and terrorist attacks. The bloody hostage-taking episode at the Munich Olympics is a resonant case in point. On 5 September 1972, a group of eight terrorists from the Black September faction of the Palestine Liberation Organisation entered the Olympic Village and took nine Israeli athletes hostage. The incident left 17 people dead, including 11 Israelis. The event received heavy media coverage and would go on to leave its mark on the history of the Games. The resulting rethink of law enforcement responses to such incidents led to the creation of special police forces in the western world.[1] At the 1996 Olympic Games in Atlanta, a pipe bombing attack in the Olympic Park left two people dead and 110 injured. More recently, the Islamic State Group carried out terrorist attacks during the 2016 Olympic Games in Rio de Janeiro.

Major sporting events, at which vulnerable members of the public gather in great numbers, therefore pose significant risks and threats.[2] They require government and the organisers to plan a range of measures to maintain public order and security, especially when crisis situations arise.[3] Yet these measures are not always planned with due weight given to how members of the public actually react. The authorities assume that spectators will act in a way that supports their work (disciplined, rational, following instructions, etc.). Nevertheless, that is not how things proceed in reality (Oberije, 2007).

Yet in the immediate aftermath of a disaster it is members of the public, themselves victims, who spontaneously volunteer to help others and are the first people to deliver first aid (Waldman et al., 2017; Lorenz, 2017). France's civil security modernisation act of 13 August 2004 made citizens a central feature of civil security. However, 14 years on, this principle is still difficult to apply in practice. Despite the emergence of various concepts such as

152 Richard, Laclémence, Senatore, Delatour

population and community resilience (Wulff et al., 2015) and initiatives attempting to restore the public's role in crisis management,[4] it is an undeniable fact that identifying and understanding how members of the public typically act, and incorporating these behaviours into operational management, remain major crisis management challenges. These challenges are a common refrain among international bodies (FEMA, 2011; United Nations Office of Disaster Risk Reduction, 2015)[5].

The authorities have yet to fully grasp these challenges because of resistance driven by a number of beliefs. The first such belief, stemming from conventional and intuitive views supported by the work of Gustave Le Bon (1895), among others, is that people invariably give in to panic when a crisis situation occurs. While this view has been questioned in recent years (Dezecache, 2015) and in various latter-day works on disaster management(Quarantelli, 1989; Tierney & Goltz, 1998), the myth that members of the public resort to panic, looting and indifference when a disaster happens continues to dominate thinking among professional rescue workers and leaders (Barsky et al., 2006; Helsloot & Ruitenberg, 2004).

The second belief is that, in the midst of a disaster, people react in volatile ways that go against the expectations of the emergency services (inhibition and collective panic, exodus, rumours, violence, etc.) and that these actions can have a destabilising and disruptive effect on the work of law enforcement and emergency services (issues around responsibility, control, coordination, effectiveness and legitimacy: Crocq, 2013; Provitolo, 2005; Provitolo et al., 2015; Tucker & O'Brien, 2011). This is compounded by the fact that many of the spontaneous actions of members of the public are unpredictable and largely incompatible with the rigidly organised, hierarchical command and control structures typical of civil security services (Helsloot et al., 2004: 104).

The third and final belief, which is more recent in nature and might go some way to explaining this reluctance, is that the risk of terrorism and secondary attacks means that every victim, witness and person involved is considered a potential threat.

Consequently, disaster preparedness plans deliberately exclude civilians and seek to keep them at arm's length. Moreover, when a disaster happens, the security services see members of the public as potential victims and sources of vulnerability rather than as assets who can be mobilised in support of crisis management and resilience-building efforts.

In light of these observations, those responsible for handling safety and security at major sporting events must consider how the public will react for crisis preparedness planning and operational purposes. The first part of this chapter will take stock of current thinking on public behaviour in disaster situations. The second part will outline further avenues of research in this field and likely changes in the French doctrine ahead of the 2024 Olympic Games.

How the public behaves when a disaster happens

A great many researchers have sought to identify and model how members of the public behave in crisis situations. Their research focuses on observing human reactions when specific events occur, or on analysing typical patterns of behaviour such as panic and looting. Both academics and professional rescue workers make a value judgement when qualifying the behaviours they observe.

Destabilising, volatile, inappropriate, pathological and dangerous patterns of behaviour

So-called destabilising behaviours are those that hinder the work of the authorities or the organising body and go against their prescriptive instructions. Such patterns of behaviour cause the victim count to rise and lead to social disorder. Examples include failing to follow evacuation instructions, evacuating in a disorderly manner, spreading rumours, and inhibition and collective panic. Some of these behaviours are caused by excessive stress when an attack is especially intense, prolonged or recurring. People react in one of four ways: they become frozen with inhibition, they become agitated and disorderly, they panic and flee in fright, or they behave like robots.

Collective panic

The term panic can be traced back to antiquity. It comes from the Ancient Greek word *"panikos"*, meaning "relating to Pan". Professor Louis Crocq (2013: 15) defines panic as follows: "Intense, collective fear felt simultaneously by all members of a population group, characterised by a descent into archaic, impulsive and herd-mentality behaviour, and causing primitive responses such as frantic flight, disorderly agitation, violence and collective suicide." These patterns of behaviour are extremely destabilising for the security forces because they cause people to act irrationally and adopt a mob mentality, thereby posing a risk of further victims. While panic and social chaos are often reported anecdotally, commentators are too quick to use these isolated incidents as evidence, without scientific proof, that this kind of behaviour is widespread (Dynes, 2008: 139). Moreover, the term "panic" is often employed incorrectly to describe situations of fear, stress and disorderly conduct by the public, without the necessary methodological precautions being taken to rigorously assess the patterns of behaviour observed. It is important to note that, here, fear and stress are adaptive responses to disaster situations.

Nevertheless, panic – insofar as it refers to the idea of herd mentality – dominates thinking among decision-makers about how the public behaves. In *L'âge des foules* (*The Age of the Crowd*), Moscovici (2005) introduces the idea of mass fear, hardening the authorities' attitudes towards the way the public responds during a crisis. The kinds of images and information[6] used in crisis management training programmes merely confirm the preconceptions of decision-makers, who believe that, 85% of the time, people's behaviour in a disaster situation is ineffective. Consequently, the view is that members of the public should be treated as soft targets.[7]

Gustave Le Bon, the leading authority on the concept of panic, pointed to how, in the right circumstances, a group of individuals follows what he calls the "law of the mental unity of crowds".

Other contemporaries of Le Bon were critical of his approach, stressing that it rides roughshod, at least in part, over both individuality and people's potential to act in isolation.

Most people do not panic in an emergency. In a crowd, individuals generally display a remarkable capacity to organise and assist (Drury et al., 2009). In *L'entraide, l'autre loi de la jungle*, Servigne and Chapelle (2017: 85) point to several scientific studies that invalidate the notion that most people panic or turn to violence when a crisis unfolds.[8] On the contrary, they argue that, in a disaster situation, most members of the public behave in an orderly manner. "All the evidence points to the same conclusion: that, when disaster strikes, people keep their cool and cooperate spontaneously." Many authors, while falling short of questioning the existence and definition of this pattern of behaviour, have made the case that collective panic occurs only rarely in crisis situations, and only when a number of conditions are met simultaneously: 1) the group's structure has disintegrated, 2) there is no clear leadership, and 3) people are no longer acting in a mutually supportive way.

Violence, looting, indiscipline

In some quarters, there is a belief – rooted in the collective psyche and stoked by media sensationalism – that, when disaster strikes and people are "left without state control, they return to their primitive, barbaric and murderous instincts, with no care for the suffering of others" (Lecomte, 2012: 72). This pessimistic viewpoint can prompt policy decisions that are detrimental to the people affected by such disasters. One example of this process in action is the rescue operations report, a piece of crisis communication that seeks to mitigate the impact of the event and limit what information is available. Moreover, according to sociologist Lee (2002: 26): "The general public acts responsibly and with civility before, during and after a disaster. Senior decision-makers often use panic as justification to prevent the public obtaining information or accessing certain places, on the pretext that people cannot handle bad news", even when the facts are something altogether different. In a disaster situation, 75% of affected people react immediately in the right manner, while 25% do not (Lee, 2002). As soon as people feel sufficiently safe, their instinct is to try to rescue the victims. Governments and the media must take account of this sense of solidarity – driven by feelings of empathy, selflessness and a shared identity in the face of adversity (Crocq, 2007 – and give citizens a stronger role in crisis and risk prevention policy. According to Appéré (2006), "decision-makers should no longer view members of the public as an exogenous or secondary factor, but rather as standalone components of the system, whose reactions to risks and decisions – whether deemed rational or irrational – are vital to the success, or otherwise, of the chosen management strategy."

There is a widely held preconception, for instance, that people affected by a crisis are helpless and dependent on outside support. Yet this is simply not true. In fact, people often take the initiative and seek out members of their community, either in person or by making phone calls. These actions have two destabilising consequences: the roads become congested as people look for their loved ones, and telephone networks become saturated. The authorities therefore need to take steps to deal with these regularly observed patterns of behaviour.[9]

Patterns of behaviour that the emergency services consider orderly or appropriate

When members of the public behave in these ways, the authorities find it easier to carry out their work and restore social order. Examples including knowing and following instructions, and evacuating when ordered to do so.

When the situation is chaotic and organised emergency services are lacking, people tend to organise themselves (Solnit, 2009; Drury et al., 2009), acting in ways designed to achieve an acceptable degree of safety according to how they perceive the situation.

Examples of these patterns of behaviour abound. In an event context, lessons learned from the Manchester Arena bombing show how the people of the city and witnesses on the scene immediately rushed to help in different ways.[10]

Moreover, people often take on new roles or enhanced responsibilities to deal with the aftermath of a disaster, set up new organisational structures, or even use existing technologies in new ways (Drabek et al., 2002).

In this distinction between "orderly" and "destabilising" patterns of behaviour, there are plenty of myths and preconceptions (Glass, 2001; Auf der Heide, 2004) that can cause crisis management professionals to make erroneous judgement calls and interpret the way in which human beings behave in disaster situations in an overly pessimistic way. Despite numerous scientific studies and lessons learned from past incidents showing that people tend to pull together and help each other out when disaster strikes, affected members of the public are still largely omitted from operational proceedings. In addition, measures such as public warning systems often fail to take account of social and psychosocial factors. In 2018, imminent threat warnings were issued in various parts of France using the national warning signal (sirens) inherited from the Second World War. Yet in 1986, Drabek pointed out those non-specific warning systems such as sirens are known to be ineffective at helping the intended recipients take protective measures. The attack warning smartphone app, launched in 2015 as part of the national public warning and information system and subsequently abandoned in 2018, shows how there is often tension between political communication demands and operational reality.[11]

Further avenues of research in this field and likely changes in the French doctrine ahead of the 2024 Olympic Games

Past and current research

A number of research projects have been launched, both in France and Europe-wide, looking at what role the public plays and how to strengthen that role. Examples include a number of European disaster risk reduction projects such as such as PrepAge, Aware & Resilient, and ReCheck, which focus respectively on disaster preparedness among the elderly, improving preparedness, and building disaster resilience with the support of local communities. Further examples include H2020 projects such as the *PeP* project (community resilience and public crisis communication) and the POP-ALERT public warning project. In France, the academic council for strategic research SCOPANUM project looked at how to engage citizens in managing the aftermath of a nuclear accident via social media. The EURIDICE research consortium's CARTO-MSGU sub-project focused on dynamic mapping based on citizen-reported information. More recent examples include the French national research agency (ANR) MACIV project looking at how social media could be used to manage citizens and volunteers in crisis situations, and the ANR Com2SiCA project, which seeks to understand and simulate how people behave in disaster situations. In addition to the production of scientific and academic literature, civil society plays a particularly prominent role in furthering knowledge on civil security issues, particularly in France.[12] Civil society organisations produce and publish awareness-raising materials explaining how citizens can take risk and crisis management back into their own hands.[13]

Changes in France's doctrine

Making citizens a central feature of operational response: an idea that still faces resistance

In addition to reluctance among managers and decision-makers stemming from preconceptions about members of the public behaving "badly" in crisis situations, citizens have only a bit-part role to play in France's major risk management policy. Looking at both theory and practice, recent institutional reports and academic articles on France's major risk management policy highlight its many limitations.[14] They show that the policy fails to take account of a range of issues around vulnerabilities and major risk prevention (Padioleau, 2012). There is a clear desire to plan and build resilience with input from all stakeholders, but the same criticism comes up time and again (Gilbert, 2013; Decrop, 2014): in practice, national policy provides little room for local policy-makers, elected officials and citizens to collaborate and act together. Central government and its devolved authorities see this policy as a sovereign matter for the welfare state, dispossessing local politicians and citizens of any power over such matters. Prevention, planning and response are viewed through a technocratic, centralist prism, and risk prevention and emergency response plans are guided by a one-size-fits-all approach. The "public", meanwhile, is treated as the poor relation in public major risk management policy-making. In her thesis *Le riverain introuvable !*, Fournier (2010) shows how the public is sidelined in flood risk management policy. Yet three key lessons can be learned from the manner in which previous crises have been managed.[15],[16],[17]

First, because it takes time for organised emergency services to arrive on the scene, there is naturally a period of time when members of the public are left to fend for themselves. Second, while inappropriate reactions do cause casualties, people tend to behave in an orderly manner and pull together to help other victims (Rodriguez et al., 2006). And third, real-time digital channels are an effective way to get information to people and to mobilise the public when an event occurs (Sullivan & Vos, 2014).

French doctrine is therefore evolving in a way that gives the public greater capacity to cope with accidents and disasters, not least following the recent terrorist attacks.

Improving public training and information

The emergency services are better able to do their job if the people on the scene of an accident or incident adopt the right behaviour[18]. At present, around 30% of French people have completed a first-aid awareness or training course. This statistic stands in stark contrast to figures in other European countries, where around 80% of citizens have completed such a course.

The 2017 Pelloux-Faure report[19] recommends a series of measures to help France catch up with its neighbours and ensure that more than 80% of its citizens have completed first-aid training:

- To propose short training courses of two hours for free, named "Introductory first aid".
- To develop tax-deductible courses.
- To develop a law that will create the Lifeguard citizen statute in France.

In 2019, many different decisions named above, have taken place reinforcing the resilience of French populations. Ongoing efforts to better train and inform the public on this issue, with input from all stakeholders, are helping to improve safety and security at major events.

In addition, new information and communication technologies are opening up new opportunities for crisis management (Adrot, 2010). For instance, the use of social media[20] and mobile apps[21] in emergencies is helping to spark and spread solidarity initiatives. Yet the sheer diversity of such technologies makes it difficult to summarise the many solidarity initiatives emerging on social media, and raises questions about how they fit into institutional systems (Douvinet et al., 2017). In late May 2018, there was a change of strategy in France's national public warning and information system, with the government signing an agreement with companies like Facebook and Twitter to make more use of social medial. Future developments will, in all likelihood, see greater use of mobile technology to better warn and inform members of the public in an affected area.

Conclusion

The Olympic Games are political events *per se*, symbolic targets, the security of these events correspond to a primordial dimension of attribution conditions. The budget attributed to this area is consistently growing upwards (the cost of the security of the Olympic Games of London 2012 was five times the cost of the security of the Olympic Games of Barcelona 1992). In this point, we can ask ourselves a prospective question for the Tokyo Olympic Games in 2020: How would sports delegations and international spectators have reacted during the earthquake, tsunami and nuclear accident of March 2011? During the event or after it, would it have triggered an annulation of the holding of the Olympic Games?

This questioning takes the organisers into a crisis of rupture. To face this major challenge, the host countries must take into account the behaviours of populations in responding to catastrophic situations.

Tokyo 2020, Beijing 2022, Paris 2024, the local organising committees for the next Games should ask themselves about the reasons and methods (why and how?) for integrating behavioural reactions of populations (inhabitants/spectators/sports delegations) in their response to serious incidents.

Certainly, we talk about populations because the heterogeneity of groups of individuals (origins, ages, languages, knowledges, territories, level of discipline) need to have a specific and different approach in the integration of behavioural reactions. (Alexander & Sagramola, 2014)

In summary, the organising countries of the Olympic Games must integrate knowledge, return of operating experiences, and the scientific states of art from the last 50 years:

- Disaster planning does not go as planned
- Victims respond with collective resourcefulness
- The majority of lives will be saved by the public. We must stimulate mutual assistance to develop safety regarding Olympic Games.
- Panic and looting is rare
- Social factors to be considered in planning

Incorporating this thinking into preparedness planning and operational response will ensure that technology developments and doctrines better reflect the reality on the ground. Current and future research projects conducted by the Crisis Management Chair, designed in partnership with experts, civil society and industry, focus on rebuilding close ties between the emergency services and the public in civil security and national security crises. This operational-focused research will support social and technological innovation that will help to improve safety and security at major events.

Notes

1 Including GSG 9 in Germany, the EKO Cobra in Austria, and the GIGN in France, the elite Police Tactical Units of those countries.
2 Examples in France include the attacks near the Stade de France in November 2015 and on Promenade des Anglais in Nice in June 2016.
3 For the purpose of this chapter, the terms "disaster" and "crisis" are used to designate a sudden, catastrophic event, irrespective of its origin (natural or man-made), that severely disrupts the normal functioning of a community or society and causes loss of human life or damage to infrastructure, the economy or the environment, and where the society or community in question lacks the capacity to cope on its own. Examples include the AZF (Azote Fertilisant–Industrie) factory explosion, the Fukushima nuclear accident, and Hurricane Irma.
4 In particular via the international standard ISO 22319:2017 Guidelines for planning the involvement of spontaneous volunteers.
5 "From a reactive to proactive then people centered approach to disaster risk reduction" (UNDRR, 2015). This document makes a contribution to the risk and disaster culture and introduces some reflections and new challenges about people's participation in disaster reduction.
6 Presented without citing scientific sources, the figures contained in various communications reveal the following statistics: when a disaster happens, 12–25% of victims and other people involved react correctly, 75% are terrified, inhibited or numb, and 10–15% behave abnormally.
7 The term "soft target" is used in counter-terrorism discourse to refer to vulnerable people who are unable to defend themselves (as opposed to a "hard target").
8 These authors cite, for instance, Lecomte (2012: 32): "panic is often invoked after the fact to explain deaths as people are crushed by the crowd. Yet, in many cases, scientific research has shown that this was not the real cause" and Johnson (1987: 171–183): "When sudden disaster strikes, individuals – whether stressed or in a state of shock – first and foremost seek safety; they therefore have little inclination to turn violent".
9 Toll-free number, partnerships with social media, family reception centre, etc.
10 Offering victims somewhere to stay, providing free taxi rides, delivering emergency care, etc.
11 Senate Information Report no. 595 presented by Senator Jean-Pierre Vogel, "Warning and people's information system: An indispensible and neglected tool".
12 "Risques majeurs: Quelles participations civiles et citoyennes?" *Risques infos* newsletter no 31 (June 2013)
    "Face aux crises, courage, changeons! Confiance et solidarité: les conditions de réussite en gestion de crise". Fondation nationale Entreprise et Performance (FNEP) 162 pages, Réf. 9782110094780, September 2013.

"Analyse Intégré de la Résilience Territoriale Groupe de réflexion « Le citoyen au cœur de la résilience »" Report of the Commissariat Général au Développement Durable, December 2013.

13 *Je me protège en famille: Plan familial de mise en sûreté (PFMS)* Leaflet, Ministère de l'intérieur et Institut des Risques Majeurs, November 2010 – ISBN 978-2-11-128165-3.

The website Faire Face 72 (www.ff72.org) allows local authorities to create their own website to prepare the population for the critical 72 hours following a disaster. Project supported by the HCFDC.

14 *Les territoires face aux catastrophes naturelles: Quels outils pour prévenir les risques?* Study presented by A. Ferreti (2015) on behalf of the Délégation à la prospective et à l'évaluation des politiques publiques. Conseil économique, social et environnemental (CESE), 133p.

Audit of programme no 181 « Prévention des risques », conseil général de l'environnement et du développement durable. Report N°007240–01 May 2012. 212p.

Chaveau, E., et al. (2011) *Les risques majeurs et l'action publique* report of the Conseil d'analyse économique. La documentation Française Paris 2012.

"Xynthia: leçons d'une catastrophe". *Cybergeo: European Journal of Geography Environnement, Nature, Pays.*

15 Calvet F., Manable C. (2015). *Xynthia, cinq ans après: pour une véritable culture du risque dans les territoires.* Senate Report 92p, *Les territoires face aux catastrophes naturelles: Quels outils pour prévenir les risques?*

16 National Assembly Report No.3922 (2016) submitted on behalf of the government counter-terrorism measures inquiry committee, set up on 7 January 2015.

17 Huet, P., Martin, X., Prime, JL., Foin, P., Laurain, C., Cannard, P., *Retour d'expérience des crues de septembre 2002 dans les départements du Gard, de l'Hérault, du Vaucluse, des Bouches du Rhône, de l'Ardèche et de la Drôme. Rapport consolidé après phase contradictoire,* 546 p, 2003.

18 Gestes de premiers secours: une responsabilité citoyenne Note d'analyse 321 février 2013 Centre d'analyse stratégique.

19 Report by the preliminary task force on rolling out first-aid training to French citizens, submitted on 20 April 2017 to Mrs. Juliette Méadel, then-Minister of State reporting to the Prime Minister, with responsibility for victim support: http s://www.gouvernement.fr/sites/default/files/contenu/piece-jointe/2017/04/rapport_ de_la_mission_de_prefiguration_sur_la_generalisation_de_la_fromation_des_ gestes_qui_sauvent_-_20_avril_2017.pdf (last accessed 29 May, 2019).

20 Shih, Gerry. 2012. Over 20 million tweets sent as Sandy struck. Reuters. [Online] 2012. [Accessed September 3 2014.] http://www.reuters.com/article/2012/11/02/ us-storm-sandy-twitter-idUSBRE8A116020121102

21 For instance, there exist apps such as Qwidam, SAIP, SignAlert, Staying Alive, SismoCom, Alertecitoyens, and services provided by web companies such as the Ushahidi collaborative mapping service, the Facebook Safety Check button, and services like Google Public Alerts and Google Person Finder.

References

Alexander, D. & Sagramola, S. (2014). *Including People with Disabilities in Disaster Preparedness and Response.* Brussels: EUR-OPA. Retrieved from www.coe.int/europarisks

Adrot, A. (2010). Quel apport des technologies de l'information et de la communication (TIC) a l'improvisation organisationnelle durant la réponse à la crise? Unpublished PhD thesis. Université Paris Dauphine.

Appéré, G. (2006). Gestion des risques et informations exogènes. *Revue française de gestion,* 162, 63–76.

Auf Der Heide, E. (2004). Common misconceptions about disasters: Panic, the "Disaster Syndrome", and Looting. In O'Leary, M. (ed.), *The First 72 Hours: A Community Approach to Disaster Preparedness*, 340–380, Lincoln, Nebraska: iUniverse.

Barsky, L., Trainor, J., Torres, M. (2006). Disaster realities in the aftermath of Hurricane Katrina: Revisiting the looting myth, Quick response Report, no. 184, University of Delaware.

Crocq, L. (2007). *Traumatismes psychiques. Prise en charge psychologique des victimes.* Elsevier-Masson.

Crocq, L. (2013). *Les paniques collectives.* Paris: Odile Jacob.

Decrop, G. (2014). Temps de crise et temps ordinaire. Un itinéraire de recherche à côté de l'institution. *Communications*, 94, 31–46.

Dezecache, G. (2015). Human collective reactions to threat. *Wiley Interdisciplinary Reviews: Cognitive Science*, 6(3), 209–219.

Douvinet, J., Gisclard, B., Kouadio, J. S., Saint-Martin, C., Martin, G. (2017) Une place pour les technologies smartphones et les Réseaux Sociaux Numériques (RSN) dans les dispositifs institutionnels de l'alerte aux inondations en France? *Cybergeo: Revue européenne de géographie/European Journal of Geography*, Document 801, doi:10.4000/cybergeo.27875

Drabek, T. E. & McEntire, D. A. (2002). Emergent phenomena and multiorganizational coordination in disasters: Lessons from the research literature. *International Journal of Mass Emergencies and Disasters* 20, 197–224.

Drabek, T. E. (1986) *Human System Responses to Disaster: An Inventory of Sociological Findings.* New York: Springer-Verlag.

Drury, J., Cocking, C., Reicher, S. (2009). Everyone for themselves? A comparative study of crowd solidarity among emergency survivors. *British Journal of Social Psychology*, 48(3), 487–506.

Dynes, R. (2008). Review of mass panic and social attachment: The dynamics of human behavior. *Contemporary Sociology*, 37(2), 139.

Federal Emergency Management Agency (FEMA) (2011). A whole community approach to emergency management: Principles, themes, and pathways for action. Retrieved from https://www.fema.gov/blog/2012-01-04/whole-community-approach-emergency-management

Fournier, M. (2010). *Le riverain introuvable! La gestion du risqué inundation au défi d'une mise en perspective diachronique.* Doctoral thesis Université de Tour François Rabelais, UMR6173 CITERE, France.

Gilbert, C. (2013). Risque. In I. Casillo*et al.* (eds), *Dictionnaire critique et interdisciplinaire de la participation.* Paris: GIS Démocratie et Participation, Retrieved from http://www.dicopart.fr/en/dico/risque.

Glass, T. A. (2001). Understanding public response to disasters. *Public Health Reports*, 116 (Suppl. 2), 69–73.

Helsloot, I., Ruitenberg, A. (2004). Citizen response to disasters: A survey of literature and some practical implications. *Journal of Contingencies and Crisis Management*, 12, 98–111. doi:10.1111/j.0966-0879.2004.00440.x

Johnson, N.R. (1987). Panic and the breakdown of social order: Popular myth, social theory, empirical evidence. *Sociological Focus*, 20(3), 171–183.

Le Bon, G. (1895). *Psychologie des foules.* Paris: Alcan.

Lecomte, J. (2012). Face aux catastrophes mortelles, la solidarité plutôt que l'égoïsme. In Przuluski, V., Hallegate, S., *Gestion des risques naturels: Leçons de la tempête Xynthia.* Editions Quae.

Lee, C. (2002). Panic: Myth or reality? *Contexts*, 1(3), 21–26.

Lorenz, F., Schulze, D. K., Voss, M. (2017). Emerging citizen responses to disasters in Germany. Disaster myths as an impediment for a collaboration of unaffiliated responders and professional rescue forces. *Journal of Contingencies and Crisis Management*, 26(3), 358–367. doi:10.1111/1468-5973.12202

Moscovici, S. (2005). *L'âge des foules*. Paris: Fayard.

Oberije, N. (2007). Civil response after disasters: The use of civil engagement in disaster abatement. Netherlands Institute for Safety.

Padioleau, J. G. (2002). *Le réformisme pervers: le cas des sapeurs-pompiers*. Presses Universitaires de France-PUF.

Provitolo, D. (2005). Un exemple d'effets de dominos: la panique dans les catastrophes urbaines. *Cybergeo: Revue européenne de géographie/European Journal of Geography*, 328, doi:10.4000/cybergeo.2991

Provitolo, D.*et al.* (2015). Les comportements humains en situation de catastrophe: de l'observation à la modélisation conceptuelle et mathématique. *Cybergeo: Revue européenne de géographie/European Journal of Geography*.

Quarantelli, E. L. (1989). The North Research on the Arkansas Tornado: A fountainhead study, Preliminary Paper #136, Disaster Research Center, University of Delaware.

Rodriguez, H., Trainor, J., Quarantelli, E. L. (2006). Rising to the challenges of a catastrophe: The emergent and prosocial behavior following Hurricane Katrina. *Annals of the American Academy of Political and Social Science*, 604, 82–101.

Servigne, P., Chapelle, G. (2017). *L'entraide, l'autre loi de la jungle*. Paris: Edition Les liens qui libèrent. 384p.

Solnit, R. (2009). *A Paradise Built in Hell. The Extraordinary Communities that Arise in Disaster*. Viking.

Sullivan, H., Vos, M. (2014) Guest Editors' Introduction. Community resilience in crises: Technology and social media enablers. *Human Technology*, 10(2), 61–152.

Tierney, K. J., Goltz, J. D. (1998). Emergency response: Lessons learned from the Kobe Earthquake, http://www.udel.edu/drc/preliminary/260.pdf

Tucker, A., O'Brien, M. (2011). Volunteers and oil spills – A technical perspective. *International Oil Spill Conference Proceedings*, 1, abs273. American Petroleum Institute.

United Nations Office of Disaster Risk Reduction (2015). *Sendai Framework for Disaster Risk Reduction*. Retrieved from http://www.wcdrr.org/uploads/Sendai_Framework_for_Disaster_Risk_Reduction_2015-2030.pdf

Waldman, S., Yumagulova, L., Mackwani, Z., Benson, C., Stone, J. T. (2017). Canadian citizens volunteering in disasters: From emergence to networked governance. *Journal of Contingencies and Crisis Management*. 26(3), 394–402. doi:10.1111/1468-5973.12206

Wulff, K., Donato, D., Lurie, N. (2015). What is health resilience and how can we build it? *Annual Review of Public Health*, 36, 361–374.

9 The microbiological quality of the Seine River

Is it compatible with open water Olympic competitions?

Françoise Lucas, Bernard de Gouvello, Jean-Marie Mouchel, Laurent Moulin, Pierre Servais and Sébastien Wurtzer

Introduction

Open water swimming includes any event organized in lakes, rivers, reservoirs and oceans, but not in a swimming pool (Gerrard & Migliorini, 2016). Marathon swims and triathlons belong to this category and were recently integrated into the Olympic Games. The first triathlon with a 1500m swim took place in Sydney Harbor in 2000 and the first Marathon swim occurred in 2008. This 10km Marathon took place in Beijing in the Shunyi Olympic Rowing–Canoeing Park. During the following Olympic Games, the triathlon and Marathon swims were held at the Serpentine Lake in Hyde Park (London, 2012) and at Copacabana Beach (Rio de Janeiro, 2016). In 2020, the Odaiba Marine Park in Tokyo will host the open water swims and, for the 2024 Olympics in Paris, the Seine River is a potential venue.

Due to water pollution, swimming in open waters can present sanitary issues and cause gastroenteritis or diverse infections. Indeed, prior to the Rio de Janeiro Olympics, early concerns regarding the quality of the water were voiced since Copacabana Beach was polluted by rivers, sewage and storm drains (Staggemeier et al., 2017). The bay waters were impacted by pathogenic microorganisms, especially human viruses and toxigenic algal blooms (Fistarol et al., 2015). Local authorities and the organizing committees of previous Olympic and Paralympic Games have been concerned by the safety of the waterways used for the competitions. In order to improve the quality of surface waters, various mitigation strategies were deployed in both Athens and Rio de Janeiro (Hadjichristodoulou et al., 2006, Staggemeier et al., 2017).

In 2024, it has been proposed that the triathlon and Marathon swims occur, for the first time, in a river, near to the Trocadero in Paris. Surface waters in heavily urbanized waterways, such as the Seine River in the Paris conurbation, may harbor a range of waterborne pathogens of fecal origin. As a consequence, the organizing committee and the local authorities are taking measures to ensure a quality of water sufficient to meet the European bathing water directive (EU, 2006). However, even this quality of water may be insufficient since water-associated health complaints have been reported previously by individuals after swimming in waters that complied with state or local water quality requirements (e.g. Prüss, 1998; Sinclair et al., 2009; Papastergiou et al., 2012).

Here, we review the recent available data on the microbial quality of the Seine River in the summer, upstream from, and at the location of, the potential site for the 2024 Olympics. We provide estimations of the infectious risk associated with these surface waters on the basis of the concentrations of pathogens in the water and the mitigation actions that will be taken to improve the quality of the water.

Pathogens of concern: origin, routes of exposure and risks

Surface waters contain complex microbial communities among which pathogenic and non-pathogenic species occur. During trials, athletes are, thus, likely to encounter human viruses, pathogenic bacteria, protozoa, and toxin-producing microalgae or cyanobacteria (Medema et al., 1997).

Exposure routes

During a swim, the entire body, most importantly the face and the trunk, frequently are immersed and/or wet by spray. As a consequence, it is likely that some water will be swallowed, inhaled or come into contact with ears, nasal passages, mucous membranes, cuts or abrasions of the skin and swimmers could contract, possibly, an illness via these exposures (ACT, 2014).

Pathogens

Enteric pathogens (parasites, bacteria and viruses) are carried by fecal contaminations (WHO, 2003). These contaminations have human and animal origins (domestic, livestock and wildlife) and can be categorized as point sources (wastewater treatment plant effluents, combined sewer overflows) or non-point sources (runoff on contaminated surfaces, sediment resuspension, soil erosion). Pathogens associated with fecal contaminations include enterohaemoragic *E. coli*, *Salmonella*, *Shigella*, *Campylobacter*, *Vibrio cholerae*, enteric viruses (Noroviruses, Adenoviruses, Rotaviruses, enterovirus, Hepatitis virus, etc.) and protozoa (*Cryptosporidium*, *Giardia*). Rodents also may carry *Leptospirae in* their urine and contaminate the surface water (Morgan et al., 2002). Moreover, some autochthonous aquatic species can become opportunistic pathogens when in contact with a suitable host (e.g. non-tuberculosis mycobacteria, *Aeromonas*, *Pseudomonas*, *Plesiomonas*). Eutrophication of surface water may stimulate the proliferation of toxigenic cyanobacteria and *Dinophyceae*. More marginally, some other pathogens could potentially cause respiratory, cutaneous or nervous system illnesses (for instance *Naegleria fowlerii, Staphylococcus aureus,* Influenza virus and Papillomavirus).

Exposed swimmers may experience diverse disease symptoms such as skin rashes, conjunctivitis, sinus infection, ear infection, fever, diarrhea, vomiting (Craun et al., 2005; et al., 2015; Mannocci et al., 2016). *Cryptosporidium, Giardia, Campylobacter* species and enteric viruses are the major cause for contracting gastroenteritis in surface waters (Schijven & de Roda Husman, 2006; Sinclair et al., 2009). Among the 24 outbreaks associated with recreational activities in surface waters that were reported in 2009–2010 in the USA, 11 were attributed to cyanobacteria toxins, *Campylobacter jejuni, E coli* O157:H7, *Shigella sonnei, Cryptosporidium* spp, *Giardia intestinalis,* norovirus and avian schistosomes (Fewtrell & Kay, 2015). Adenovirus, human enterovirus and type A rotavirus were detected in several sites at venues used during the Rio de Janeiro Olympics (Staggemeier et al., 2017). In Copenhagen (Denmark), after a triathlon swim in the harbor waters, stool samples of several athletes were reported positive for *Campylobacter jejuni, Giardia lamblia* and/or diarrheagenic *E. coli* (Harder-Lauridsen et al., 2013). A few *Leptospira* outbreaks also have been reported after triathlon events (e.g. Morgan et al., 2002; Radl et al., 2011).

Risks

Prolonged exposure of triathletes during training and competition increases the risk of contracting a disease (British triathlon, 2008). Indeed, several outbreaks associated with swimming events, such as the triathlon, have been reported in the literature (e.g. Harder-Lauridsen et al., 2013; Parkkali et al., 2015; Hall et al., 2017). The risk of illness and the number of reported symptoms were directly correlated with the concentrations of pathogens in the water (Dwight et al., 2004). For instance after a 3.8 km open water swim in Copenhagen, 42% (2010) and 8% (2011) of the triathletes reported diseases (Harder-Lauridsen et al., 2013). Randomized, controlled studies which assessed the risks of infectious disease following bathing in recreational freshwaters showed that bathers had 0.4 to 27.7% more risk of contracting gastroenteritis as compared to non-bathers (Prüss, 1998; Wiedenmann et al., 2006).

The risk also is associated with several other factors which depend upon the swimmers and the pathogens (the time spent in the water, the time of head immersion, the volume of water swallowed, the immune system of the swimmer and the infectious dose of the pathogen) (Kay et al., 1994; Wiedenmann et al., 2006). Although Olympic participants could be considered to be in good health, intense and prolonged physical activity combined with intensive mental stress can lower the immunological defenses (Friman & Wesslen, 2000). During 15–40 minutes of swimming, 75% of the triathletes reported ingestion of surface water (Medema et al., 1997). Although the exact volume ingested is difficult to evaluate, previous studies on recreational swimmers reported volumes ranging from 10–34 ml per event for adults (Dufour et al., 2006; Schets et al., 2011). It is not always possible to evaluate the potential risk of infection based on the concentration of the pathogen in the water and the volume of water swallowed since the infectious doses are available in the literature for only some pathogens (e.g. Couch et al., 1969; Ward et al., 1986; Graham et al., 1987; Teunis et al., 1996; Teunis et al., 2008; Zambriski et al., 2013). However, enteric viruses have low infectious doses, since small numbers of viral particles are sufficient for 50% of the exposed population to contract gastroenteritis (e.g. Couch et al., 1969; Graham et al., 1987).

There exist only a few sound epidemiological studies on recreational bathing in the literature (e.g. Prüss, 1998; Wiedenmann et al., 2006). Cohort studies on swimmers are difficult to perform since swimming-related outbreaks may be missed easily due to unidentified sources or pathogens and due to the fact that gastroenteritis is mostly asymptomatic and rarely reported in disease surveillance systems. However, the epidemiological studies that are available have been used to develop guidelines and standards in order to limit the risks associated with swimming in marine and fresh waters (e.g. US EPA, 2012; EU, 2006).

What is the minimum quality of water required for swimming competitions in open waters?

The international federations for swimming (FINA, Fédération internationale de natation) and for triathlons (ITU, International Triathlon Union) have adopted the World Health Organization (WHO) minimum requirements for water quality (WHO, 2003). These standards also have been agreed to by the International Olympic Committee (IOC) Medical Commission. Also, race organizers and host committees remain obligated to apply the state and local safety rules and regulations at every FINA- and ITU-sanctioned event (Gerrard & Migliorini, 2016). Since 2010, the ITU has used the European community standards for bathing water quality (EU, 2006) and recommends organizing triathlons in waters with an "Excellent" quality (Migliorini, 2017). The WHO's guidelines (2003) suggest that water quality is best described by a combination of sanitary inspection and microbial water quality assessment using standardized procedures.

Water quality standards are based upon measurements of the concentrations of fecal indicator bacteria (FIB) such as *Escherichia coli* and intestinal enterococci (IE). Although based on the same epidemiological studies, the guidelines vary from one country to another (Table 9.1). Standards for the USA and Canada use the geometric means of the FIB concentrations, whereas EU and New Zealand regulations rely on the 95–90th percentiles of the FIB concentrations (Table 9.1). The swimming associated gastroenteritis risk is 0.8% per event in the USA, 1–2% in Canada, and 5–8% in the EU regulations (Coffey et al., 2015). A 95th percentile >500 IE/100 mL indicates an average probability of more than 10 cases of gastroenteritis in every 100 exposures and the acute febrile respiratory illness rate would be greater than 1 in 25 exposures (WHO, 2003).

Water quality tests (pH, FIB, cyanobacteria, eventually pathogens) should be conducted prior to determining the course site (at least 15 months before the first competition date). Subsequently, quality tests need

Table 9.1 Water quality standards established for *E. coli* in recreational freshwaters

Region	Guideline value (*E. coli*/100 mL)	References
United States	[a]Geometric mean concentration ≤126	US EPA (2012)
	[b]Single sample maximum concentration 235	
European Union	[c]<500 (excellent)	EU (2006)
	[c]<1000 (good)	
	[d]<900 (sufficient)	
Canada	Geometric mean concentration 200	Health Canada (2012)
	Single sample maximal concentration 400	*Cryptosporidium parvum*
New-Zealand	[d]A < 130 (very good)	New Zealand Ministry for the Environment (2003)
	[d]B 131–260 (good)	
	[d]C 261–550 (fair)	
	[d]D >550 (poor)	

[a] 0% violation rate
[b] <10;5% violation rate
[c] based upon 95th percentile evaluation
[d] based upon 90th-percentile evaluation

to be performed at the same period as the event, one year prior, two months and seven days before the competition (Mirioglini, 2017). Samples should be collected, at a minimum, from three different locations on the swimming course, since spatial variations in water quality are largely determined by the hydrodynamic characteristics of the water body, confluences and effluent discharges (WMO, 2013).

Cohort studies have shown a positive correlation between the densities of IE and the risk of contracting gastroenteritis (Kay et al., 1994; van Asperen et al., 1998). However, these studies also have demonstrated that the current standards may be insufficient to protect bathers (Kay et al., 1994; van Asperen et al., 1998; Wiedenmann et al., 2006). A cohort study of bathers and non-bathers in Greek coastal waters with excellent quality, according to the EU guidelines, showed that bathers have a significantly higher risk of symptoms related to gastrointestinal infections, respiratory infections, eye and ear infections as compared to non-bathers (Papastergiou et al., 2012). As a consequence, it should be kept in mind that although these regulations aim at limiting the sanitary risk, they are not designed to reach a zero level of risk.

What is the current microbiological quality of the Seine River in the summer?

Bathing has been prohibited since 1923 in the Seine River in Paris, however swimming is occasionally practiced (e.g. "Triathlon de Paris" or the "Traversée de Paris à la nage"). The City of Paris has monitored the microbiological quality of the surface waters for several years by collecting samples at the locations of several bridges including the Ièna Bridge which is close to the location of the future Olympic venue in 2024 (Figure 9.1).

We used this database for the summer periods (June to September) of 2016 and 2017 to evaluate the quality of the potential Olympic waterways. The 90th percentiles of the concentrations of *E. coli* and IE were calculated according to the EU bathing directive and compared to the guidelines (EU, 2006; Table 9.2).

Although the *E. coli* concentrations are quite low at the Iéna bridge as compared to the other sampling sites (Figure 9.2), all of the 90th percentile values are above the threshold 900 *E. coli*/100 mL (Figure 9.2). For IE, the results are similar with 90th percentiles values of 1369 IE/100 mL. If we focus only on July and August, which correspond to the months of the 2024 Olympics, the results are similar. The 90th percentile values reach 6483 *E. coli*/100 mL, and 1146 IE/100 mL. During dry weather periods, FIB concentrations may display values below the "sufficient quality" requirements at the Iéna bridge, however these concern only 44% of the sampled dates. Only 25% of the samples had FIB concentrations below the "very good" guidelines

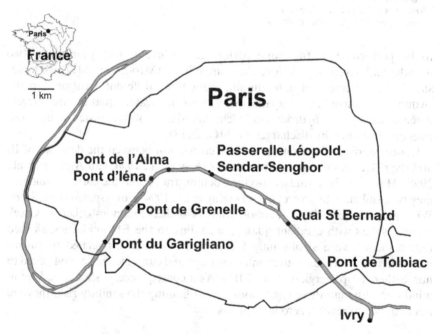

Figure 9.1 Location of the sampling points (circled dots) in Paris (Quai St Bernard, Passerelle Léopold-Sédar-Senghor, and Alma, Iéna, Grenelle, Garigliano and Tolbiac Bridges)
Modified from http://www.glz.com

Table 9.2 European bathing guidelines for inland waters (source : EU, 2006)

Class of quality	Excellent	Good	Sufficient
Intestinal enterococci (N/100 mL)	200[a]	400[a]	330[b]
Escherichia coli (N/100 mL)	500[a]	1000[a]	900[b]

[b] based on 90th-percentile evaluation

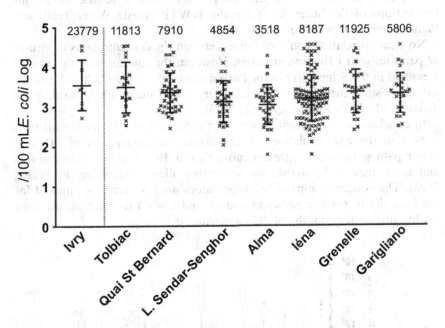

Figure 9.2 Escherichia coli concentrations in the Seine River in the Paris area during the summers of 2016 and 2017 at the different sampling points. The numbers represent the 90th percentile values (*E. coli*/100 mL)

during dry weather. The water quality was, thus, insufficient for bathing activities at the Iéna bridge during the summers of 2016 and 2017.

Major pathogens have been monitored also in the Seine River for the last ten years by Eau de Paris. The Seine River is impacted by parasitic pathogens, and more specifically by *Giardia* (mean concentration of 60 cysts/10L, with almost 100% positive samples), and *Cryptosporidium* (about 5 oocystes/10L and 50% positive samples) (Mons et al., 2009). The origin of the parasitic pathogens is mostly from diffuse pollution and probably linked to agricultural practices in the upstream watershed (Mons et al., 2009). Viruses also were monitored in the surface waters using real time PCR (Polymerase Chain Reaction), with adequate controls and an intercalating agent to detect infectious non-defective particles (Prevost et al., 2015). Four major virus families are present in the Seine River – Noroviruses GI and GII, Adenoviruses and Rotaviruses with average concentrations of about 1000 genomes units/L (Figure 9.3). Other families are present in lower frequencies or concentrations (Prevost et al., 2015). Almost 100% of the samples were positive in the water collected at Ivry-sur-Seine. In comparison, the water of the Bay of Rio de Janeiro was also contaminated with 10^3 to 10^9 viral genome units/L, with 95,9% of positive samples. Major contributors to the viral contaminations of the Seine River are the WWTP (Waste Water Treatment Plant) effluents (Prevost et al. 2015).

No clear correlation could be found between the concentrations of viruses or parasites with FIB concentrations. However, the concentrations of viruses measured in the Seine River in the Paris area could represent a health risk for swimmers since their infective dose is very low (Couch, 1969; Ward, 1986; Teunis et al., 2008; Zambriski et al., 2013).

In conclusion, the current quality of the Seine River is insufficient with respect to the EU regulations. The measured concentrations of FIB and major pathogens could represent more than a 10% risk for gastroenteritis and more than a 3.9% risk for respiratory illness (according to WHO, 2003). The concentrations of fecal indicators need to decrease ninefold for the Iéna site to reach a sufficient quality and 20-fold to reach an excellent quality during the months of July and August.

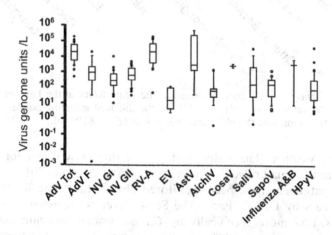

Figure 9.3 Concentrations of non-defective viruses (genome units/L) in positive water samples collected at Ivry-sur-Seine just upstream of the confluence of the Seine/Marne rivers

ADV tot: Adenovirus total; AdV F: Adenovirus F; NV GI: Norovirus group I; NV GII: Norovirus group II; RV-A: Rotavirus A; EV: Enterovirus; ASTV: Astrovirus; AichiV: Aichivirus; CosaV: Cosavirus; SaliV: Salivirus; SapoV: Sapovirus; HPyV: Papillomavirus

How to comply with the guidelines?

Over the past 50 years, considerable expenditures have been devoted to improving the sewer systems and the treatment of wastewater in all developed nations. These efforts have resulted in a clear improvement in the quality of the surface waters. However, in spite of all these efforts, the quality of Olympic venues are not always up to the standards. For instance, in 2017, the concentration of *E. coli* at the future venue of the 2020 Tokyo Games was 20 times higher than the accepted limit (Tokyo2020, 2018). The same concern arises for the 2024 Olympic Games. Although the quality of the Seine River upstream from Paris has considerably improved since the late 1980s (Figure 9.4), the quality is still not sufficient in downtown Paris. This poor quality could be related to residual microbial loadings from sewerage systems after rainfall events, improper cross-connections to the sewerage system and/or absence of disinfection in wastewater treatment plants.

As a consequence, for previous Olympic Games, additional mitigation measures were taken in order to comply with the international water quality standards (Hadjichristodoulou et al., 2006; Staggemeier et al., 2017). For the 2020 Olympics, triple layer screens will be used to filter the water in the Odaiba Marine Park (Tokyo2020, 2018).

Improving the quality of surface waters can be achieved by reducing the pollution at three levels: 1) removal of direct point source pollutions, 2) decrease of intermittent pollution, 3) decrease of catchment pollution (WHO, 2003). To improve the quality of the Seine River water in Paris to a level compatible with bathing activities, a plan of action has been established for the period 2016–2023. This plan aims to strengthen wastewater treatment plants, improve wastewater collection, reduce storm water effluents and suppress any direct discharge from boats.

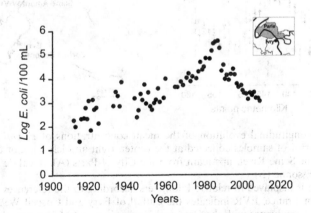

Figure 9.4 Evolution of the concentration of *E. coli* in the Seine River from the beginning of the 1900s to the present period (data from Eau de Paris) at Ivry-sur-Seine (Val de Marne) upstream of Paris

Direct point source pollution abatement

Upstream from Paris, several point sources have been identified: three waste-water treatment plants (Corbeil-Essonnes, Evry, and Seine Amont at Valenton), three tributaries (the Marne, Orge and Yerres Rivers), and several separate sewer outfalls with cross-connections. The main tributary is the Marne River. At the confluence with the Seine River (kilometric point 163, Figure 9.5), the quality of the Marne River is fair, with 445±282 *E. coli*/100 mL and 97±92 IE/100 mL, (n=39, June to September 2017 at Alfortville, data from the Syndicat Marne Vive). Figure 9.5 shows the impact of the wastewater treatment plant Seine Amont (Valenton, Val de Marne), the main sewer Fresnes-Choisy outfall and the Orge River. The results were obtained during dry weather during a single campaign in the summer of 2017 (Mouchel et al., 2018). To improve the Seine quality upstream from the Iéna bridge, one of the mitigation strategies will be to equip the WWTPs Seine Amont (Valenton) and Marne Aval (Noisy-le-Grand, Val de Marne) with tertiary disinfection treatments. There are 380,000 sewer connections upstream from the future Olympic waterways (upstream from the Iéna bridge), among which about 10% have inappropriate connections. Urban watersheds to be treated in priority have been identified by a working group involving the operational actors and local authorities. Actions should start beginning in 2018 to identify the non-compliant connections and fix them.

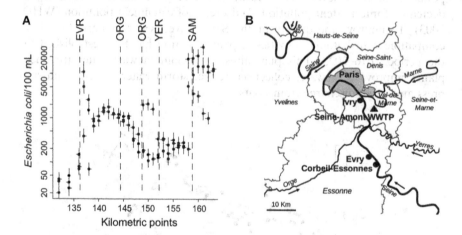

Figure 9.5 Longitudinal evolution of the mean concentrations of *E. coli* (±standard error of samples collected at the center, right and left bank of the river) in the Seine River, upstream from the City of Paris (A) in Val de Marne and Essonne (B)

The distance is displayed in relative kilometers according to the references of the Voie Navigable for France. EVR indicates the outfall of Evry and Corbeil WWTPs, ORG and YER the confluence with the Orge and Yerres rivers, SAM indicates the outfall of Seine Amont WWTP

Adapted from Mouchel et al., 2018 and Spedona (http://www.gnu.org/copyleft/fdl.htm l)

Intermittent pollution

Event driven pollution can seriously impair the quality of surface water for short periods. Summer campaigns on the Marne River in 2015 showed that the quality of the surface water was mainly impacted by the rainfall on the eve of the sampling and not by rainfall three days prior to the sampling (Lucas & Servais, 2016). To limit the discharge of polluted effluents into the Seine and Marne Rivers during storm events, the deployment of best management practices (BMPs) of stormwater will be reinforced in Ile de France. A reduction of about 5% of the impervious surfaces connected to the sewerage system (600 ha) seems sufficient to improve the quality of the Seine surface water (Safege, Hydratec & Prolog, 2017). Different techniques can be used including porous pavements, vegetated drainage swales, filter strips or rain gardens. They are designed to reduce stormwater volume, peak flows and/or nonpoint source pollution. Four watersheds are being tested to access their land cover and to plan the implementation of BMPs. In addition, three water storage structures will be built to improve the management of polluting storm sewers during heavy rains.

Besides rain runoff, wastewater discharges from commercial and private boats constitute a non-negligible source of pollution. Boats owners have two years to comply with an obligation to connect their sewage tanks to a sewer system. Equipment of harbors with collection systems connected to the sewers is in progress.

Watershed

Coordination and prioritization of the mitigation actions at the scale of the watershed are being engaged in Ile de France. Working groups were constituted in 2016 and regular debriefings are held to assess the advancement of the projects and to plan the course of actions for the Seine and the Marne Rivers. Such an undertaking requires cooperation among multiple actors and extensive financing. Several monitoring campaigns have been conducted during the summer of 2017 on the Seine and the Marne Rivers and additional campaigns are going to be carried on each summer. Routine monitoring of the water quality in Paris will be reinforced during the summer period. This monitoring program will provide an evaluation of the impact of the different mitigation actions from 2018 to 2023.

Conclusion

Concerns about the microbial quality of open waters arose during the preparations for previous Olympic and Paralympic competitions and are valid for future competitions. Considering the concentrations of FIB, the quality of the Seine River in Paris is currently not suitable for bathing activities according to EU regulations and there is a risk of gastroenteritis for swimmers. Moreover, the presence of human pathogens (viruses and gastro-intestinal parasites) supports this conclusion and highlights the connection between both approaches.

Mitigation strategies are currently deployed all over the Ile de France in order to improve the quality of the surface waters in the Seine and Marne Rivers. These efforts will be an important legacy of the Olympic Games to the Paris area which will allow the planning of future permanent swimming sites in downtown Paris.

To monitor the impact of these mitigation actions, FIB should not be the sole parameter to be measured and pathogens also should be studied. Indeed, there is a poor correlation between the FIB and the pathogens' concentrations. As a consequence, a body of water that complies with the EU regulation may still carry high levels of pathogens. This finding shows the importance of new research studies which take into account the direct risks linked to human pathogens and, thus, overcome the limitation of indicators. In the Paris area, such research projects are included in two interdisciplinary research programs: Observatoire des Polluants Urbains (OPUR) and PIREN-Seine. Together with the Zone Atelier Seine, these programs offer the possibility of long term studies of the Seine River which are clearly needed in order to monitor the long term evolution of the quality of the river.

Temporal and spatial variations of FIB and pathogen concentrations are also crucial points that need to be studied in detail using hydrodynamic models and high resolution sampling. Approaches that combine modeling, experimentation and *in situ* monitoring could help to improve the compre-hension of FIB and pathogen dynamics. Such studies are taking place all over the world in different cities in order to promote swimming in urban waterways both for sport and recreational activities.

Acknowledgments

We are grateful to the City of Paris and the Syndicat Marne Vive for granting their approval to use their data. We thank all the local authorities and stake-holder members of the Working Group "Qualité de l'eau et baignade" man-aged by the City of Paris for providing useful insights. We are grateful to Lawrence Ackerbeck, who kindly performed a proofreading and a linguistic revision of the chapter.

References

ACT (2014). *ACT Guidelines for Recreational Water Quality.* ACT Government, Environment Protection Authority, Health Protection Service, HPS-00–0434.

British Triathlon (2008). *Open Water Swimming Safety Guide for Multi-Sport Events.* http://www.triandenter.com/wp-content/uploads/2010/02/British-Triathlon-Open-Water-Swimming-Safety-Guidelines-08.pdf (accessed 02. 01. 2019).

Coffey, R., Benham, B., Kline, K., Wolfe, M. L., & Cummins, E. (2015). Potential microbial load reductions required to meet existing freshwater recreational water quality standards for a selection of mid-century environmental change scenarios. *Environmental Processes*, 2(4), 609–629.

Couch, R. B., Knight, V., DouglasJr, R. G., Black, B. H., & Hamory, S. H. (1969). The minimal infectious dose of adenovirus type 4: The case for natural transmission by viral aerosol. *Transactions of the American Clinical Climatological Association*, 80, 205–211.

Craun, G. F., Calderon, R. L., & Craun, M. (2005). Outbreaks associated with recreational water in the United States. *International Journal of Environmental Health Research*, 15(4), 243–262.

Dufour, A. P., Evans, O., Behymer, T. D., & Cantú, R. (2006). Water ingestion during swimming activities in a pool: A pilot study. *Journal of Water and Health*, 4(4), 425–430

Dwight, R. H., Baker, D. B., Semenza, J. C., & Olson, B. H. (2004). Health effects associated with recreational coastal water use: Urban versus rural California. *American Journal of Public Health*, 94, 565–567.

EU (2006). *Directive 2006/7/EC of the European Parliament and of the Council of 15 February 2006 concerning the management of bathing water quality and repealing Directive 76/160/EEC as amended by Regulation 596/2009/EC.*

Fewtrell, L., & Kay, D. (2015). Recreational water and infection: A review of recent findings. *Current Environmental Health Reports*, 2(1), 85–94.

Fistarol, G. O., Coutinho, F. H., Moreira, A. P. B., Venas, T., Cánovas, A., de Paula Jr., S. E. M., Coutinho, R., de Moura, R. L., Valentin, J. L., Tenenbaum, D. R., Paranhos, R., do Valle, R. A. B., Vicente, A. C. P., Filho, G. M. A., Pereira, R. C., Kruger, R., Rezende, C. E., Thompson, C. C., Salomon, P. S., & Thompson, F. L. (2015). Environmental and sanitary conditions of Guanabara Bay, Rio de Janeiro. *Frontiers in Microbiology*, 6, 1232.

Friman, G., & Wesslen, L. (2000). Infections and exercise in high-performance athletes. *Immunology and Cell Biology*, 78, 510–522.

Gerrard, D., & Migliorini, S. (2016). Testing the waters: Highlighting the safety of open water swimmers. *ASPETAR* 5, 58–63.

Graham, D. Y., Dufour, G. R., & Estes, M. K. (1987). Minimal infective dose of rotavirus. *Archives of Virology* 92(3–4), 261–271.

Hadjichristodoulou, C., Mouchtouri, V., Vousoureli, A., Konstantinidis, A., Petrikos, P., Velonakis, E., Boufa, P., & Kremastinou, J. (2006). Waterborne diseases prevention: Evaluation of inspection scoring system for water sites according to water microbiological tests during the Athens 2004 pre-Olympic and Olympic period. *Journal of Epidemiology and Community Health*, 60(10), 829–835.

Hall, V., Taye, A., Walsh, B., & Maguire, H. (2017). A large outbreak of gastrointestinal illness at an open-water swimming event in the River Thames, London. *Epidemiology & Infection*, 145, 1246–1255.

Harder-Lauridsen, N. M., Kuhn, K. G., Erichsen, A. C., Mølbak, K., & Ethelberg, S. (2013). Gastrointestinal illness among triathletes swimming in non-polluted versus polluted seawater affected by heavy rainfall, Denmark, 2010–2011. *PLoS ONE*, 8(11), e78371.

Health Canada (2012). *Guidelines for Canadian Recreational Water Quality*, 3rd edn. Ottawa, Minister of Health.

Kay, D., Fleisher, J. M., Salmon, R. L., Jones, F., Weyer, M. D., Godfree, A. F., et al. (1994). Predicting likelihood of gastroenteritis from sea bathing: Results from randomized exposure. *The Lancet*, 344(8927), 905–909.

Lucas, F. S., & Servais, P. (2016). *Etude de la qualité bactériologique de la zone aval de la Marne*. Rapport d'étude. Saint-Maur: Syndicat Marne Vive

Mannocci, A., La Torre, G., Spagnoli, A., Solimini, A. G., Palazzo, C., & De Giusti, M. (2016). Is swimming in recreational water associated with the occurrence of respiratory illness? A systematic review and meta-analysis. *Journal of Water Health*, 14(4), 590–599.

Medema, G. J., van Asperen, I. A., & Havelaar, A. H. (1997). Assessment of the exposure of swimmers to microbiological contaminants in fresh waters. *Water Science and Technology*, 35(11–12), 157–163.

Migliorini, S. (2017). ITU triathlon water quality statement. ITU Medical Committee Report. https://www.triathlon.org/uploads/docs/Triathlon_Water_Quality_Statement.pdf (accessed 02. 01. 2019).

Mons, C., Dumètre, A., Gosselin, S., Galliot, C., & Moulin, L. (2009). Monitoring of Cryptosporidium and Giardia river contamination in Paris area. *Water Research*, 43(1), 211–217.

Morgan, J., Bornstein, S. L., Karpati, A. M., Bruce, M., Bolin, C. A., Austin, C. C., Woods, C. W., Lingappa, J., Langkop, C., Davis, B., Graham, D. R., Proctor, M., Ashford, D. A., Bajani, M., Bragg, S. L., Shutt, K., Perkins, B. A., & Tappero, J. W., for the Leptospirosis Working Group (2002). Outbreak of Leptospirosis among triathlon participants and community residents in Springfield, Illinois, 1998. *Clinical Infectious Diseases*, 34(12), 1593–1599.

Mouchel, J. M., Colina-Moreno, I., Kasmi, N. (2018). *Évaluation des teneurs en bactéries indicatrices fécales en Seine dans l'agglomération parisienne par temps sec*. Rapport final. Paris: Ville de Paris.

New Zealand Ministry for the Environment (2002). *Microbiological Water Quality Guidelines for Marine and Freshwater Recreational Areas*. Manatu Mo Te Taiao, Wellington: Ministry for the Environment.

Papastergiou, P., Mouchtouri, V., Pinaka, O., Katsiaflaka, A., Rachiotis, G., & Hadjichristodoulou, C. (2012). Elevated bathing-associated disease risks despite certified water quality: A cohort study. *International Journal of Environmental Research and Public Health*, 9(5), 1548–1565.

Parkkali, S., Joosten, R., Fanoy, E., Pijnacker, R., van Beek, J., Brandwagt, D., & van Pelt, W. (2015). Outbreak of diarrhoea among participants of a triathlon and a duathlon on 12 July 2015 in Utrecht, the Netherlands. *Epidemiology & Infection*, 145(10), 2176–2184.

Prevost, B., Lucas, F.S., Goncalves, A., Richard, F., Moulin, L., & Wurtzer, S. (2015). Large scale survey of enteric viruses in river and waste water underlines the health status of the local population. *Environment International*, 79, 42–50.

Prüss, A. (1998) Review of epidemiological studies on health effects from exposure to recreational water. *International Journal of Epidemiology*, 27, 1–9.

Radl, C., Müller, M., Revilla-Fernandez, S., Karner-Zuser, S., de Martin, A., Schauer, U., Karner, F., Stanek, G., Balcke, P., Hallas, A., Frank, H., Fürnschlief, A., Erhart, F., Allerberger, F. (2011). Outbreak of leptospirosis among triathlon participants in Langau, Austria, 2010. *Wiener Klinische Wochenschrift*, 123, 751–755.

Safege, Hydratec, & Prolog (2017). *Mise à jour du SDA du SIAAP pour l'atteinte de l'objectif baignabilité en Seine et en Marne: Hypothèses de simulation de Prose*. Rapport d'étude, Syndicat Intercommunal d'Aménagement de l'Agglomération Parisienne.

Schets, F. M., Schijven, J. F., & de Roda Husman, A. M. (2011). Exposure assessment for swimmers in swimming waters and swimming pools. *Water Research*, 45(7), 2392–2400.

Schijven, J., & de Roda Husman, A. M. (2006). A survey of diving behavior and accidental water ingestion among Dutch occupational and sport divers to assess the risk of infection with waterborne pathogenic microorganisms. *Environmental Health Perspectives*, 114, 712–717.

Schijven, J., Derx, J., de Roda Husman, A. M., Blaschke, A. P., & Farnleitner, A. H. (2015). QMRAcatch: Microbial quality simulation of water resources including infection risk assessment. *Journal of Environmental Quality*, 44(5), 1491–1502.

Sinclair, R. G., Jones, E. L., & Gerba, C. P. (2009). Viruses in recreational water-borne disease outbreaks: A review. *Journal of Applied Microbiology*, 107, 1769–1780.

Staggemeier, R., Heck, T. M., Demoliner, M., Ritzel, R. G., Röhnelt, N. M., Girardi, V., Venker, C. A., & Spilki, F. R. (2017). Enteric viruses and adenovirus diversity in waters from 2016 Olympic venues. *Science of the Total Environment*, 586, 304–312.

Teunis, P. F., Moe, C. L., Liu, P., Miller, S. E., Lindesmith, L., Baric, R. S., Le Pendu, J., & Calderon, R. L. (2008). Norwalk virus: How infectious is it? *Journal of Medical Virology*, 80(8), 1468–1476.

Teunis, P. F. M., van der Heijden, O. G., van der Giessen, J. W. B., & Havelaar, A. H. (1996). *The Dose–Response Relation in Human Volunteers for Gastrointestinal Pathogens*. RIVM Report 284550002. Bilthoven, The Netherlands: RIVM.

Tokyo2020 (2018). *Odaiba Marine Park Water Test Results Published*. https://tokyo2020.org/en/news/notice/20181005-02.html (accessed 02. 01. 2019).

US EPA (2012). *Recreational Water Quality Criteria*. Washington DC, United States: Environmental Protection Agency, Office of Water. http://water.epa.gov/scitech/swguidance/standards/criteria/health/recreation/upload/RWQC2012.pdf (accessed 02. 01. 2019).

van Asperen, I. A., Medema, G., Borgdorff, M. W., Sprenger, M. J., & Havelaar, A. H. (1998) Risk of gastroenteritis among triathletes in relation to faecal pollution of fresh waters. *International Journal of Epidemiology*, 27(2), 309–315.

Ward, R. L., Bernstein, D.I., Young, E. C., Sherwood, J. R., Knowlton, D. R., & Schiff, G. M. (1986). Human rotavirus studies in volunteers: determination of infectious dose and serological response to infection. *Journal of Infectious Diseases*, 154(5), 871–880.

WHO (2003). *Guidelines for Safe Recreational Water Environments. Volume 1, Coastal and Fresh Waters*. Geneva, Switzerland: World Health Organization.

Wiedenmann, A., Krüger, P., Dietz, K., López-Pila, J. M., Szewzyk, R., & Botzenhart, K. (2006). A randomized controlled trial assessing infectious disease risks from bathing in fresh recreational waters in relation to the concentration of Escherichia coli, intestinal enterococci, Clostridium perfringens, and somatic coliphages. *Environmental Health Perspectives*, 114, 228–236.

WMO (2013). *Planning of Water Quality Monitoring Systems*. Technical report series N° 3. Geneva: World Meteorological Organization, WMO-N°1113.

Zambriski, J. A., Nydam, D. V., Wilcox, Z. J., BowanD. D., Mohammed, H. O., & Liotta, J. L. (2013). Cryptosporidium parvum: Determination of ID_{50} and the dose-response relationship in experimentally challenged dairy calves. *Veterinary Parasitology*, 197(1–2), 104–112.

10 Paris 2024 Olympic/Para-Olympic Games and air quality

Gilles Foret, Matthias Beekmann, Olivier Ramalho, Martin Koning, Martial Haeffelin, Etienne de Vanssay, Rachel Nadif, Isabella Annesi-Maesano, Pietro Bernardara and Jean-David Bernard

Introduction

Olympic and Para-Olympic Games (OPG) draw the world's attention to a specific region and on its environmental situation. Since 1992, "Sport for sustainable development" is published in the framework of the agenda 21 movement which also takes into account air quality. Hence, air quality is of importance in the bidding process and for the image of organizing countries and cities, which can impact tourism. Poor air quality also presents a health issue for athletes and their staff and can affect their performance (McKenzie and Boulet, 2008). Exposure to pollution during OPG is also an acute question for local inhabitants and tourists, especially due to the huge increase in transport demand during the event (Currie and Shalaby, 2012; Kassens-Noor, 2013).

In most cases, OPG are held in major urban centers where population density is high (Los Angeles, Athens, Atlanta, London, Rio, Beijing and Tokyo). Therefore, pollutant emissions associated with human activities in crowded areas are intense and pollution levels can be very high. In these big cities, main air quality issues are associated with ozone (O_3) and airborne particles (and their precursors). These pollutants have the most important harmful effects on human health (REVIHAAP, 2013) with particulate matter and outdoor air pollution classified as carcinogenic to humans by the International Agency for Research on Cancer (2013). As a consequence, air pollution represents a significant socio-economic cost for the society particularly in France considering both outdoor (Husson and Aïchi, 2015) and indoor exposure (Boulanger et al., 2017). Moreover, it should be noted that weather/meteorology is playing a key role in the buildup of pollution and the occurrence of pollution peaks. Since OPG 2024 takes place during the summer, anticyclonic situations associated with low winds, clear sky, and weak precipitations consequently favor pollutant accumulation and enhanced photochemistry driven by solar radiation. The higher incidence of heat waves in summer could also significantly worsen the overall air pollution.

The Qi^2 (for "Qualité de l'air, Impacts sanitaires, Innovations technologiques et politiques") research network has planned to take advantage of the 2024 OPG to initiate research actions and projects around the air quality key questions. This research network is supported and funded by the Île-De-France region (IDF) in the framework of its DIM (Domaine d'intérêt majeur) policy that aims at developing top research networks in the Paris region. The network is focused on air quality related research with a transdisciplinary approach including atmospheric chemistry and physics, health impacts, transportation sciences, urban planning, economics, and sociology. Another strong point of the network is the inter-sectoral approach involving academics, operational actors, agencies business partners and local authorities.

This chapter describes the problem of air quality during Olympic Games in the first section, the state of atmospheric pollution in the Paris area in the next section, and then the final section describes the research plan conceived by the Qi^2 network for OPG 2024.

Air quality and past Olympic Games

In the past, air quality has already been directly or indirectly a concern for OPG organizers: Indirectly with the objectives to reduce traffic congestion and to facilitate "clean" mobilities during the event (Los Angeles, Seoul, Barcelona, and Atlanta), in particular through an acceleration of investments in public transport facilities (Currie and Shalaby, 2012; Kassens-Noor, 2013); directly by developing programs specifically tailored to tackle air quality issues (Sydney, Athens, and Beijing).

A particularly striking example is the case of the 2008 OPG in China, even if institutional features clearly limit results' transferability. There was a lot of concern about Beijing's air quality and it was one of the main concerns of the OPG allocation committee during the bidding process (He et al., 2016). As illustrated in Figure 10.1 (that shows annual mean concentrations for particles with diameter less than 2.5 μm), Beijing pollution levels were among the highest in the world (see Figure 10.1) and both national and local authorities were pushed to propose solutions to improve air quality. Since pollutant concentrations in air are largely driven by emissions related to anthropogenic activities, authorities chose to impose drastic reductions on several of these sources. As industry and energy production can be highly polluting activities, efforts were made to close factories (at least during the event) and impose new furnaces and desulfurization equipment for coal combustion. In addition, emission standards were set up for private vehicles, as well as stringent traffic control and reduction (Zhang et al., 2016) and massive investments in public transport infrastructures (Currie and Shalaby, 2012). This set of actions proved partly successful in reducing air pollution during the event (Caie and Xie, 2011; Chen et al., 2013; Zhang et al., 2016; He et al., 2016; Ma and He, 2016). However, meteorological conditions also played a favorable role in reducing concentrations during the Beijing OPG (Wang et al., 2009).

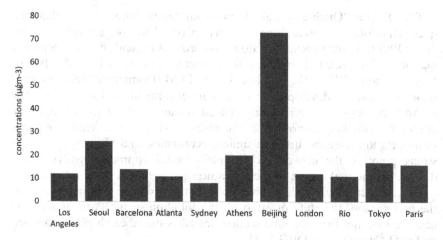

Figure 10.1 Annual mean PM2.5 concentrations measured in previous and future
Olympic cities in 2014 (Tokyo), 2015 (Rio de Janeiro) and in 2016 (all
other cities). Data have been compiled from the WHO database for air
quality[1]

From the research point of view, Beijing OPG was a tremendous living field
experiment to assess the efficiency of emission reduction policies either on
concentrations (Chen et al., 2013; Wang et al., 2009) or on health impacts
(He et al., 2016). As a result, this approach has been used for other Asian big
events. It should be noted, however, that the improvement of air quality
observed during the event has been partially offset after the OPG, due to the
transient character of several measures like factory closings and traffic
reduction (Caie and Xie, 2011). Nevertheless, the scientific experiment in itself
can be considered as an important legacy of the OPG. Considering other
Olympics events, available literature on the assessment of air quality is scarce
due to the unique (negative) character of Beijing 2008, as compared to other
past or future Olympic cities (Figure 10.1).

The management of urban air quality obviously depends on a city's idio-
syncratic characteristics. Since, however, private cars often represent the
dominant source of urban pollutants, traffic planning and control as well as
investments in public transport infrastructures are common measures proposed in OPG programs in order to mitigate traffic congestion (and associated emissions) (Currie and Shalaby, 2012). This has been the case, at
different levels, in Los Angeles, Athens, Sydney, Atlanta, London and Rio.
The Brazilian event (magnified by the 2014 football World Cup) has been
characterized by the launching of several metro lines, streetcars, or bus-rapid
transit systems (Lindau et al., 2016) that have strongly promoted public
transport usage (Bovy, 2017), even after OPG and hence improving air quality in the future. British authorities have chosen to improve existing infrastructures and to implement "transport demand management" strategies for

both households and freight operators, especially via the "4Rs" paradigm (reducing, re-timing, re-routing, re-moding; see Parkes et al., 2016; Browne et al., 2014). Since transport and specifically traffic congestion are closely related to pollutant emissions, an impact on air quality was expected everywhere, especially for pollutants like NO_2 and PM2.5 (particles with diameter lower than 2.5 μm). The procedure set up to reduce traffic was sometimes effective but in general it has been difficult to attribute the observed changes in concentrations to these actions. Most often meteorological variability has been identified has the main driver of pollutant burden, either in a favorable way like in Atlanta 1996 (Peel et al., 2010) or with a negative impact like in Sydney 2000 (Palese et al., 2000). Moreover, while the London experience has shown that modifications in travel behaviors may be prolonged after OPG (even if to a modest extent, see Parkes et al., 2016; Browne et al., 2014), virtuous changes observed during the event quickly vanished in Los Angeles (Giuliano, 1988) or in Sydney (Brewer and Hensher, 2001), thus softening any potentially positive impacts on air quality.

Air quality within the Paris area

For the Paris Region, where about 12 million inhabitants live, pollution burdens are similar to those observed in Western Europe, for example London, or even in northern America. For the particle levels, annual means observed in the Paris area are similar to previous Olympic cities (Figure 10.1) except for Beijing where much higher concentrations were observed. Recent decennial trends indicate a slow decrease of most regulated pollutants and especially particle burden. Close to the traffic, EU air quality standards are still exceeded (AIRPARIF, 2018). As a consequence, like several other European countries, France is still under the threat of penalties for the infringement of European recommended levels. Moreover, more stringent values recommended by the World Health Organization (WHO), such as an annual PM2.5 guideline value of 10 μg.m^{-3}, still have not been reached. Compared to other pollutants, ozone has a particular trend pattern. Like in Europe, peak values observed during summer have decreased significantly since 2000. Thus the number of exceedances of the indicator for health protection was 13 in 2016, i.e. lower than the 25 days threshold prescribed by the European Community that was systematically reached between 2000 and 2006. On the other hand, for several years mean daily concentrations observed in urban centers indicate sometimes a slight increase of a few μg.m^{-3} (about 5% in 2016 and 2017 compared to 2010) as observed in the Paris area (AIRPARIF, 2018). This is explained partly by the sharp reduction of NO and the nonlinear relationship between nitrogen oxides and ozone in urban centers where these oxides are found in excess (Seinfeld and Pandis, 2006).

During summer periods, the main pollution concerns in Europe are particles and ozone, and their precursors. In the Paris area, industrial emissions do not represent a very large fraction and transport dominates the emissions of primary pollutants such as NO, NO_2, VOCs (Volatiles Organic compounds among which hydrocarbons are counted), and primary particles (largely composed of organic matter and soot). Within the atmosphere, driven by photochemistry, secondary species, mostly ozone and Secondary Organic Aerosol (SOA), are formed during summer. It should be noted that an important fraction of this pollution is formed outside the Paris area and then transported inside (70% at annual scale). Also, concerning VOCs, precursors of ozone and SOA, biogenic sources such as trees are important sources and have to be considered.

Air quality Research Action Plan for Paris 2024 Olympic Games

As previously described, air quality remains an important topic in the Paris area and a question that needs to be addressed in the OPG context both to protect citizens and tourists, and to provide athletes safe and optimal conditions for the competition. Moreover, as shown for the Beijing 2008 case, it is an opportunity for the research community and authorities to conduct experiments to improve air quality or to set up measures and management policies that extend beyond the sole question of the OPG. We describe here the research topics that we propose to address to improve our knowledge of air quality and its management in the context of the OPG.

Planning mobility and traffic with air quality perspectives

As previously described, mobility and traffic congestion are systematic major concerns for OPG. Experience from previous events showed that it is often difficult to evaluate the impact of these air quality policies, but it provided the opportunity to set up more efficient monitoring and attribution systems and strategies based on observations and numerical tools with finer spatial resolution and targeting more specific tracers like black carbon for traffic. The question of the impact on air quality is almost always raised especially when sustainable transportation modes are encouraged.

An ambitious plan is needed on these aspects for Paris 2024. OPG should be the opportunity, the accelerator of a perennial plan for IDF mobility and transport policies. To do so, we are now in position to develop and use new tools to design such planning which will fully take into account air quality concerns. More importantly, the emphasis should not only be put on passenger transport but also on the freight sector, a major contributor to air quality in IDF (Coulombel et al., 2018) which will be the focus of various research programs, notably in line with off-peak deliveries that can induce large emissions savings (LaBelle et al., 2015). Moreover, it is also important to be able to design multidisciplinary research projects to evaluate the health impact of air pollution during large gatherings of people associated with such unique events.

Ambient air quality by 2024 in the Paris region

If the general context in France, and more specifically in the IDF region, leans toward a decrease of pollution levels in ambient air (associated to strong emission reductions), we have underlined the fact that pollutant concentrations remain at levels potentially harmful for health and that urban mean ozone could still increase. On the other hand, meteorology strongly drives these pollution levels. Potential increase of stagnation situations and heat waves would be of importance for future air quality by allowing pollutant accumulation. Such a situation would also have an impact on VOC emissions from vegetation which are dependent on temperature and solar radiation. Enhanced biogenic VOC emissions would have an impact on ozone and aerosol (SOA) budgets. For such topics, we still need to improve our knowledge for which an international observation campaign in IDF would provide beneficial opportunities both for documenting the complex interplay between urban and surrounding biogenic plumes and set-up efficient mitigation policies for air quality. Indeed, air quality models used for air quality forecasting and planning are lacking most of this complex chemistry. The objective of such an initiative would be also to provide a mid/long term forecast of the air quality by 2024 and specifically during the OPG in August 2024. Projections themselves are subject to potential methodological development using deterministic air quality models in synergy with statistical modelling (Monte Carlo approaches, etc.) in the context of emissions mitigation and climate change. Addressing such questions exceeds the sole OPG question and would be of great help for air quality management in IDF, and in other urbanized areas in general where densely populated areas are also under the influence of more rural/forested areas.

Air quality in Olympic arenas and facilities

Until now there have not been specific efforts made to estimate the air pollution inside Olympic facilities during OPG events. This is of high interest to address the next point of athletes' exposure, but also to estimate exposure of spectators inside and outside Olympic arenas. This interest for indoor environments during OPG is very new and reflects the general interest to estimate air quality as close as possible to the occupants, either spectators or athletes.

Air pollution is very specific in the different indoor places such as gymnasiums, swimming pools as both sources, activities and exposure conditions differ from place to place, and can be sometimes enhanced by poor ventilation conditions. Moreover, it is also important to maintain good indoor air quality inside Olympic villages to ensure the well-being of athletes during both their training and their rest periods. Our objective is to provide air quality estimates for Olympic sites based on both innovative numerical models working at unprecedented fine resolution and innovative measurements provided by air quality sensors. Such environments are also perfect to test innovative technology of atmospheric cleanup.

Air quality and athletes

Athletes are healthy citizens a priori unlike vulnerable groups (like elderly people or children), but they become particularly vulnerable to air pollution during exercise because of higher respiratory rates and higher tidal volumes, that increase their personal pollutant intake (Helenius et al., 1998; Lumme et al., 2003). Pollutants can induce airway inflammation especially for athletes with asthma and practicing endurance (McKenzie and Boulet, 2008). Pollution can also affect their performance. Studies on this topic are still scarce and often restricted to short periods or based on a small number of persons (Fu and Guo, 2017, Giles and Koehle, 2014; Mullins, 2018).

In collaboration with INSEP (the French national institute for sport and performance), it would be of interest to develop research projects to estimate impacts of air quality on athletes' performance and health. To do so, we aim at establishing athletes' cohorts to obtain a longitudinal follow-up of athletes' health, physiology, performance, and exposure to air pollution.

Air quality and citizens

Finally, this event is a unique opportunity to share knowledge on air quality and its impacts on citizens. IDF territories are very keen to study these environmental questions and there is a strong movement to develop experiments on this topic. The Paris OPG will be a unique opportunity to set up participatory science projects around the air quality questions. Such actions are of course favorable to increasing citizen's perception and knowledge of air quality issues.

Conclusion

Air quality is an important concern of megacities due to the high level of pollutant emissions associated with high population densities. During OPG, the issue takes on a particular importance since the attention of the whole world is focused on the region hosting the events.

This issue of air pollution has been raised in most recent Olympics but in a more intense way during the Beijing Olympics where pollution levels were, by far, the highest. In this case, the measures taken were spectacular and very effective in reducing air pollution with the help of favorable weather conditions. Although we cannot say that there has been a legacy associated with the Olympics in the field of air quality management, in some cases, as in Beijing, it has allowed us to raise citizen's awareness.

In the case of Paris, the issue of air pollution remains sensitive even though significant progress has been made in recent decades. The question of the levels of ozone and particles and their impacts at the time of the OPG 2024 therefore arises. The Qi^2 air quality research network proposes an ambitious project to address this issue. This project tackles the issues of mobility and transport, projections of air quality by 2024, individual exposure and its impacts, athlete performance and citizen perception.

In this case, the Games can be an opportunity to improve quality management in a sustainable way through the production of new knowledge and tools. Thus, more than a contribution to the management of air quality in major events, the OPG 2024 must make it possible to provide answers for the management of the air quality of megacities in general.

Note

1 Data for fine particles (PM2.5) are generally not available at the time of the Olympics for these cities. It has been chosen to display more recent values from the same WHO database.

References

AIRPARIF (2018). *Bilan de la qualité de l'air: année 2017. Surveillance et information en Île-De-France*. https://www.airparif.asso.fr/_pdf/publications/bilan-2017.pdf

Boulanger, G., Bayeux, T., Mandin, C., Kirchner, S., Vergriette, B., Pernelet-Joly, V., Kopp, P. (2017). Socio-economic costs of indoor air pollution: A tentative estimation for some pollutants of health interest in France. *Environment International*, 104, 14–24.

Bovy, P. (2017). *Rio 2016 Olympic Games Public Transport Development outstanding Legacy and Mobility Sustainability*. http://www.mobility-bovy.ch/resources/Resources/D.-RIO-Transport.legacy.2017.pdf

Brewer, A.M., Hensher, D.A. (2001). *The Impact of Staging a Major Event on Commuters' Travel and Work Behaviour: The Sydney 2000 Olympic Games*. Hobart: Australasian Transport Research Forum (ATRF).

Browne, M., Allen, J., Wainwright, I., Palmer, A., Williams, I. (2014). London 2012: Changing delivery patterns in response to the impact of the Games on traffic flows. *International Journal of Urban Sciences*, 18(2), 244–261.

Caie, H., Xie, S. (2011). Traffic-related air pollution modeling during the 2008 Beijing Olympic Games: The effects of an odd–even day traffic restriction scheme. *Science of Total Environment*, 409, 1935–1948.

Chen, Y., ZheJin, G., Kumar, N., Shi, G. (2013). The promise of Beijing: Evaluating the impact of the 2008 Olympic Games on air quality. *Journal of Environmental Economics and Management*, 66, 424–443.

Coulombel, N., Dablanc, L., Gardrat, M., Koning, M. (2018). The environmental social cost of urban road freight: Evidence from the Paris region. *Transportation Research Part D: Transport and Environment*, 63, 514–532.

Currie, G., Shalaby, A. (2012). Synthesis of transport planning approaches for the world's largest events. *Transport Reviews*, 32(1), 113–136.

Giles, L.V., Koehle, M.S. (2014). The health effects of exercising in air pollution. *Sports Medicine*, 44(2), 223–249.

Giuliano, G. (1988). Testing the limits of TSM: the 1984 Los Angeles Summer Olympics. *Transportation*, 15, 143–161.

Guo, M., Fu, S. (2017). Running with a mask? The effect of air pollution on marathon runners' performance. *Journal of Sports Economics*, doi:10.2139/ssrn.2978302.

He, G., Fan, M., Zhou, M. (2016). The effect of air pollution on mortality in China: Evidence from the 2008 Beijing Olympic Games. *Journal of Environmental Economics and Management*, 79, 18–39.

Helenius, I.J., Tikkanen, H.O., Sarna, S., Haahtela, T. (1998). Asthma and increased bronchial responsiveness in elite athletes: Atopy and sport event as risk factors. *Journal of Allergy and Clinical Immunology*, 101(5), 646–652.

Husson, J.F., Aïchi, L. (2015). *Rapport de la commission d'enquête sur le coût économique et financier de la pollution de l'air*, 610(I), (2014–2015) Sénat, http://www.sena t.fr/rap/r14-610-1/r14-610-11.pdf

International Agency for Research on Cancer (2013). *Outdoor Air Pollution*, IARC Monographs on the Evaluation of Carcinogenic Risks to Humans 109.

Kassens-Noor, E. (2013). Transport legacy of the Olympic Games, 1992–2012. *Journal of Urban Affairs*, 35(4), 393–416.

LaBelle, J., Frève, S., Gottschling, E. (2015). *Off-peak Delivery – A Pilot Project for the Chicago Region*. Research report for NURail.

Lindau, L.A., Petzhold, G., Tavares, V.B., Facchini, D. (2016). Mega-events and the transformation of Rio de Janeiro into a mass-transit city. *Research in Transportation Economics*, 59, 196–203.

Lumme, A., Haahtela, T., Öunap, J., Rytilä, P., Obase, Y.Helenius, M., Remes, V., Helenius, I. (2003). Airway inflammation, bronchial hyperresponsiveness and asthma in elite ice hockey players. *European Respiratory Journal*, 22, 113–117. doi:10.1183/09031936.03.00112403.

Ma, H. & He, G. (2016). Effects of the post-Olympics driving restrictions on air quality in Beijing. *Sustainability*, 8, 902. doi:10.3390/su8090902.

McKenzie, D.C. & Boulet, L.-P. (2008). Asthma, outdoor air quality and the Olympic Games. *CMAJ*, 179, 543–548. doi:10.1503/cmaj.080982.

Mullins, J.T. (2018). Ambient air pollution and human performance: Contemporaneous and acclimatization effects of ozone exposure on athletic performance. *Health Economics*, 27(8), 1189–1200.

Palese, B., Millais, C., Posner, R., Koza, F., Mealey, E., McLaren, W., *et al.* (2000). *How Green the Games?* Greenpeace's environmental assessment of the Sydney 2000 Olympics. Sydney: Greenpeace International & Greenpeace Australia Pacific.

Parkes, S.D., Jopson, A., Marsden, G. (2016). Understanding travel behavior change during mega-events: Lessons from the London 2012 games. *Transportation Research Part A: Policy and Practice*, 92, 104–119.

Peel, J.L., Klein, M., Flanders, W.D., Mulholland, J.A., Tolbert, P.E. (2010). *Impact of Improved Air Quality during the 1996 Summer Olympic Games in Atlanta on Multiple Cardiovascular and Respiratory Outcomes*. HEI Research Report 148. Boston, MA: Health Effects Institute.

REVIHAAP (2013). *Review of Evidence on Health Aspects of Air Pollution*. Copenhagen, Denmark: World Health Organization.

Seinfeld, J., PandisS. (2006). *Atmospheric Chemistry and Physics*. New York: John Wiley and Sons Inc.

Wang, X., Westerdahl, D., Chen, L. C., Wu, Y., Hao, J., Pan, X., GuoX., Zhang, K. M. (2009). Evaluating the air quality impacts of the 2008 Beijing Olympic Games: On-road emission factors and black carbon profile. *Atmospheric Environment*, 43, 4535–4543.

Zhang, J., Zhong, C., Yi, M. (2016). Did Olympic Games improve air quality in Beijing? Based on the synthetic control method. *Environmental Economics and Policy Studies*, 18, 21–39. doi:10.1007/s10018-015-0109-2.

Conclusion

Towards Olympic public–private partnerships

Jean-Loup Chappelet

Staging the Olympic Games requires close cooperation between the host city and country, on the one hand, and the national and international sports movement, on the other. That is between the public authorities (both local and national) and private organisations such as the host country's National Olympic Committee (NOC) and national sport federations, international federations and the International Olympic Committee (IOC). But can these arrangements be considered public–private partnerships (PPP), a way of delivering goods and services that has been widely embraced since the turn of the century in response to the difficulties of public investment and the large risks associated with some projects (OECD, 2008)?

From their resurrection in Athens in 1896 to the Los Angeles Games in 1932, the modern Olympics were essentially a private affair, attributed by the IOC, a club of international dignitaries founded in 1894, and organised by local para-public but highly independent bodies known as Organising Committees of the Olympic Games (OCOGs). Of course, the IOC made sure the Games were opened by the local head of state and that the OCOG, which financed the actual staging of the Games, mostly through ticket sales, obtained the agreement of the host city (or, in some cases, patrons) to build the facilities needed.

This mostly private approach was abandoned with the 1936 Berlin Olympics, when Hitler's government took over the organisation of the Games, which it used to project an image of a "new Germany" that had risen from the ashes of defeat in the First World War. To achieve its goal, the Nazi government provided almost unlimited finance for both the Summer Olympics in Berlin and the 1936 Winter Olympics in Garmisch-Partenkirchen. This trend continued after the Second World War, albeit more modestly at first, because the Games had become an unparalleled media event and were one of the few places where East and West came together during the Cold War. Thus, even though the 1948 London Olympics came to be known as the "Austerity Games", they provided Great Britain with an opportunity to show the country's resilience to the war, while Rome 1960, Tokyo 1964 and Munich 1972 marked Italy's, Japan's and Germany's (still the Federal Republic) return to the "concert of nations" after the defeat of the Axis powers. The Olympics were also becoming more global, with editions in Melbourne (1956), Mexico City (1968), Montreal (1976) and Seoul (1988), all of which received substantial funding from their national and/or regional authorities.

Such government support was also a feature of the Moscow 1980 Olympics, but it resulted in the United States boycotting the event for geopolitical reasons – the Soviet invasion of Afghanistan – that had nothing to do with sport, as it felt the Soviet Union was making excessive use of the Games for propaganda purposes. The 1984 Olympics, which had been awarded to Los Angeles long before this boycott, did not pose the same problem because they were organised by an independent, not-for-profit OCOG that claimed not to need public finance from either the local or federal authorities. Despite a Soviet boycott, in retaliation for the US boycott four years earlier, Los Angeles 1984 was a great success, with 140 participating nations, compared with 81 nations at Moscow 1980. Los Angeles's OCOG made an operating profit of US$225 million (mostly used to finance the LA84 Foundation, which continues to promote sport in Southern California to this day). Furthermore, it had almost no investment costs because it used either existing sports arenas, rented from their owners, or convinced sponsors to build any facilities that were not already available. Nevertheless, a study by the US General Accounting Office (GAO) showed that the federal government contributed US$78 million to the 1984 Olympics (GAO, 2001: 12).

The success of Los Angeles 1984 led to a huge increase in the number of Olympic bids, which had dropped to just one following the massive deficit posted by Montreal 1976 and the gigantism that was beginning to affect the Games. But very few regions are as well equipped with sports facilities as Southern California. All the host cities that followed Los Angeles 1984 required considerable investment by the local, regional and national authorities in order to build the numerous facilities needed for the Games (around 40), many of which were underused after the Olympic fortnight because they were oversized and/or built to house sports with only small local followings.

Atlanta, in the United States, hoped to follow Los Angeles's example when it was chosen to host the centenary Games in 1996. However, the need to build several stadiums, many temporary, put a strain on the OCOG's budget, which it only managed to balance thanks to record ticket sales (a record that still stands). But here too the Games received significant federal government funding (US$193 million), to which must be added the US$234 million provided by the local authorities housing the Olympic venues, including the city of Atlanta (GAO, 2001: 15). How much the state of Georgia contributed was still unknown when the GAO published its report.

It appears, therefore, that contemporary editions of the Games cannot be staged without significant input from all levels of government (local, regional, sub-national, national). In addition, ensuring Games security, which has become increasingly strict since the September 11 2001 terrorist attacks, requires input from state bodies such as the army, police and secret services. Diplomatic services are also involved as, under IOC rules, Olympians selected for the Games and holding an "Olympic identity card" (issued by the IOC with its partners) must be able to enter the host territory without a visa. Moreover, host governments are responsible for many other issues affecting the Games, including food security, work permits and brand protection.

Every host city and host NOC must sign the IOC's "Host City Contract" (333 pages long for Paris 2024!), which stipulates that the host city and NOC must set up an OCOG, generally as a not-for-profit body (association, public interest group, foundation, etc.), within a few months of the Games being awarded. In some countries, the OCOG is tied very closely to the public authorities (or may even be a public agency, as for Sydney 2000). Since the 2000 Olympics, many OCOGs have also worked alongside a public body formed to build the facilities needed for the Olympics (OCA for Sydney 2000, ODA for London 2012, Olympstroy for Sochi 2014, Solideo for Paris 2024, etc.). These bodies are created under "Olympic laws", drafted by the host country for this purpose and in order to cover a wide range of issues relating to intellectual property, taxation and transportation, etc.

In addition to these public and para-public Olympic bodies, numerous private companies contribute to organising the Game, including agents of the OCOG or of the body responsible for building work, international and domestic sponsors, broadcasters, Olympic Broadcast Services SA (OBS SA, the IOC company that produces television pictures of the Olympic competitions), and IOC Television and Marketing Services SA (IOCTMS SA), etc.

Hence, organising the Olympic Games now involves a partnership between three types of bodies: private commercial companies, public bodies and private not-for-profit organisations. To ensure the various partners work together effectively, their efforts are coordinated by a supervisory body, such as London 2012's Olympic Board, which included representatives of the London 2012 Organising Committee (LOCOG), the Olympic Delivery Authority (ODA), the British Olympic Association (BOA), the Mayor of London (city authorities), the Greater London Authority (regional authorities) and the British government's Department of Media Culture and Sport (DMCS). The IOC has its own, *ad hoc* coordination commission, which regularly brings together the OCOG and bodies within the IOC group (IOC, Olympic Museum, OBS SA, IOCTMS SA, etc.).

Thus, hosting the Games clearly requires a close partnership between the public and private (both commercial and not-for-profit) sectors. But is this a true public–private partnership (PPP)? Although there is no consensus definition of a PPP, the Organisation for Economic Co-operation and Development (OECD) defines a PPP as

> an agreement between the government and one or more private partners (which may include the operators and the financers) according to which the private partners deliver the service in such a manner that the service delivery objectives of the government are aligned with the profit

objectives of the private partners and where the effectiveness of the alignment depends on a sufficient transfer of risk to the private partners.

(OECD, 2008)

The Games can be considered a service delivered by private partners whose profit objectives (in the case of the IOC: obtain the funds needed to finance the Olympic movement for four years, mostly from television and marketing rights; in the case of the OCOG: finance its operations, mostly from domestic sponsorship and ticketing) are aligned with the host government's aims at different levels (primarily regional development and promoting the host territory, while ensuring the Games' legacy). On the other hand, the risks incurred during all four of the classic phases of a PPP (design, build, finance, operate) are shouldered entirely by the OCOG and its local partners (notably the public authorities), and not by the IOC or local NOC.

In response to a worrying fall in the number of Olympic bids (Chappelet, 2017), the IOC now plays a more active role in helping potential host cities draw up Candidature Files (so-called "invitation" phase, recommendations 1 and 3 of the IOC's Agenda 2020, 2014) and has agreed to contribute more to the OCOG's budget for the operational phase of the Games (preparation and staging). For example, the IOC will contribute at least US$1265 million, in cash and in-kind, to the Paris 2024 OCOG's operating budget. Services in-kind, such as producing television pictures and providing IOC consultancy services, will be worth an estimated US$435 million (IOC, 2017: 12–15).

In addition, the IOC now recommends using existing facilities (unless there is a real need for new facilities after the Games), which reduces construction costs to almost nothing. On the other hand, it does not contribute to the cost of operating Olympic facilities after the Games. Logically, these costs have to be borne by the facilities' owners (usually local authorities), but national sport federations and the NOC could also contribute as future users of these facilities. As a result, these private partners should be involved in the design and construction of facilities, possibly alongside commercial partners, in order to ensure they are, for example, sized appropriately and therefore viable to operate after the Games, as called for by PPP theory.

Nevertheless, following the huge deficit incurred by Montreal 1976, the Host City Contract's primary aim is to avoid any financial liabilities for the IOC and NOC (articles 4.1 and 4.2, IOC, 2017: 11–12) and to ensure the "joint and several liability" of the host city and OCOG. Because most host cities do not have the financial capacity needed to guarantee a deficit, since 2017 the IOC has accepted additional signatories (for example, a sub-national authority) to the Host City Contract. Hence, for the 2028 Games, the state of California has approved a deficit guarantee equal to that of the city of Los Angeles (maximum of US$250 million each), but the US federal government has not provided any financial guarantees. Nevertheless, the OCOG for Los Angeles 2028 would like to do without this deficit guarantee, just like Los

Angeles 1984. Time will tell whether this is possible and whether the soft form of PPP adopted by Paris 2024 will be a success.

References

Chappelet, J.-L. (2017). L'avenir des candidatures Olympiques. *Jurisport, la revue juridique et économique du sport*, 177, July–August, 42–45.

GAO (2001). *Olympic Games: Costs to Plan and Stage the Games in the United States.* Report to the Ranking Minority Member Subcommittee on the Legislative Branch Committee on Appropriations, US Senate, November, 12–15.

IOC (2014). *Olympic Agenda 2020, 20+20 Recommendations.* Lausanne: International Olympic Committee.

IOC (2017). *Host City Contract – Principles – Games of the XXXIII Olympiad in 2024.* Lausanne: International Olympic Committee, 13–15.

OECD (2008). *Public–Private Partnerships: In Pursuit of Risk Sharing and Value for Money.* Paris: Organisation for Economic Co-operation and Development.

Index